Missionaries to the Skeptics

Missionaries to the Skeptics

Christian Apologists for the Twentieth Century

C. S. Lewis, Edward John Carnell, and Reinhold Niebuhr

John A. Sims

Mercer University Press
Macon, Georgia

ISBN 0-86554-496-4

Missionaries to the Skeptics.
Christian Apologists for the Twentieth Century:
C. S. Lewis, E. J. Carnell, and Reinhold Niebuhr
by John Alfred Sims

BT
1117
.S55
1995

Copyright © 1995
Mercer University Press
6316 Peake Road
Macon, Georgia 31210-3960

Library of Congress Cataloging-in-Publication Data

Sims, John Alfred (John A.), 1942–
    Missionaries to the skeptics. Christian apologists for the twentieth
century: C. S. Lewis, E. J. Carnell, and Reinhold Niebuhr / John A.
Sims.
    x + 235 pp.   6 x 9" (15 x 23 cm.)
    Includes bibliographical references and index.
    ISBN 0-86554-496-4 (alk. paper)
    1. Apologetics—History—20th century. 2. Lewis, C. S. (Clive
Staples), 1898–1963. 3. Carnell, Edward John, 1919–1967.
4. Niebuhr, Reinhold, 1892–1971. I. Title.
BT1117.S55 1995
239'.0092'2—dc20   95-41832
                                                                CIP

                                                                CIP

Contents

Part Two: Edward John Carnell

Part Three: Reinhold Niebuhr

Photography Credits

The photograph of C. S. Lewis appearing on the cover is by Wolf Suschitzky and is from the The Marion E. Wade Center, Wheaton College, Wheaton, Illinois. The photograph of Lewis appearing on page 18 is also from The Marion E. Wade Center. Both photographs are used here with the permission of The Marion E. Wade Center.

The photograph of E. J. Carnell appearing on the cover and on page 93 is from the Archives of Fuller Theological Seminary, Pasadena, California, and is used with permission of the seminary's office of communications and public affairs.

The photograph of Reinhold Niebuhr appearing on the cover and on page 151 is from the Archives of The Union Theological Seminary in the City of New York and is used with permission of the seminary's development office.

Acknowledgments

The writing of a book does not begin when an author first puts a pen to the paper or keyboards information into a computer. Its beginnings generally go back much farther to those influencing persons, processes, and events that instill an enduring interest and desire to share that which "has been shut up as fire in one's bones." One cannot always readily recall or articulate the rightful source of one's inspiration and encouragement, but there are usually those whose influence and strength have been unmistakably real.

I take this opportunity to mention a few. Special gratitude is owed to those women in my life who were always there when I needed them: my mother, my sister Freda, and my wife Pat. My first course in apologetics was under Professor Don Bowdle, an inspiring teacher who imparted a love for the subject and with whom I have been privileged to teach at Lee College for the past twenty-five years. Professor Charles Wellborn supervised my doctoral dissertation, which had an apologetic theme, and displayed a special patience and grace during that tedious process. Reverend Charles Conn, a former president at Lee College, was a special friend and father-figure who gave me every opportunity and encouragement to do scholarly work. And then there are my three sons, John Patrick, Mark, and Matthew, whose exemplary strength of character has been a great source of inspiration. Many thanks as well to Mercer University Press, and particularly to Scott Nash, for their special contribution to this work.

I have taught Christian apologetics at Lee College now for twenty-five years, and many fine students have passed through my classes. I express my love and appreciation to them for what they have taught me, and for their commitment to the truth of the gospel, which has been so evident in their lives. My prayer is that this volume will be received as one small way through which I may give something in return.

John Sims
Lee College
Fall, 1995

Affectionately dedicated to Pat,
my best friend,
mother of our children
(Matthew, Mark, and John Patrick),
and loving wife.

With loving gratitude
for being a constant source
of inspiration and encouragement.

Introduction

The Case for Christianity in a Secular World

Christian apologetics is all about the way Christians commend and defend the Christian faith to their contemporaries. It is not a new task but one that Christians have assumed throughout the centuries. Christians have always done what they could to give an account of their faith. A Christian community that neglected this task would be something less than a genuine Christian community, just as a theology that neglected the apologetic imperative would be something less than a genuine Christian theology. It has always been natural for Christians to feel some obligation to integrate human truth and value into the unified vision of the Christian faith.

Origen's *Contra Celsum*, Augustine's *City of God*, Aquinas's *Summa contra Gentiles*, Butler's *Analogy of Religion*, and Paley's *Natural Theology* are classic examples. In more modern times such diverse thinkers as Friedrich Schleiermacher, John Henry Newman, Emil Brunner, Paul Tillich, Wolfhart Pannenberg, J. Gresham Machen, G. W. Berkouwer, and Carl F. H. Henry have made comparable contributions to the field of Christian apologetics. The mere grouping of these diverse apologists serves as a reminder that Christian apologetics mirrors historical change, cultural diversity, and different confessional commitments. Apologetic diversity has always existed in the Christian church. Irenaeus, Justin Martyr, Augustine, and Aquinas, for example, were all prominent Christian apologists, but their apologetic strategies as well as their theological perspectives were different. After the Reformation, apologetics took on a more confessional style. Apologists were naturally prone to defend the Christian faith from the perspective of their Catholic, Lutheran, Reformed, or Anglican point of view. The whole tenor of enlightenment thinking encouraged a more ecumenical understanding and defense of the Christian religion, but theologians, in general, did not abandon their confessional commitments. There were no neutral apologists, just as there were no official methods or normative ways of doing apologetics.

In more recent times, however, the emergence of the secular mind has provided Christian apologists with a common challenge. C. S. Lewis, Edward John Carnell, and Reinhold Niebuhr were from different theological traditions, but they all responded to a common need to make the case for Christianity in a secular world. They were not theological bedfellows, nor did they employ the same strategies for doing apologetics. As persons and as apologists they were distinctly different types. What they shared in common were creative and seminal minds and a passionate desire to defend the Christian faith against the "intellectual despisers" of the twentieth century. They were the pacesetters in the great apologetic traditions of this century.

Twentieth-Century Apologetic Traditions

In the preface to *Mere Christianity* C. S. Lewis warned his readers not to expect him to help them decide whether they ought to become an Anglican, a Methodist, a Presbyterian, or a Roman Catholic. "Ever since I became a Christian," Lewis said, "I have thought that the best, perhaps the only, service that I could do for my unbelieving neighbors was to explain and defend the belief that has been common to nearly all Christians at all times."[1]

Lewis's refusal to offer help to those hesitating between Christian "denominations" should not be construed to mean that he did not know who he was or what it meant to be a Christian. Lewis belonged to the Church of England, a communion that did not consider itself to be essentially Protestant or Roman Catholic. As John Donne noted in the seventeenth century, Anglicans preferred to think of their tradition as the "Middle Way." It was a tradition whose continuity was guaranteed more by the episcopacy and the Prayer Book than it was by a particular theological commitment. It did not lack a theology, but it was not a dogmatic church—at least not in the sense that many Catholics and Protestants are dogmatic. What was more important in the Anglican tradition was the sense of belonging to a communion of saints. So long as they could agree on the most fundamental of Christian beliefs, it was generally acceptable for Anglican Christians to have their theological differences.

Lewis thought of himself simply as a Christian. He preferred to talk about the enormous common ground that most Christians share—what Lewis called "mere" or essential Christianity. He did not like to wear theological labels, but he was not afraid of theological commitments. His one overarching commitment was to the doctrines of historic Christianity as defined by the New Testament and the creeds of the church. He never avoided doctrines because they were difficult or repellant to modern assumptions. Lewis was not particularly interested in "moving with the times"; he was much more interested in timeless truth. For Lewis, this entailed a defense of a supernatural worldview—a commitment that was not intellectually acceptable to most of his colleagues in the academic world. It is the Christian plot that gives the most illuminating account of the story of our lives, Lewis argued, and that plot makes no sense at all apart from its supernatural content.

C. S. Lewis is not generally thought of as an Anglican apologist, however, but rather as a literary figure who used his writings as a vehicle for conveying and defending Christian truth. He is numbered among an impressive group of Christian writers, including G. K. Chesterton, W. H. Auden, T. S. Eliot, Charles Williams, Dorothy Sayers, and J. R. R. Tolkien—all of whose writings contain some kind of apology for the Christian faith. These writers were not theologians who pushed for one religious concept or doctrine, or even developed a formal apologetic. Their primary concern was for a commonsense theology that is applicable to life, conducive to morality, and reasonable to thinking persons. What these literary figures were most eager to defend were those permanent truths and values, rooted in the Christian tradition, that were endangered by the secular forces of modernity. Christianity was obviously important to these writers because they believed it to be true, but they were also concerned about the future of the Christian faith because they believed that it was indispensable to the preservation of those truths and values that have sustained our western civilization.

C. S. Lewis's influence upon intellectuals is well-known. But his continuing importance as a Christian apologist rests even more on his work as a translator of truth into language that common people could understand and appreciate. The great mass of Lewis's fellow countrymen either heard the Christian message in the highly emotional form offered by revivalists or in the unintelligible language of learned clergymen. At the expense of ridicule and rejection by many of his professional colleagues at Oxford, Lewis took up the apologetic task of communicating and commending the Christian faith to common people. In response to a Bible scholar who had criticized his work for being overly simplified, Lewis replied: "One thing at least is sure. If the real theologians had tackled this laborious work of translation about a hundred years ago, when they began to lose touch with the people (for whom Christ died), there would have been no place for me."[2] The wide-spread reception of Lewis's work throughout the English-speaking world affirmed the need for his lively and imaginative presentation of Christian truth. Storekeepers, lawyers, realtors, policemen, artisans, students, and children around the world bought Lewis's works in record numbers because they spoke to them in a manner that they could understand and affirm. Because of his work of *translation,* C. S. Lewis's reasoned and imaginative influence spread far beyond the academic confines of Oxford and Cambridge into a wider world that needed the simple truth of the Christian message.

About the time that C. S. Lewis was becoming a well-known advocate and defender of the Christian faith in England, a movement was emerging in this country that sought to reclaim and defend the truths of evangelical Christianity. The early leaders of this evangelical renaissance were Harold John Ockenga, Carl F. H. Henry, Bernard Ramm, Gordon Clark, and Edward John Carnell—all of whom had strong apologetic interests. From its inception the movement has been blessed with outstanding leaders who have made substantial contributions to the field of Christian apologetics. One immediately thinks of outstanding apologists like Francis Schaeffer, John R. W. Stott, Josh McDowell, John Montgomery, Ronald Nash, Clark Pinnock, and J. I. Packer. Virtually all of these men would be worthy representatives of the evangelical apologetic tradition. E. J. Carnell has been chosen to represent this rich apologetic tradition for one overarching reason. He embodied the evangelical spirit and set a bright example for young evangelicals to follow at a crucial time when many wondered if there would be a future for evangelical theology. He set the apologetic standard against which his peers and future evangelical apologists would measure their own contribution. Carnell, more than any other single individual, is recognized for making the case for evangelical conservatism in this century.

Today, the movement has grown to the point that the term "evangelical" is virtually a household word. One constantly hears about evangelical churches, seminaries, colleges, and publishing houses. The evangelical message is daily aired across the country by means of radio and television. Youth and campus ministries are active at most major universities. The evangelical influence is felt in Congress and in statehouses across the nation. Presidential candidates compete for the large evangelical vote by assuring their audiences that they are "twice born" and eager to support traditional religious values.

Carl F. H. Henry, the movement's most prominent systematic theologian, has defined an evangelical as "one who believes the evangel." Henry explained that "the Good News is that the Holy Spirit gives spiritual life to all who repent and receive divine salvation proffered in the incarnate, crucified and risen Redeemer." The Christian message "is what the inspired Scriptures teach—no more, no less—and an evangelical is a person whose life is governed by the scriptural revelation of God and His purposes."[3] Henry's definition accentuates the evangelical commitment to Scripture and doctrine as well as a personal relationship to Christ and the need to spread the gospel. It would be a mistake to assume too much homogeneity among evangelicals. They do not all share a common theological background or believe exactly the same thing, but it is probably safe to assume that most evangelicals embrace the commitments that Henry mentions.

Theologically informed evangelicals, on the other hand, are usually quick to differentiate their belief system from that of other theological traditions. But they do not see themselves as a reactionary movement. On the contrary, evangelicals regard themselves as belonging to the mainstream of Christian orthodoxy. They trace their roots back through nineteenth-century American Protestantism, the Reformation tradition of Luther and Calvin, to the historic roots of New Testament Christianity. Evangelicalism understands itself as nothing more, nor less, than the attempt to restore the lost heritage of historic Christianity.

The primary problem that evangelicals have with Roman Catholicism is the Catholic sacerdotal system that emphasizes a salvation mediated by sacraments and a theology that is erected on tradition and papal infallibility rather than the word of God. Their differences with liberal Protestantism, on the other hand, stem from the naturalistic and melioristic assumptions that liberals adopted from the Enlightenment and the cultural climate that it had produced by the turn of the twentieth century. They were definitely at odds with the liberal rejection of a supernatural metaphysic, their endorsement of radical forms of biblical criticism, their substitution of human experience for the authority of Scripture, and their interpretation of salavation in this-worldly moral, social, and progressive terms. Liberalism, in the minds of most evangelicals, represented a capitulation to the assumptions of modern culture.

Evangelicals were encouraged by the neo-orthodox reaction to liberalism and its attempt to correct many of the liberal errors. But they could never fully support the neo-orthodox agenda because they could not accept their views on Scripture. Evangelicals were more at home with fundamentalists on matters relating to doctrine and the authority of Scripture. After all, most of the early evangelical leaders had come from fundamentalist backgrounds. But they increasingly found themselves at odds with fundamentalist attitudes toward the nature of the church and the Christian's relation to culture.

As fundamentalists attempted to hold the line against the modernists during the early decades of this century, they increasingly found themselves on the losing side in denominational squabbles. The fundamentalist reaction was erroneously to identify the true church with those of their own kind who were "pure in doctrine" and "separatist" in their ethic. The result was that fundamentalists soon came to be identified with distasteful attitudes such as separatism, phariseeism, obscurantism, and an indifference to social problems. The growing consensus in the mainstream of American society was that fundamentalists no longer deserved to be taken seriously. The new evangelicals of the post World War II era supported the fundamentalist defense of the inerrancy of Scripture and the fundamental doctrines of the Christian faith, but they soon distanced themselves from the fundamentalist understanding of the church. Evangelicals were also insisting that Christians not forsake their responsibility to the culture but actively work toward its transformation.

In place of the separatist attitude of fundamentalists the new evangelicals emphasized the need for evangelical fellowship and cooperation. This new evangelical attitude was expressed through the formation of the National Association of Evangelicals in 1942. The NAE served as a fellowship where the evangelical position could be articulated by members from diverse theological traditions. In place of the seige mentality of fundamentalism the evangelicals emphasized the need for a new offensive in evangelism, misssions, and Christian education. This concern was visibly expressed in men like radio minister Charles Fuller and evangelist Billy Graham. Youth for Christ rallies, campus ministries, radio evangelism, and evangelistic crusades soon became standard fare in the evangelical community. The training of evangelical ministers who could preach and defend the gospel was also a high priority in the movement. New colleges and seminaries were soon established in response to this need. Prominent among these new institutions was Fuller Theological Seminary in California, which intended to exemplify the high scholarly standards, academic freedom, and evangelistic outreach that was so highly valued by the leadership of the movement. Finally, a journal was established so that evangelical theological views could be solidified and spread to pastors and laypersons throughout the world. It was called *Christianity Today,* and Carl F. H. Henry was selected to be its first editor.

Fundamentalists and evangelicals were not alone in their conviction that liberalism had failed and that something more "realistic" and "biblical" had to be found. A theology of crisis began to appear during the 1920s that expressed serious differences with the moral optimism espoused by the liberals. This movement endorsed the liberal openness to modern science and biblical criticism, but it rejected liberalism's emphasis on the immanence of God and its defective understanding of human nature that failed to account for the sinful depths of human life. Liberal optimism, with its roots in the Enlightenment, saw the Christian religion as the soul of culture—as representing society's finest ideals, its noblest institutions, its truest philosophy. Liberals were intent on realizing the kingdom of God on earth through the combined efforts of human achievement and divine grace.

The new movement, with its roots in the Reformation, was soon being called neo-orthodoxy. It understood life more in terms of its ambiguous and tragic depths. Karl Barth, the leading theologian in the movement, regarded liberalism as a form of "culture-Protestantism," as a vain effort on humanity's part to achieve what could only be fulfilled through divine intervention and grace. Humanity's real relation to the world, Barth insisted, was more akin to a "crisis" out of which it had to make a radical choice. Emil Brunner, Friedrich Gogarten, and Karl Barth were the leaders of the new movement on the European continent. As theologians they had some serious differences, but they all agreed that Liberalism is not Christianity. That concession, more than any other, bonded their efforts to dismantle liberalism.

During the early 1930s serious questions about the viability of liberal Christianity began to emerge in America. In 1931 Henry P. Van Dusen, a young and promising professor at Union Theological Seminary, was writing about "The Sickness of Liberal Religion." An article by John C.

Bennett in 1933 entitled, "After Liberalism—What?" was anticipating a post-liberal era. Even Harry Emerson Fosdick, the great defender of Liberalism, published an article entitled "Beyond Modernism." The most serious attack, however, appeared in 1932 when Reinhold Niebuhr challenged Liberalism's most cherished assumptions in *Moral Man and Immoral Society*. This work established Niebuhr as the major post-Liberal theologian in the English-speaking world. A decade before all of these men had been ardent defenders of liberal Christianity. Now they were writing about its shortcomings and its demise.

Niebuhr, in particular, argued for a more realistic understanding of human nature and destiny. Like the continental theologians, Niebuhr turned to the personal, dramatic, and historical thought-forms of biblical revelation rather than to philosophical reflection for his answers. Niebuhr's apologetic concerns, however, alienated him from Barth and allied him more closely with the thinking of Emil Brunner. The most striking difference between Niebuhr and the continental theologians in general, however, was one of focus. The continental theology was primarily addressed to the church; Niebuhr turned his theology outward upon the world. More than any other post-Liberal theologian, Niebuhr played the role of the prophet in bringing social and cultural institutions under the critical reflection of Christian truth. Niebuhr was critical of Barth's preoccupation with transcendence and eschatology, which, he believed, made Barth's theology ineffective in challenging the assumptions of modern secularists. Niebuhr's efforts to persuade secularists to re-examine and reconsider the content and significance of Christian belief, however, was matched by his passion to unmask religious illusions and pretensions within the church. The application of biblical realism, he believed, must be extended to the church as well as the world.

Reinhold Niebuhr's effectiveness as a prophetic apologist, both within the context of the culture and the church, eminently qualifies him to represent the post-Liberal apologetic tradition. Emil Brunner and Edwin Lewis, the American Methodist theologian, were also notable defenders of the faith in the Neo-orthodox tradition, but it is generally accepted that Niebuhr spoke with the stronger voice and exercized the greater apologetic influence upon the skeptics and secularists of his day.

A Full-orbed Apologetic

C. S. Lewis, Edward John Carnell, and Reinhold Niebuhr represent an impressive aggregate because they bring together a full-orbed (comprehensive) defense of the Christian faith. Each contributed something different but essential to the whole life perspective of the Christian religion. Together, they addressed virtually every major dimension of human concern—the moral and the practical as well as the cognitive and the affective.

C. S. Lewis's effectiveness as a Christian communicator was largely due to his ability to combine reason with imagination in a manner that made him the great imaginative apologist of this century. Before his conversion Lewis's life was pulled in opposite directions by his rationalist and romantic interests, but after his conversion these faculties were united as complementing organs of truth and meaning in Lewis's understanding of the Christian vision. The factual and the historical, Lewis believed, needs the mythical and imaginative element that makes the knowable meaningful. The function of myth is to enable one to appreciate the power and beauty of truth.

As an apologist Lewis emphasized the importance of objective truth and value. His primary concern was always the truth question. He repeatedly found that popular audiences seldom understood that he was recommending the Christian faith because its claims were objectively true. Most were more concerned with whether or not the faith was comforting, inspiring, or socially useful. Lewis often found it necessary to remind his audiences that he was not recommending the faith because he "approved of it" but because it is *true*. The imagination is vital, however, because it provides a picture that enables the reason to grasp what the objective truth is and what it means. Lewis's reasoned efforts to demonstrate the truth of the Christian faith found wide acceptance because he almost always depicted the truth in some form of concrete imagery or metaphor that captivated the reader. Even when he was speaking about theological and philosophical issues that readers normally find dull and prosaic, Lewis seemed always to know how to present them in an imaginative way. Instead of saying things like, "We must be spiritually regenerated," he said: "We're like eggs at present. And you can't go on indefinitely being an ordinary, decent egg. We must be hatched or go bad."[4]

Lewis was almost never accused of being irrelevant because he consistently presented the truth in a manner that was related to life. He knew how to give secular forms a sense of sacredness and transcendence. There was a kind of "pagan holiness" in Lewis that drew common things into the radiance of the transcendent and made secular persons desire them. The great literary evangelist skillfully used his craft as a satirist, allegorist, novelist, and fiction writer to cultivate in his readers a "taste for the other." We can never be truly fulfilled, he claimed, apart from God and others. It is the "taste for the other" that draws us out of ourselves and restores us to our true humanity.

C. S. Lewis was a modern sage who skillfully and convincingly introduced the wisdom of the ages into the human condition. The power of the true, the good, and the beautiful were so persuasively interrelated in Lewis's writings that skeptics and "half-believers" were often won over as much by his manner as by the substance of his thought.

Edward John Carnell, on the other hand, was more of a Christian philosopher and theologian. His primary objective was to convince his students and readers that it was reasonable to accept the tenets of orthodox Christianity in the twentieth century. In his defense of biblical Christianity Carnell appealed primarily to the law of non-contradiction and secondarily to the facts of science and history in the attempt to demonstrate that the faith is systematically consistent. He appealed to axiology, however, as well as logic in order to show that those who reject the evidence are foolish as well as inconsistent. The strength of the Christian claim is that it can satisfy both the heart and the mind; it is grounded in a coherent perspective that provides a basis for both consistency and wisdom.

In his later work Carnell broadened his apologetic beyond the realm of facts and truth claims in order to make room for a form of knowledge that he described as "the third method of knowing" and "the judicial sentiment." The apologetic that Carnell developed on the basis of these concepts acknowledged the epistemic limitations of philosophy and science as a source of truth and moved into a more subjective analysis of humanity's moral predicament. The significance of this transition was that it shifted the emphasis from truth as systematic consistency to truth as "being"—truth in the heart that allows the existing individual to relate to God in personal fellowship. It is infinitely more important, Carnell acknowledged, to "be the truth" than it is simply to "know the truth." The real person is the moral person who comes into being as he or she mediates eternity in time through passionate ethical decision. This kind of truth, "truth as moral rectitude," comes into being, however, only when God—not humans—closes the the gap between what one is and what one ought to be. The moral imperative then has only one adequate answer. That answer is the righteousness of Jesus Christ.

Christianity is always relevant, Carnell stressed, because it addresses the whole person in the totality of one's fourfold environment. It speaks to humans and their needs as physical, aesthetic, rational, and moral/ spiritual creatures. God has so tempered truth together, Carnell argued, that no single locus may say to another, "I have no need of you." The Christian answer is convincing because it allows the whole person to be harmoniously related both to the universe that is over and against one and to the totality of one's own person within.

Few, if any, apologists spoke to the open heart more forcibly than C. S. Lewis and Edward John Carnell about the enduring standards of the true, the good, and the beautiful. Brilliant as they were, however, there was a missing motif in both of these apologists that prevented them from addressing the social and economic problems that masses of people face every day. Peter Kreeft put his finger on that missing element in a critical essay on Lewis that took note of Lewis's weaknesses as well as his strengths. Kreeft noted that, "Eldils are irrelevant to subway strikes and fair housing laws, however much more interesting. It is difficult to imagine a Harlem slum dweller 'relating' to Lewis," Kreeft said, "though whether this is too bad for Lewis or too bad for Harlem is another question. Lewis tells us how to live in his fictional worlds, in the medieval world, even in any world, but not how to live in *this* world. He offers no Christian sociology, politics, or economics."[5]

The same criticism could just as well be directed at Carnell. Worldviews should fit what we know about the external world as well as what we know about ourselves. But there is another test. They must work in the laboratory of life. Like yeast in bread, true religion must permeate political and social structures and demonstrate its capacity for prophetic criticism and social change. A full-orbed apologetic must do more than engage in or even reformulate thinking about the social role of religion. It must, as one social critic observed, be able to "translate theologies of social change into active, practical movements which engage the energies and resources of traditional religious institutions and their popular constituencies."[6]

The strength of Reinhold Niebuhr's apologetic was that it contained an incentive for Christian social action as well as an intellectual defense of the Christian perspective. On the one hand, Niebuhr recognized the importance of bringing the theological and ethical insights of the Christian faith to bear upon the thought processes of modern society. On the other hand, he realized that the traditional manner of doing intellectual apologetics and engaging in philosophical debate would not be enough. The forces of prejudice, exploitation, and injustice that depersonalize persons in a modern industrial society cannot be engaged wholly on the intellectual level. Christians are not merely called to explain the world but to change it.

Against those who said that biblical religion had outlived its function in the modern world, Niebuhr argued that Judeo-Christian suppositions always remain vital because they are what preserve the integrity of human personality. Naturalism, the presupposition of modern society, depersonalizes humans, the universe, and nature. In order to preserve the sanctity of human personality, however, Christians must do more than defend their belief in a personal God. They must demonstrate their concern for personality by bringing their resources to bear upon the forces that seek to rob humanity of its humaneness. The concept of a personal God is only viable to modern persons so long as those who believe in God give credence to that view by working for a more just and humane society. In one of his earliest works, Niebuhr wrote:

> The fact is that more men in our modern era are irreligious because religion has failed to make civilization ethical than because it has failed to maintain its intellectual respectibility. For every person who disavows religion because some ancient and unrevised dogma outrages his intelligence, several become irreligious because the social impotence of religion outrages their conscience.[7]

Niebuhr recognized that meaningful social action called for a realistic understanding of the depth and complexity of sin both in man and society. Liberalism's illusions and self-deceptions regarding the essential goodness of humanity and inevitable social progress had to be punctured. The key to understanding the ethical situation was a more adequate view of the human condition. The Social Gospel movement was hopelessly grounded in a liberal optimism that expected social relations to be progressively brought under the law of Christ on the basis of education and goodwill. The realistic view, Niebuhr urged, was the biblical understanding of humans as sinners. This does not mean that humans are necessarily sinful in all that they do for they are created in the image of God and capable of rising above their natural limitations through the use of their God-given freedom. In their freedom, however, the creatures inevitably refuse to acknowledge their creatureliness and assert their independence from God through pride of power, intellect, and moral superiority. Therein lies humanity's sin and an understanding of the self-interest and will to power that persons exercize in order to dominate others. Sin arises out of humanity's insecurity and expresses itself through the misuse of human freedom. It cannot be rightfully attributed to environment, the devil, or any influence outside of the self. Persons must take responsibility for their own sin and the social problems that it creates. The same biblical source that provides a realistic insight into the human dilemma, however, also provides the realistic answer to the problem. That answer is the grace for transformation and change that God has revealed in Jesus Christ.

In Christ Christians find the resources of love, wisdom, and power through which they can be restored to God, self, and others. Christ is the "center of history," the disclosure of God's kingdom and purpose. In him, God discloses the law of love that provides both the norm and the motive for all of life and for social action. Love, as the ethical ideal, is never fully realized in this world. No amount of human achievement can ever realize what God must fulfill from "beyond history." But neither is it possible for true love to allow tyranny and social injustice to go unopposed. In an unloving and unregenerate world love must be transposed into a perpetual quest for approximate social justice. Love continually raises systems of justice to new, more demanding, heights. Justice, as the embodiment of love in a sinful world, keeps love practical and unsentimental. Because every struggle for justice involves efforts to secure a more equal distribution of power in society, it usually entails the use of political and economic means of power in order to achieve its ends. It is the willingness to use power and interest in the service of an end dictated by love that saves the Christian ethic from complacency and despair. The recognition that one's own best intentions are always tainted by sinful self-interest, on the other hand, saves the Christian realist from self-righteousness.

Addressing the Mood of the Times

Historians tell us that at the time of the Bolshevik revolution in Russia the leadership of the Russian Orthodox Church was assembled at a conference called to discuss liturgical vestments. The topic being discussed was, of course, important and relevant to the clergy of the church, but it was hardly the pressing issue that needed to be addressed at that critical time in Russian history. It is conceivable that Russian Christians might well have made more of a mark on the direction of their country, and perhaps the world, had they been more attuned to the mood of the time.

If Christians are to be the "light" and the "leaven" that Christ charged them to be, they must take responsibility for shaping the faith and mission of the church in the world. Christians cannot claim the center for their faith when they are living and working on the boundaries of the real world. They must be sensitive to the thoughts, needs, anxieties, and temptations of those who need their message. Paul Tillich was never more on target than when he suggested that the church must be a listening as well as a speaking body. It has to be sensitive to the mood of the times, to listen intently to the questions that are being asked, and feel the anxieties and injustices that real people experience. When it does not listen, when it does not feel, the church inevitably isolates itself into a spiritual ghetto of its own making—cut off from those for whom Christ died and who need his message of hope. Relevance, as an apologetic imperative, does not mean that the Christian message has to be presented through contemporary idioms, or that Christian action has to be channeled through godless secular means. It simply means that the Christian apologist must come to grips with problems as they are being experienced, and questions that are currently being asked by those who sincerely desire a reason for the hope that lies within the believer (1 Pet 3:15).

C. S. Lewis, Edward John Carnell, and Reinhold Niebuhr were truly contemporary Christian apologists in this sense. They were contemporary because they were in touch with their time and stood ready to speak the historic Christian message into the situations they encountered. They were Christian because their primary concern was to be faithful to the message of the Christian revelation that they knew to be the answer to the human dilemma. The three apologists did not have the same understanding of the character of biblical authority (we will have more to say about that later), but they were all secure enough in their convictions concerning its truth claims that they were willing to subject it to the demands of public verification. They were convinced that Christians can enter into the problematics of philosophy, the social and natural sciences, and all other academic and social challenges with the full assurance that no real contradiction will ever exist between what true reason discovers and the truth that has been revealed through the Christian faith.

When Augustine spoke of our hearts being restless until they find their rest in God, he was primarily speaking about the longings of love in the depths of our being. But it is also true that our intellectual restlessness can only be fulfilled in God. As Bernard Lonergan has noted, the quest of the intellect, no less than that of the heart, is the quest for God. Anselm spoke of theology as "faith seeking understanding," but the search of the modern truth-seeker could perhaps be more aptly described in terms of "understanding in search of a faith."[8]

Lewis, Carnell, and Niebuhr were in essential agreement as well that human existence is itself a witness to the truth of the Christian message. It is no denigration of revelation, nor a reduction of theology to anthropology, to admit that God's answers are meaningful to human experience. Revelation is not some truth falling into an empty space, but into a space that is already filled with human searching. From the apologetic point of view the image of God in humanity means that a point of contact has already been established between God and persons. The gospel does not turn to a person who knows nothing about God, but it speaks to one who already knows that the gospel proclamation is saying something that has to be taken seriously. The Christian does not have to throw answers at the listener's head. The Christian can confidently start with the listener, with the human situation, allowing one's skepticism, helplessness, and despair to make evident the need for an answer than lies outside oneself. The Christian's encounter with doubt and unbelief is not like a debate in which it is assumed by both sides that the other knows nothing of the truth. It is more like a discussion in which it is assumed that the other party already knows something of the truth.

The twentieth century has been a critical time for Christian apologetics. The challenge of setting forth the Christian message in as relevant a manner as possible, without compromising its unchanging truth, has been as great an apologetic challenge as Christians have faced in the history of the Christian church. What has been a time of unparalleled challenge, however, has also been one of great opportunity for the missionary theologians of the church. Scores of outstanding apologetic evangelists have stepped forward to meet this tremendous challenge. All of them deserve our gratitude. C. S. Lewis, Edward John Carnell, and Reinhold Niebuhr have been chosen to represent those richly varied apologetic traditions that were committed to the communication and defense of the Christian faith to the sincere truth-seekers of their generation. They were major voices who deeply influenced their own time and who will continue to be heard as we move into the twenty-first century.

Notes

[1]C. S. Lewis, *Mere Christianity* (New York: Macmillan Co., 1971) 6.

[2]Lyle W. Dorsett, ed., *The Essential C.S. Lewis* (New York: Macmillan Co., 1988) 348.

[3]Bob E. Patterson, *Carl F. H. Henry* (Waco TX: Word Books, 1983) 14, 15.

[4]Peter Kreeft, *C. S. Lewis: A Critical Essay* (Front Royal VA: Christendom College Press, 1988) 17.

[5]Ibid. 65.

[6]Roger A. Johnson, *Critical Issues in Modern Religion* (Englewood Cliffs NJ: Prentice Hall, 1989) 234.

[7]Reinhold Niebuhr, *Does Civilization Need Religion?* (New York: Macmillan, 1928) 12.

[8]John Polkinghorne, *Science and Creation: The Search for Understanding* (London: SPCK, 1988) 32.

Part One: C. S. Lewis

Introduction

1. From Atheist to Christian Scholar

   A. The Journey
   B. Loss of Faith
   C. Atheism Reinforced
   D. The Oxford Experience
   E. Toward Conversion
   F. The Oxford Don

2. In Defense of Supernaturalism

   A. The Great Communicator
   B. Clues to the Meaning of the Universe
      1. The Moral Law
      2. The Quest for Fulfillment
   C. The Miraculous
   D. The Grand Miracle
   E. The Fitness of Miracles
   F. Miracles Old and New
      1. Miracles of the Old Creation
      2. Miracles of the New Creation
   G. The Problem of Pain
      1. Natural Evil
      2. Moral Evil
   H. Lewis's Personal Experience with Grief

3. In Defense of Permanent Things

   A. The Loss of Permanent Truth and Value
      1. Evolutionism
      2. Historicism
   B. The Poison of Subjectivity
   C. The Magician's Bargain
   D. Men without Chests
   E. A Theology for Monday Morning

Selected Bibliography

Introduction

The assasination of John F. Kennedy on 22 November 1963 over-shadowed all else that happened on that fateful morning. C. S. Lewis's death the same afternoon at his home in the Kilns, just outside of Oxford, went virtually unnoticed.

Twenty-five years after his death, however, Lewis's legacy as a Christian writer, scholar, and apologist refuses to die. Today, he is widely regarded as one of this century's most effective Christian apologists. Every Lewis enthusiast remembers him for some special piece of litera-ture. Some are especially fond of the Narnia stories, while others are drawn to his science fiction trilogy. Many were introduced to Lewis through the *Screwtape Letters, Mere Christianity*, or some other favorite work. Regardless of their literary preference, however, Lewis's readers continue to find his writings fresh and relevant. This is borne out by the fact that he is still the most popular Christian writer being published.

The old "dinosaur," as he called himself, has escaped extinction. Trendy theologies and pop theologians have come and gone, but Lewis's works retain an ongoing vitality. He is still being read because he addressed the central issues—the things that matter most about the Christian faith.

A Christian apologist is often popular because he is able to make some sympathetic contact with the thought of his age and commend the Christian faith to his contemporaries on the merits of its relevance. That was only true for Lewis, however, to a limited extent. He was too critical of the presuppositions of his age to play much of a priestly role. His work as an apologist was more like that of a relentless prophet, unmercilessly exposing and condemning the inadequacy of contemporary thought forms.

Lewis seriously questioned whether Western civilization could even survive under its present set of assumptions. How could any civilization survive without enduring standards? It is easy enough to live in an age of scientific "positivism" where science and technology promise to supply all of our wants, but can they ensure humanity's survival in the absence of permanent truths and values? Lewis did not think so.

C. S. Lewis confessed to being both an "old fashioned" Christian and an "old Western man." He did not confuse one with the other, but he did contend that there was a necessary relationship between the two. The survival of worthwhile Western values depended on the preservation of the core assumptions in the Christian worldview. He recognized that Western man had come to a time when God and permanent things had been relegated to the past as some kind of antiquated irrelevancy. Belief in objective truth and value was as extinct as the dinosaurs. But it was time, he believed, for a case to be made for the legitimate place of dinosaurs in the modern world.

For all their differences, Lewis noted, Christians and pagans at least shared important predispositions that are lacking in modern man. Both believed in the supernatural, were conscious of sin and divine judgment, and had some kind of redemptive hope. "In the last hundred years," he said, "the public mind has been so radically altered . . . that we must try to convert [a world] that shares none of those predispositions." Lewis had no desire to return to some idyllic past. That was neither possible nor desirable. But he did believe that the mental climate in which the modern evangelist has to work is such that a re-conversion to the basic assumptions of the pagan may be a preliminary first step in pointing modern persons back to Christianity.

I.
From Atheist to Christian Scholar

Walter Hooper, C. S. Lewis's biographer and longtime friend, called Lewis "the most thoroughly converted man he had ever met." He was not referring to a solitary religious experience but to Lewis's unselfish manner of living and his conversion to a wholistic vision of life.

There was, however, another aspect of Lewis's conversion that was more like a religious experience. It was not as dramatic as the Apostle Paul's Damascus road experience, as emotionally charged as John Wesley's Aldersgate, or as intellectually transforming as Augustine's experience in the garden at Milan. But it was the climactic event on a spiritual journey that Lewis had been traveling for some time. Lewis described his conversion as being like an unexpected arrival at a place for which one had longed, or, more precisely, like meeting a person whom one longed to meet but was not sure existed.

This final moment in his conversion took place on a sunny fall morning in 1931 as Lewis and his brother Warren set out by motorcycle for a visit to a nearby zoo. In his autobiography, *Surprised by Joy*, Lewis described what happened:

> I know very well when, but hardly how, the final step was taken . . . When we set out I did not believe that Jesus Christ is the Son of God, and when we reached the zoo I did. Yet I had not exactly spent the journey in thought. Nor in great emotion. . . . It was more like when a man, after long sleep, still lying motionless in bed, becomes aware that he is now awake.[1]

The story of Lewis's intellectual odyssey from atheism to Christianity, from being a literary scholar to becoming this century's most renowned Christian apologist, is one of the great stories of the twentieth century.[2]

The Journey

Clive Staples Lewis was born in Belfast, Ireland, the second son of Albert and Flora Lewis, on 29 November 1898. The Lewis home was nominally Christian but lacked the warmth and vitality that one usually expects from Christian experience. The two boys were made to say their prayers, were taken to church, and were expected to accept the tenets of the Christian faith that they had been taught. But neither expressed much interest in religion. What Lewis favorably remembered from his childhood were not religious experiences but good parents, good food, a garden he enjoyed playing in, and a kind and gentle nurse named Lizzie Endicott who kindled his imagination with stories and fairy tales. His brother Warren was his closest friend and became his lifelong confidant.

One of the strongest early influences on Lewis was "Little Lea," his boyhood home. Lewis wrote about "Little Lea" as though it had personality. "I am the product," he wrote," of long corridors, empty sunlit rooms, upstair indoor silences, attics explored in solitude . . . also of endless books."[3] His powers of imagination were stirred very early by fairy tales told by his nurse and from books he read in the family library. The works of Beatrix Potter, Lewis Carroll, Edith Nesbit, and animal cartoons from old volumes of *Punch* gave Lewis endless pleasures when inclement weather prevented the boys from exploring the surrounding countryside. His first introduction to romance, the literary genre he loved most, was Mark Twain's *A Connecticut Yankee in King Arthur's Court* and the *Arthurian* stories. Lewis wrote his first stories in the attic of "Little Lea" and illustrated them with his own drawings or pictures cut from magazines. His chief literary pleasures were "dressed animals" and "knights-in-armour."

Shortly before his tenth birthday, Lewis's mother died of cancer. He never forgot the shock of learning about her illness, and the disappointment that followed a period of hopeful convalescence seemed to destroy his faith in the power of the "magician" God that he prayed would save her. Neither Albert Lewis or the boys ever fully recovered from her death. "All settled happiness, all that was tranquil and reliable disappeared from my life," Lewis recalled. "The great continent had sunk like Atlantis."[4] Lewis's father was devastated. He became moody and no longer seemed capable of providing a pleasant atmosphere in the home. His cold mannerisms soon distanced him from the boys and made them to feel rebuffed. The estrangement they felt from their father seemed to draw the boys closer to each other and, no doubt, contributed to the bonds of brotherly love and loyalty that lasted throughout their lives.

The following September Albert sent young Lewis across the Irish Sea to England where he began his studies at Wynyard in Hertfordshire. Wynyard was the first of his educational experiences in a succession of boarding schools. This one, however, turned out to be the worst of all. The instruction was straightforward and factual but boring and lacking in challenge. To make matters worse, the headmaster was a brutal uncaring man who was later declared insane. Lewis referred to this school in his autobiography as the "concentration camp." He did remember Wynyard, however, as the place where he first began to pray seriously and read his Bible.

Shortly thereafter Lewis entered Campbell College near his home in Ireland, but his stay there was even shorter. An early illness forced him to return home for recuperation, and the next year he returned to England to study at Cherbourg, a preparatory school in Malvern. His school experiences there were more pleasant. As he immersed himself in Latin and English Lewis began to experience the joys of learning. His capacity for scholarship was becoming more evident but so too was the weakening of his faith. Young Lewis was entering early adolescence, and he was beginning to experience the full range of adolescent problems. He was adding intellectual muscle, but other experiences were moving him further and further away from his childhood faith.

Loss of Faith

John Wisdom, a well-known contemporary philosopher, noted that reasons for faith are more "like the legs of a chair than links of a chain."[5] One's faith, in other words, usually rests upon something more than a single support. Consequently, it is not as likely to be lost through a single break in the reasoning process as it is through the collapse of several supports. This was particularly true for young Lewis. During the two years that he spent at Malvern the shaky legs that supported his faith began to collapse under the weight of doubt and youthful experiences.

Thirteen-year-old boys are impressionable. Lewis was no exception. The matron at Malvern was a kind and gentle woman, a motherly type, whose influence strongly impacted the students. She was, however, an occultist, and Lewis became enthralled by her "spiritual" lust. There was no deliberate attempt to destroy Lewis's faith; her esoteric manner of religious searching simply seemed so speculative and exciting that conventional religion, by comparison, seemed dull and unattractive. The thrill of religious excitement without any corresponding behavioral demands had its appeal. Lewis described the experience:

> Little by little, unconsciously, unintentionally, she loosened the whole framework, blunted all the sharp edges, of my belief. The vagueness, the merely speculative character, of all this occultism began to spread—yes, and to spread deliciously—to the stern truths of the creed. The whole thing became a matter of speculation. I was soon . . . altering "I believe" to "one does feel." And oh, the relief of it.[6]

It was, in essence, more of an emotional than an intellectual attack on young Lewis's faith. At this point in his life he hardly knew how to separate "truth" from an emotional appeal to novelty and charm. He only knew that it felt good to be free from prescribed beliefs and behaviors.

Lewis was, at the same time, undergoing a crisis with guilt reminiscent of young Martin Luther's experience in the sixteenth century. One will recall that Luther experienced more guilt than he could bear as he painfully discovered that he could not do enough good works to please God. The more he did, the more he realized what he had left undone. He always felt guilt over not having done enough. Lewis had a similar experience at Malvern. He was plagued by such high expectations of himself that the practice of his religion became burdensome, even impossible. Prayer, for example, became an impossible task because he always questioned whether or not he was really thinking about what he was saying as he should. There was no peace, no joy, in the practice of his religion. It had become a laborious, guilt-ridden exercise.

Lewis's exposure to non-Christian religions also began to challenge his faith in the uniqueness of Christian truth. As he delved more deeply into the classical authors, especially Virgil, he encountered a mass of religious ideas that seemed strikingly similar to those of the Christian faith. What most Christians assumed was that even though the myths and themes of the pagans were similar to those contained in the Bible, the pagan stories could be dismissed as illusory and nonsensical. Christianity, of course, was accepted as an exception. What troubled Lewis was that no one bothered to offer a reasoned explanation of why Christianity should be regarded as a true exception. As Lewis put it,

No one ever attempted to show in what sense Christianity fulfilled Paganism or Paganism prefigured Christianity. The accepted position seemed to be that religions were normally a mere farrago of nonsense, though our own, by a fortunate exception, was exactly true.[7]

The evidence, at the time, led Lewis to a different conclusion. He concluded, with many others who did comparative studies of religion, that Christianity was not unique. It, too, was a mere product of religious evolution and belonged to the relativity of its time and place in human history. "It obviously was in some general sense the same kind of thing as all the rest. Why was it so differently treated? Need I," Lewis asked, "continue to treat it differently? I was very anxious not to," he said.[8]

Lucretius, the Latin author, confirmed Lewis's growing conviction that no religion could save man from a menacing and unfriendly universe. His so-called "Argument from Undesign" had a convincing ring:

Had God designed the world, it would not be
A world so frail and faulty as we see.

Lewis's own adolescent clumsiness seemed to confirm his conviction that we live in a world where everything does what one does not want it to do. Humanity's struggle in a faulty world seemed to be evidence enough that no friendly, perfect Deity stood behind such shoddy workmanship.

Adolescence is usually the time when one first feels the full force of worldly temptation, what is often described as the "world," the "flesh," and the "devil." The effectiveness of such temptation is doubled when it happens to occur in conjunction with one's willful withdrawal from divine protection. This was precisely what happened to Lewis. A young teacher at the preparatory school, whom Lewis called "Pogo," introduced the boys to vulgarity and worldly wisdom through off-color jokes and his questionable lifestyle in the local town. Lewis confessed,

What attacked me through Pogo was not the flesh (I had that of my own) but the world: the desire for glitter, swagger, distinction, the desire to be in the know. He [Pogo] gave little help, if any, in destroying my chastity, but he made sad work of certain humble and childlike and self-forgetful qualities which (I think) had remained with me till that moment. I began to labor very hard to make myself into a fop, a cad, and a snob.[9]

Lewis felt the full weight of the world's pull and the adversary's temptation, but in retrospect he never attributed his loss of faith to external forces. He always took seriously the responsibility for personal choice. The root problem, he admitted, was his desire to be emancipated from God, to rid himself of God's intervention in his life. Lewis wanted no divine intrusion into his private world. He would later learn from George MacDonald, one of his favorite authors, that the one principle of hell is—"I am my own." This lesson became one of the central themes in Lewis's writings. He never regarded hell as a threat or heaven a bribe. They are the consequence of the choices that we make. Lewis later wrote in *Mere Christianity* that

> every time you make a choice you are turning the central part of you, the part of you that chooses, into something a little different from what it was before. . . . [A]ll your life long you are slowly turning this central thing either into a heavenly creature or into a hellish creature: either into a creature that is in harmony with God, and with other creatures, and with itself, or else into one that is in a state of war and hatred with God, and with its fellow creatures, and with itself.[10]

The latter state was the one that Lewis felt he had begun to create for himself at Malvern.

Almost simultaneously with the loss of his faith Lewis discovered the music of Wagner through an illustrated copy of *Seigfried and the Twilight of the Gods*. He became fascinated with Norse and Celtic mythology. His discovery of "Northernness" revived earlier romantic longings, and a search for "Joy" intensified. The myths and romance of the North contained an element of mystery and depth that Lewis found lacking in many religions, including Christianity. After he became a Christian he used this point of comparison to suggest to the Socratic Club at Oxford that the Gospels were surely more than myth and legend. If they were not history, they were certainly inferior forms of myth. "If Christianity is only a mythology," he said, "then I find that the mythology I believe in is not the mythology I like best. I like Greek mythology much better: Irish better still: Norse best of all."[11] On another occasion he described himself as one who "loved Balder before he loved Christ." Lewis was a professional literary critic with a keen sense for myth and legend. These sensibilities made him leery of biblical critics who were prone to regard any biblical narrative as unhistorical simply on the grounds that it included the miraculous. Most biblical critics, he argued, were not really good at recognizing myth or legend. Lewis contended that "the Gospels were certainly not legends (in one sense they are not good enough): if they are not history then they are realistic prose fiction of a kind which actually never existed before the eighteenth century."[12]

During his youth Lewis's imagination was vivid. He created imaginative stories about the political history of an animal land called "Boxen" and even tried his hand at writing a tragedy in Greek form about Norse gods. *Loki Bound*, as it was called, reflected his atheistic and pessimistic mood at the time. Lewis assures us in his autobiography, however, that he never mistook imagination for reality. Northernness and nature were simply mediums through which he aspired for real Joy. It was essentially a desire, partly a creation, through which he hoped to find a fulfilling object. But it was not to be—at least, not yet.

Atheism Reinforced

Lewis's teachers at Cherbourg recognized his creative and scholarly abilities. When he completed his work at the preparatory school he was offered a scholarship to study classics at Malvern College. He entered the college, but his stay there only lasted one year. His father had bigger plans. He decided to send him to "Kirk," a close family friend and scholar, whom he trusted to get young Lewis ready for the entrance examination at Oxford. The next two years of Lewis's life would be spent with W. T. Kirkpatrick, the Scotsman, who was affectionately called "the Great Knock."

In many ways it was a fortunate experience for Lewis. Kirkpatrick was an excellent scholar and a stern logician who expected a reasoned explanation for even the most casual statement. Under the "Great Knock's" tutelage Lewis learned to balance imagination with reason. "If ever a man came near to being a logical entity," Lewis recalled, "that man was Kirk." Born a little later, Lewis was convinced, the "Great Knock" would have been a Logical Positivist. "The idea that human beings should exercise their vocal organs for any purpose except that of communicating truth was to him preposterous,"[13]

Lewis learned from Kirkpatrick the importance of insisting on the question of truth. He never allowed his young student to succumb to the twentieth-century fallacy of substituting questions of desire or goodness for the question of truth. This lesson later helped Lewis recognize that Christianity presents us with a truth claim that, if false, is of no importance. But if it is true, it is of infinite importance. The one thing it cannot be is moderately important, and it cannot possibly be desirous or good if it is not true.

Kirkpatrick, however, was more than a logician. He was a disciplinarian who demanded good work habits from his students. It was the greatest intellectual challenge Lewis had faced, but he welcomed the challenge. He arrived at the Kirkpatrick home on a Saturday; on Monday he began reading Homer in the original Greek. Lewis made steady progress in Greek and was soon tackling original works in Latin, German, and Italian as well. In the evenings Mrs. Kirkpatrick was tutoring Lewis in French, and before long he was reading French novels on his own. He had a love and aptitude for learning languages, and the scope of his reading, for a sixteen year old, was remarkable. Within a short while he was reading Demosthenes, Cicero, Lucretius, Catullus, Tacitus, Herodotus, Virgil, Euripides, Sophocles, and Aeschylus in the original languages. Compositions in Greek and Latin were expected regularly. He never felt that he had crossed his proverbial Rubicon, however, until he discovered that he was beginning to "think" in Greek.

All the while Lewis was also immersing himself in the great classics of English and American literature. During this period he read George MacDonald's *Phantastes*, which he said "baptised" his imagination. He had always been waist deep in romanticism, but now he plunged into *Sir Gawain and the Green Knight, Beowulf, Tristan, The Song of Roland, The Faerie Queen*, and other works in the romantic genre.

Lewis was a young atheist before he went to Bookham, but he found a great deal in Kirkpatrick's thinking that reinforced his unbelief. Kirkpatrick's atheism was an atheism born from Schopenhauer's pessimism and Frazier's *Golden Bough*. The current opinion of anthropologists like Frazier was that Christianity was like all other primitive religions. It had no real uniqueness. Its myth about a dying and rising God was merely humanity's primitive invention and could be accounted for on evolutionary, naturalistic grounds. Lewis wrote to his close friend Arthur Greeves that "All religions, that is all mythologies, to give them their proper name, are merely man's own invention—Christ as much as Loki."[14]

The Oxford Experience

The two years that Lewis spent under the tutelage of Kirkpatrick were rigorous but pleasant. In later years he looked back on them with a deep sense of appreciation for what he had learned from the "Great Knock." When Kirkpatrick thought he was ready, it was arranged for Lewis to sit for an examination for a scholarship at Oxford.

Oxford university is made up of many colleges. Each college selects its own students, subject only to minimal educational qualifications laid down by the university. Lewis was well prepared to work toward his goal of becoming a poet and romance writer, but, as he later admitted, the two sides of his brain did not work equally well. He won a scholarship to University College but failed to pass the mathematics requirement for general admission to the university. Fortunately for Lewis, however, the university was making some exceptions because it was wartime.

In 1916 things were not going well for the allies. Because he was an Irishman, Lewis had the privilege of claiming exemption from wartime service, but he wanted to enlist. By entering Oxford he could join the Officer's Training Corps and obtain a commission. In 1917 Lewis entered the famed university where he would spend most of his adult life. Oxford was an ideal place for a scholar with Lewis's sensibilities and intellect. He was awed by its cluster of spires and towers and the almost endless row of bookstores that lined the main street. The Bodleian library was ideal for the serious student, and nearby pubs provided a cozy atmosphere for friends to meet for stimulating talk. Oxford was surrounded by natural pastoral beauty. It was a world of gardens, forests populated with deer, the famed Addison's walk, and rivers and ponds for swimming and boating. It would become Lewis's second "Little Lea."

When he first arrived, half of the college had been converted into a hospital. A small community of undergraduates was living in the other half. Lewis's battalion was quartered at Keble College, so he did not have to leave the university for his training. In a few short weeks Lewis completed his training, was commissioned a second lieutenant, and sent directly to the warfront. He arrived at the trenches in France on his nineteenth birthday but soon fell ill with trench fever and had to be hospitalized. After a period of recuperation he returned to the front lines but was wounded by an exploding shell. None of his wartime experiences, however, shook Lewis's unbelief. He had none of the propensities for "foxhole" religion. During this time he wrote that "he was convinced the gods hate me—and naturally enough considering my usual attitude toward them."[15]

Lewis's belief in moral responsibility was not wedded to his belief in God. Long before he became a Christian, or even a theist, Lewis felt an obligation to moral duty. It was as though he viewed moral responsibility as something woven into the very fabric of the universe. His own sense of moral responsibility was manifested through the death of a wartime friend. His roommate during army training was a young soldier named "Paddy" Moore. Through Paddy, Lewis had become acquainted with Paddy's widowed mother and her daughter Maureen. When Paddy was killed in the war, Lewis committed himself to care for Paddy's mother and sister as though they were his own family. It was a truly remarkable act of loyalty toward a friend to whom Lewis felt a moral obligation. For thirty years he cared for Paddy's dependents as he would his own mother and sister.

When Lewis returned to Oxford after the war, it was as though he had returned to his natural habitat. But there were some surprises in store for Lewis, not the least of which was the postwar presence at Oxford of a number of outstanding scholars and intellectuals who were committed Christians. Many of them were thoroughgoing supernaturalists. Men like Nevill Coghill, J. R. R. Tolkien, A. K. Hamilton Jenkins, and Owen Barfield soon kindled a desire in Lewis to look more deeply into an intellectual basis for theism. Throughout the decade of the twenties Lewis remained an atheist, but it was a time of searching and discovery. The Christian thinkers he met at Oxford helped clear away some of the intellectual obstacles that had hindered his spiritual progress. Perhaps more than anything else, they presented a formidable challenge to his unexamined atheism.

Toward Conversion

The college years are a time when many turn away from their faith in God. For Lewis, it was a gradual movement in the opposite direction. He had already plumbed the depths of doubt; he was now ready at least to consider the possibilities of faith. Lewis was a mature enough thinker to know that the priviledge of holding bold doubts carries with it the responsibility of pursuing the facts. The "facts," however, are not always readily obvious; they often take time to emerge.

Some persons think of conversion as a moment, a point in time, when spiritual birth occurs. Lewis experienced such a moment the day he and Warren visited the zoo. But many Christians recognize that conversion is also a process. C. S. Lewis had been prepared for his conversion sometime before it actually happened. Lewis was fond of swimming in the local ponds, and his writings note that the summer before his conversion he learned to *dive*. He used the metaphor of "diving" as a way of saying that he had to learn how to "let go" and hold nothing back. Letting go is the last thing one does before the plunge. The struggle is in the process before the moment. One has to dive in order to experience the reality of the water, but only a fool would dive into an empty pond. In order to believe, Lewis needed the consent of all his faculties. But he also had to learn how to let go and trust in God as a fathomless mystery beyond rational analysis.

Lewis was being seriously challenged by Christian intellectuals at Oxford to reconsider some of his views. What he discovered was that much of what he had accepted as fact was little more than biased opinion. Many of the so-called facts that mitigated against the Christian faith were based on an uncritical acceptance of the "climate of opinion" that permeated academic circles.

The most pervasive overarching view in academia at the time was naturalism. As a philosophical and scientific worldview, naturalism held that nature is the "ultimate fact, the thing you cannot go behind," a "process in space and time that is going on of its own accord." Since, in this view, nature is the whole of reality, what we call "spirit" really belongs to the data of nature.[16] All religion, from a naturalistic perspective, is part of a natural phenomenon. Since there is no God, or anything outside of nature, human imagination takes the place of God and becomes the object of human worship. The new disciplines of archaeology and anthropology that were beginning to exert such a powerful influence were grounded in these naturalistic assumptions. They gave no creedence to special revelation or belief in the supernatural. Events that had formerly been accepted as supernatural happenings were explained as mythopoetic accounts of a primitive worldview. Students of comparative religion placed the biblical account of Jesus' death and resurrection in the same category as myths from other religions that told of "dying" and "rising" gods.

Lewis's acceptance of naturalism, with all of its implications for the Christian religion, began to be shaken through his own studies and a process of critical assessment sparked by his Oxford friends. At times, the criticism came from unsuspected sources. Lewis was surprised, for example, when the hardest boiled atheist he knew suggested that the Gospels seemed to be historically sound. "It almost looks as if it really happened once" [referring to Jesus' death and resurrection], his friend remarked. His unbelief was really shaken when he read G. K. Chesterton's *Everlasting Man*. For the first time he saw the Christian outline of history set out in a manner that made sense. He later spoke of Chesterton as one of the most sensible men alive.

In his reading of English literature Lewis discovered a Christian vision in men like Johnson, Spenser, Milton, and Herbert that made the worldview of skeptics like Shaw, Wells, Mill, Gibbon, and Voltaire seem "thin" by comparison. It began to dawn on him that there might be some relationship between theism and sound reasoning. His suspicion was reinforced by the fact that the most brilliant men he knew at Oxford were scholars who believed in supernatural religion.

At Oxford Lewis was being challenged to take another look at the facts, but just as importantly he was discovering a fellowship of believers that gave him the emotional and psychological support he needed to accept the new facts he was discovering. He learned that the strength one finds in a community of believers can be particularly important for those who are struggling with doubt and unbelief.

Those who are familiar with the history of Christian thought will recall that Augustine's search for truth led him through several schools of thought before he finally found what he was searching for in the Christian faith. His intellectual journey took him from Manichaeism to skepticism. From the emptiness of skepticism he moved to Neoplatonism, and finally he came under the influence of Ambrose who led him to Christianity. C. S. Lewis's journey likewise led him through a series of intellectual stages. One of the important turns in his pilgrimage occurred when he realized that what he yearned for was not some subjective state of mind but a reality that lay outside himself. Reading Samuel Alexander's *Space, Time, and Deity* helped convince him that the joy he longed for was not an end in itself but was merely a pointer to the absolute. Lewis first looked for the absolute in philosophy. His search started with Idealism; from there he moved to Pantheism. But he was never satisfied because the "God" he found through philosophy was not one with whom he could enter into personal relationship. "I thought," Lewis said, that "He projected us as a dramatist projects his characters, and I could no more 'meet' Him, than Hamlet could meet Shakespeare. I didn't call Him 'God' either; I called Him 'Spirit.' "[17]

The first part of Lewis's journey then was from atheism to theism. That part of his journey ended during the Trinity term of 1929 when he knelt in his room at Magdalen College and prayed. He admitted that God was God, but his conversion was not complete. He had not yet surrendered to the Christian truth of the Incarnation. From the beginning of his conversion to theism, however, Lewis respected the sovereignty of God. He insisted that we are under obligation to keep the moral law because God is God; His commands are inexorable. "If you ask why we should obey God, in the last resort," Lewis said, "the answer is, 'I am.' To know God is to know that our obedience is due to Him. In His nature His sovereignty *de jure* is revealed."[18] Lewis counted it among God's greatest mercies to have allowed him to know God and to attempt obedience for some time before he even raised the question of rewards or a future life.

In theism Lewis found what Rudolf Otto called the experience of the "numinous," the sense of awe that is common to all religions. He also found the source of the moral law, the sense of "oughtness" that is universally experienced. What he could not find through abstract thought was that truth in history in which all other historical truths are fulfilled. "The question," Lewis concluded, "was no longer to find the one simply true religion among a thousand religions simply false. It was rather, 'Where has religion reached its true maturity? Where, if anywhere, have the hints of all Paganism been fulfilled?' "[19] Of all possible answers, it seemed that there were only two viable alternatives: Hinduism or Christianity.

Lewis reduced to absurdity all other claims. Islam, he reasoned, was the greatest of the Christian heresies. Buddhism was the greatest of the Hindu heresies. Real paganism was dead. And the best in Judaism and Platonism survive in Christianity. Lewis divided all religions, like soups, into "Thick" and "Clear." By Thick he meant those religions that are grounded in earthly realities—religions that are strong on orgies, ecstasies, mysteries—religions of the heart and the belly. Africa, for example, is full of Thick religions. By Clear he meant those that are philosophical, ethical, and universalizing. Stoicism and Buddhism are Clear religions. Lewis concluded that one would expect the true religion to be both Thick and Clear "for the true God must have made both the child and the man, both the savage and the citizen, both the head and the belly."[20]

Christianity, he believed, fulfills this condition much more perfectly than Hinduism: "It takes a convert from central Africa and tells him to obey an enlightened universalist ethic: it takes a twentieth-century prig like me and tells me to go fasting to a Mystery, to drink the blood of the Lord. The savage convert has to be Clear: I have to be Thick. That is how one knows one has come to the real religion."[21]

Lewis's personal need was to thicken up, to come closer to the enfleshed historical Jesus. This, Lewis realized, was the direction the Holy Spirit had been taking him: "Every step I had taken, from the Absolute to 'Spirit' and from 'Spirit' to 'God,' had been a step toward the more concrete, the more immanent, the more compulsive. To accept the Incarnation was a further step in the same direction."[22]

Soon after he became a theist Lewis began to attend the college chapel on weekdays and his parish church on Sundays. He felt some obligation, he said, to signal his belief. This was when he began a serious reading of the Gospels. What he found there was not what most of the critics were saying. Instead of myths, he found an undiluted Christian faith grounded in historical fact. Lewis was a literary critic who had been immersed in myth since childhood. He had a feel for it. As a literary critic he could not pass the Gospels off as myths. "They had not the mythical taste," Lewis said. And yet, the very matter they conveyed "was precisely the matter of the great myth." He described the irony of what he found:

> If ever a myth had become fact, had been incarnated, it would be just like this. And nothing else in all literature was just like this. Myths were

like it in one way. Histories were like it in another. But nothing was simply like it. And no person was like the Person it depicted; as real, as recognizable, through all that depth of time, as Plato's Socrates or Boswell's Johnson . . . yet also numinous, lit by a light from beyond the world, a god. But if a god—then not a god, but God. Here and here only in all time the myth must have become fact; the Word, flesh; God, Man. This is not "a religion," nor "a philosophy." It is the summing up and actuality of them all.[23]

Mere belief in God carried with it no demands. Lewis liked that because what he had always desired was not to be "interfered with." Theism was safe, he declared, because it was immovably "there," but "It would never come 'here,' never (to be blunt) make a nuisance of Itself. . . . There was nothing to fear; better still, nothing to obey."[24] It was, in the words of Dietrich Bonhoeffer, a form of "cheap grace." Lewis discovered that a commitment to the incarnate Lord, on the other hand, brought more concrete demands. The most concrete demand of all was the surrender of self. It was a door that he would have to open from the inside, and in some mysterious way that Lewis never quite understood he managed to open it that morning on the way to the zoo.

When he did, he was surprised by joy. He was surprised because he never suspected any connection between God and his longing for joy. "I had hoped that the heart of reality might be of such a kind that we can best symbolize it as a place," Lewis said. "Instead, I found it to be a Person."[25] Lewis had expected joy to be some kind of subjective experience, some state of mind. He discovered instead that joy was the way out of a life turned inward on itself. His conversion was not so much an emotional or subjective experience as it was an awareness that he had been the object of a divine decision. Lewis knew that he had been offered a moment of "wholly free choice," and yet it really did not seem possible to do the opposite. When the ultimate reality of the incarnate Christ closed in on him, Lewis reluctantly surrendered. He was always glad for the way it turned out, but at the moment, he said, it was as though he heard God saying: "Put down your gun and we'll talk."

God had found C. S. Lewis. It was not "his" religion, something he could claim as his own. He confessed that his search for God had been no more intent than that of the mouse's search for the cat. Consequently, he never tried to communicate some personal experience or sell the wares of a particular denomination. His burden was simply to communicate the truth of essential Christianity.

The Oxford Don

Lewis's teaching career began in 1924 when he was invited to tutor philosopy students at University College. The following year, however, the faculty of Magdalen College elected him a fellow, and he gave up philosophy for his true love, English language and literature. Lewis's knowledge of the English language was prodigious, but he chose to specialize in the literature from Middle English to Milton. Both his teaching and his work as a writing scholar were soon being praised by his students and peers. Like most Oxford dons, Lewis spent most of his time tutoring students and giving lectures. He was very conscientious about his work and soon gained a reputation as the best lecturer at Oxford. When he lectured, the lecture room was usually filled and oftentimes students had to be turned away. His stimulating lectures made Lewis the biggest draw in the English department. His reputation as a literary critic also grew as he published scholarly articles and book length works on literary history and criticism. Two of his best works were published early in his career and helped to establish Lewis as one of England's finest literary scholars. They were his *Allegory of Love* and a larger volume entitled *English Literature in the Sixteenth Century Excluding Drama*. The latter was done for the collection called the *Oxford History of English Literature.*

Lewis's conversion in 1931 coincided with his purchase of a home on the edge of Oxford that came to be known as the Kilns. Mrs. Moore, her daughter Maureen, and the gardener (Paxford) took care of the house, the family cats and dogs, and eight acres of land. Lewis's time there was usually limited to the weekends and holidays. During the week he stayed in his apartment at Magdalen College that the university provided. From one window Lewis had a view of the university's splendid gothic architecture and from another a beautiful forest inhabited by deer that often fed just below. Lewis looked forward to his daily encounter with nature. Walks through the woods and an occasional swim in a nearby pond were cherished experiences. On those days when Maureen or Paxford could come and drive him back to the Kilns for lunch, Lewis usually took a stroll through the woods on his own land. When he stayed over at the university, he enjoyed the meditative silence of the famed Addison's Walk.

Monotony was never a problem for Lewis. He thrived on it. His daily regimen varied very little. He had a set time for rising in the morning, for eating, correspondence, tea, writing, and preparing lectures. Tutorials lasted from nine o'clock in the morning until one o'clock in the afternoon (except on Mondays), and he had students again from five until seven o'clock in the evenings. When Lewis was not busy with students or lectures, he filled his life with friends and good conversation. J. R. R. Tolkien, best known as the author of *Lord of the Rings*, usually stopped by on Monday mornings. Their custom was to go to a nearby pub for beer and conversation on matters that ranged from politics, poetry, and theology to matters no higher than "bawdy" or "puns." From 1939 until William's death in 1945 Lewis met regularly with Charles Williams, an editor from London who had moved to Oxford during the war. Lewis regarded Williams as one of his closest personal friends. He especially admired William's selfless character and his capacity for stimulating conversation.

Lewis detested cliques and artificial gatherings, but he had an amazing facility for friends on a personal level. He thoroughly enjoyed discussing matters of substance, but he also enjoyed the excitement of a smoke filled room where friends simply enjoyed one another's company. His interests were wide-ranging, and so were his friends and colleagues. Most of his evenings were taken up with undergraduates discussing drama, Anglo-Saxon literature, Icelandic sagas, and philosophical issues. From 1941 to 1954 Lewis was president of the Socratic Club, a group that met every Monday evening to discuss the pros and cons of the Christian religion. The normal procedure was for a believer to read a paper one evening, to be followed by a paper from an opposing point of view the following Monday. The opposing side was often taken by a resident atheist or agnostic. It was an unusual forum for differing points of view. One could hardly hold to an unexamined faith in this atmosphere of serious intellectual inquiry.

The most creative and challenging group that Lewis belonged to was the "Inklings," a group of scholars and intellectuals that regularly met to critique each other's writings and discuss topics of interest. From 1933 to 1950 they met on Thursday evening in Lewis's apartment. On Tuesday mornings they gathered again at the "Eagle and Child" pub, affectionately called the "Bird and Baby." The most frequent attenders were C. S. Lewis, Warren Lewis, J. R. R. Tolkien, R. E. Havard, and Charles Williams. Neville Coghill, Hugo Dyson, Owen Barfield, and Adam Fox were there on occasion. The Inklings had a reputation for lively discussion and candid critiques. The Tuesday morning gatherings continued until Lewis's death.

In September of 1947 *Time* magazine devoted its cover story to C. S. Lewis. By this time Lewis had written his book on miracles, and the editors of *Time* took special note of the Oxford scholar who dared to advocate supernatural Christianity in the world of academia. Lewis was not embarrassed in the least. On the contrary, he considered it one of the highest compliments that he had ever received. Lewis believed that there were times when a bold defense of the faith was necessary and appropriate. Many of his own works were in response to such a need. It was always rewarding for him to feel that his work as a scholar had lent some creedence to Christian belief and perhaps made it easier for others to believe who had been struggling with their faith.

Lewis believed, however, that one of the fruits of true Christianity was quality work. He once advised an assembly of Anglican priests and youth leaders to write good books on subjects other than Christianity. There is a *latent* Christianity, he said, that can be most effectively communicated through the quality of one's work. The Hindu or the materialist would surely be shaken, he remarked, if the best work they could find on science, or any other subject, was one written by a Christian. Scholarly work that is intellectually honest can itself be a powerful witness to Christian truth. "The first step to the reconversion of this country," Lewis told the gathering, "is a series, produced by Christians, which can beat the *Penguin* and the *Thinkers Library* on their own ground. Its Christianity would have to be latent, not explicit: and of course its science perfectly honest. Science twisted in the interests of apologetics would be sin and folly."[26]

E. H. Harbison, in his work entitled *The Christian Scholar in the Age of the Reformation*, noted that "The Christian scholar—like the Christian poet, the Christian musician, or the Christian scientist—has always run the risk of being dismissed as an anomaly."[27] There have always been deep currents of anti-intellectualism in the Christian tradition. Men like Tertullian have asked, "What has Athens to do with Jerusalem, the Academy with the church?" But there have also been Augustines who insist that there can be no such thing as a purely secular search for truth. The true philosopher, they say, is a "lover of God" for He is the source of all wisdom and truth. Lewis was in the latter tradition, the tradition of men like Augustine, Abelard, Aquinas, Erasmus, Luther, and Calvin who viewed scholarship as a Christian calling.

What endeared Lewis to so many different publics was his ability to translate scholarship and imagination into narratives, metaphors, and analogies that common readers could understand and appreciate. Lewis published more than forty volumes in his lifetime, on such varied subjects as science fiction, children's stories, literary criticism, poetry, philosophy, and theology. It was not all of the same quality; he was a much better literary critic, for example, than he was a poet. But throughout all of his work there is a sense that one is reading an author whose scholarship is his calling—one who could be rightly called a literary evangelist. And yet, he carried his learning lightly. He understood that an effective scholar must also be a good communicator. His desire to translate essential Christianity into language that the common person could understand, coupled with his unique ability to persuade effectively, enabled C. S. Lewis to become the most widely read defender of the Christian faith in the twentieth century.

Notes

[1]C. S. Lewis, *Surprised by Joy* (New York: Harcourt, Brace, Jovanovich, Inc., 1955) 237.

[2]A number of good biographies are available. The best known is probably Walter Hooper and Roger Green's *C. S. Lewis, A Biography* (New York: Harcourt, Brace, Jovanovich, 1974). One can, of course, read Lewis's own account of the events and struggles leading up to his conversion in *Surprised by Joy* and *Pilgrim's Regress*.

[3]Lewis, *Surprised by Joy*, 10.

[4]Ibid., 21.

[5] John Hick, *Faith and Knowledge* (Glasgow: William Collins Sons and Co., 1966), 81.

[6]Lewis, *Surprised by Joy*, 60.

[7]Ibid., 62.   [8]Ibid., 63.   [9]Ibid., 68.

[10]C. S. Lewis, *Mere Christianity* (New York: Macmillan Co., 1971) 86.

[11]Roger Lancelyn Green and Walter Hooper, *C. S. Lewis: A Biography* (New York: Harcourt, Brace, Jovanovich, Inc., 1974) 33.

[12]Walter Hooper, ed., *God in the Dock* (Grand Rapids MI: Eerdmans Publishing Co., 1970) 101.

[13]Lewis, *Surprised by Joy,* 135.

[14]Hooper, *A Biography,* 48.

[15]Clyde Kilby, *C. S. Lewis: Images of His World* (Grand Rapids MI: Eerdmans Publishing Co., 1973) 9.

[16]Virtually all introductory philosophy texts present and explain the basic tenets of naturalism. Lewis's perspective on it can be found in the opening chapters of *Miracles.*

[17]Lewis, *Surprised by Joy,* 223.

[18]Ibid., 231.   [19]Ibid., 235.

[20]Hooper, *God in the Dock,* 102.

[21]Ibid.

[22]Lewis, *Surprised by Joy,* 237.

[23]Ibid., 236.   [24]Ibid., 210.   [25]Ibid., 230.

[26]Hooper, *God in the Dock,* 93.

[27]E. Harris Harbison, *The Christian Scholar in the Age of the Reformation* (New York: Charles Scribner's Sons, 1956) 1.

2.
In Defense of Supernaturalism

By the beginning of the Second World War Lewis had begun to establish his reputation as a writer throughout Great Britain. He had already published *Pilgrims Regress, The Problem of Pain* and *Out of the Silent Planet.* During the war he virtually became a household name through the attention his radio addresses received over the BBC. Millions heard him expound and defend the basic claims of the Christian faith over the air waves, and many of those who heard him were moved by what he had to say. His radio talks were published in three parts entitled *The Case for Christianity* (1943), *Christian Behaviour* (1943), and *Beyond Personality* (1945). These three short publications were soon compiled into one volume entitled *Mere Christianity.*

The war was a trying time for the English people, particularly for the men and women in the armed forces. In the interest of spiritual and moral support Lewis visited units of the army and the RAF, lecturing and dialoguing on basic tenets of the Christian faith. Talking about theological matters in non-theological language that the common soldier could understand and relate to was one of the biggest challenges Lewis had faced. But he proved to be more than equal to the task. His wartime experiences in communicating the Christian faith to the common people of Great Britain gained Lewis a reputation for being a rare scholar who knew how to communicate with the general public.

In the post-war era Lewis became well-known outside of Great Britain as well through his writings, television specials based on the Narnian chronicles, and increasing numbers of testimonies from those whose lives had been changed through Lewis's influence. Many who had drifted away from their faith or had only been half-convinced returned to the faith and the church. Others who were caught up in a "climate of opinion" that regarded Christianity as a relic of the past were challenged to rethink their "facts" and assumptions. Large numbers of those who read Lewis confessed that Christianity still made sense in the twentieth century. Lewis's name soon became synonomous with a reasoned faith that a thinking person could accept with the consent of all his faculties.

The Great Communicator

The favorable reaction that Lewis received from readers around the world during the decades of the 1940s and 1950s did not stem from a "pop" mentality toward theology. Lewis was above catering to public taste. He had no interest in vulgarizing the gospel by passing it off as some form of Pollyannaish optimism or as a panacea for all personal or social ills. It would have been tempting to do so because there were millions of people in Europe and America who were suffering from wartime anxieties who would have, no doubt, welcomed such a message. On the contrary, Lewis suggested that those who were merely looking to Christianity for happiness or comfort should look elsewhere. What Christianity offers, Lewis insisted, is not comfort but death to self and a complete opening of the will to God. One never knows in advance what that will mean. Oftentimes it turns out to be something pleasant; sometimes it entails pain and suffering.

Lewis was candid about Christianity's demands, and yet he was able to present the faith in a manner that made it appealing on its own terms. He insisted that theologians were obligated to be effective communicators. One must first have something to say and then use good communication skills in order to effectively say it. All clergymen, he said, should be able to translate their theology into language that those not trained in theology can understand. "I have come to the conviction," Lewis said, "that if you cannot translate your thoughts into uneducated language, then your thoughts were confused. Power to translate is the test of having really understood one's own meaning. A passage from some theological work for translation into the vernacular ought to be a compulsory paper in every Ordination examination."[1]

Lewis did not demean or patronize the uneducated. He simply contended that those who are not accustomed to sustained argument must proceed slower. Popular speech requires more explanation. What one can say with brevity to an educated person may require more explanation when presented to the unlearned. "Talk the same language as your readers or hearers," he advised. "Avoid vogue-words that may be understood by those within one's own circle but not by those outside." Lewis was himself a layman, and a former atheist. These were assets to him in communicating the gospel to "outsiders." He had a special knack for anticipating his reader's questions, and he knew how to give an honest straightforward answer. He was a master at finding the right word, at using a striking metaphor, or illustrating a point through an easy-to-understand analogy. His brilliant use of allegory was one of his finest literary achievements—one that can only be appreciated through a careful reading of his *Screwtape Letters, Pilgrims Regress, and The Great Divorce.*

Literary skills were important, but they were not the only factor in Lewis's success as a communicator of the Christian message. Paul Holmer, a prominent theologian and interpreter of Lewis, rightly suggests that Lewis's success was largely due to his willingness to accept the Bible on its own terms and follow its logic and the shape of its thought.[2] Lewis took seriously the direct and ordinary manner in which the Bible addresses the human heart and mind. He preferred the plain and simple assertions of the gospel over that of an imposed "reason" and "meaning" from philosophical or theological interpretations. Modernists had tried to make the gospel "intellectually respectable" by accommodating it to prevailing philosophical and scientific currents. In doing so, they had lost or given up the elementary truths that constitute the core of its message. Lewis was content to let the Bible do its own compelling in its own language and thought forms and in the strength of its own demands. After all, the purpose in reading the Bible is not to arrive at an acceptable theology but to conform oneself to the truths that are presented.

It should be noted that Lewis was not a literalist who thought that knowing the "facts" merely meant parroting words or memorizing Scriptures. His attitude toward Scripture was similar to his view of how one should read poetry. It must be read on its own terms. If one is to see things from the inside and be moved by its passions and thought-life, it must come directly from the source. It is our own thoughts that must be converted if we are to again see things in a manner that makes sense.

The problem with the biblical critics, Lewis insisted, was not that they were engaged in a bogus discipline but that they too often drew unwarranted conclusions from biased assumptions. Many of the better known critics, for example, were philosophically committed to naturalistic presuppositions that ruled out *a priori* the possibility of miracles. Consequently, when they encountered an account of a miracle in the Gospels, they simply concluded that it must be a myth or a legend. Miracles could not, from their point of view, be factual historical events. Naturalistic conclusions inevitably led then to historical skepticism. Having denied the historical basis of the text, the critic was expected to reconstruct its origin and determine its purpose and influence. What usually resulted were highly speculative reconstructions. What the biblical authors presented as historical events and concrete demands the critics viewed as the naive faith of the early church. Most laypersons never bother to question the critics, Lewis noted. They respect the critics' learning and judgment. The critics' learning and judgment, however, were precisely what Lewis challenged. "If he [the Bible critic] tells me that something in a Gospel is legend or romance," Lewis said, "I want to know how many legends and romances he has read, how well his palate is trained in detecting them by the flavour; not how many years he has spent on that Gospel."[3]

It is particularly perturbing when a critic asks one to believe that they have some special ability to read between the lines of the text when, Lewis said, "the evidence is their obvious inability to read (in any sense worth discussing) the lines themselves. They claim to see fern-seed and can't see an elephant ten yards away in broad daylight."[4] In looking for what is hidden or missing from the text they miss the obvious. Lewis used, as an example, Rudolph Bultmann's contention that there was no personality of Christ presented in the New Testament. What is common to virtually all believers, and even to many unbelievers, Lewis argued, is the conviction that in the Gospels they have met a personality. Lewis found it mind-boggling that any critic could miss such an obvious divulgement.

Lewis was not so concerned about the influence that the higher critics would have on trained scholars. They were supposed to be equipped to recognize a critic's assumptions and conclusions and sort that out from the text. He was more concerned about the unlearned common person whose orthodoxy the critic completely undermined. In an article on the subject, Lewis vented his scorn:

> A theology which denies the historicity of nearly everything in the Gospels to which Christian life and affections and thoughts have been fastened for nearly two millennia—which either denies the miraculous altogether or, more strangely, after swallowing the camel of the Resurrection strains at such gnats as the feeding of the multitudes—if offered to the uneducated man can produce only one or other of two effects. It will make him a Roman Catholic or an atheist. What you offer him he will not recognize as Christianity. If he holds to what he calls Christianity, he will leave a church in which it is no longer taught and look for one where it is. If he agrees with your version he will no

longer call himself a Christian and no longer come to church. In his crude, coarse way, he would respect you much more if you did the same.[5]

Lewis was not inclined toward the extremes of either the modernist or the fundamentalist. On fundamental matters of doctrine he taught what most conservative Protestants believe—the historical fact of the Incarnation, the Resurrection, the Ascension, the Return of Christ, and Christ's miracles. He referred to modernism's optimistic tone of "a good God in heaven and all's well in the world" as Christianity-and-water. Modernism is a "boy's philosophy," he said. It leaves out all of the difficult and terrible doctrines about sin and hell, the devil, and redemption. On the other hand, he was not particularly concerned with many of the issues that mattered so much to the fundamentalist or the evangelical. He was never embroiled, for instance, in any "battle for the Bible." Consequently, he had no axe to grind on the well-worn subject of revelation and inspiration. And, he raised more than a few evangelical eyebrows with his Catholic leanings on subjects like purgatory, prayers for the dead, and regular confessions to the priest. In another vein, American fundamentalists never quite knew how to reconcile his strong Christian beliefs with certain personal habits like pipe-smoking and beer-drinking.

Denominational distinctives were not very important to Lewis. He was more interested in those Christian truths that have the potential to unite Christians than he was in the non-essentials that divide them. Lewis admitted that he had no advice to offer anyone hesitating between Christian denominations or to those involved in dog-fights over differing points of view. He understood the word "Christian" in its original sense, as one who accepted the teaching of the Apostles (Acts 11:26). This enormous common ground was what Lewis called "mere" Christianity. Essential Christianity was surely the diet that Jesus had in mind when he commanded Peter to "Feed my Sheep!"

Lewis did not believe that the logic and shape of biblical thought could be reduced to rational propositional language. An infinite God could not be comprehended or explained in terms of finite rational concepts. He felt that this was why so much that is in the Bible comes to us in mytho-poetic form. The purpose of Scripture is not simply to lead one to logical conclusions but to open up a whole new world of meaning that can take root in the reader. Myth is not, as some suppose, a type of deception or a misrepresentation of facts but a kind of picture-making that helps one understand the reality that is at the core of things. Poetry and mythology help us to see and participate in the reality itself. They are comparable to the Eucharist, Lewis said, in that they use symbols and yet they are more than the symbols. They are mediums capable of creating communion.

Lewis defined myth as "a real though unfocused gleam of divine truth falling on human imagination."[6] He believed that the Hebrews, like other ancient people, had their mythology. But Hebrew mythology was unique in that it was the one chosen by God as a "vehicle of the earliest sacred truths." In the New Testament these sacred truths become more focused, more concrete and historical. Lewis used an analogy from the Incarnation to explain the phenomenon:

> Just as God, in becoming Man, is "emptied" of His glory, so the truth, when it comes down from the "heaven" of myth to the "earth" of history, undergoes a certain humiliation. Hence the New Testament is, and ought to be, more prosaic, in some ways less splendid, than the Old; just as the Old Testament is and ought to be less rich in many kinds of imaginative beauty than the Pagan mythologies.
>
> Just as God is none the less God by being Man, so the myth remains Myth even when it becomes Fact. The story of Christ demands from us, and repays, not only a religious and historical but also an imaginative response. It is directed to the child, the poet, and the savage in us as well as to the conscience and to the intellect. One of its functions is to break down dividing walls.[7]

The imaginative chord that runs through the Bible found a ready response in Lewis. That response, which Lewis had been attuned to since childhood, was vividly expressed in his Space Trilogy and the Narnian stories. He spent much of his time producing modern myths through which gleams of divine truth could be grasped by modern readers who no longer read the old prosaic forms of theology.

Many Lewis readers regard his works of fiction as his best work. They are, without doubt, among the most creative and effective forms of fiction that have been used to communicate the Christian faith in this century. T. S. Eliot, the well-known Christian poet, shivered at the "cold, interstellar spaces," but Lewis, the mythmaker, filled "deep heaven" with a presence that made the vast distant spaces of the universe more tolerable to the imagination.[8] Chad Walsh, who called Lewis the "Apostle to the Skeptics," said that Lewis's space trilogy shows in dramatic fashion the necessity of our involvement in the struggle between good and evil. Even more important, he asserted, Lewis created a mythology in which the whole solar system has been baptized and filled with the presence of God.[9] In many ways Lewis's myths and fairy tales are more effective than his realistic stories for they "arouse longing for more ideal worlds and . . . give the real world a new dimension of depth."[10] The longing for Aslan's land, the great lion who is a personification of Christ, is a recurring theme. It moves the reader in a way that more "realistic" accounts of the Gospels cannot by taking them off guard and allowing them to "feel" the truth in an uninhibited way.[11]

Clues to the Meaning of the Universe

The search for an adequate explanation of oneself and the world in which one lives has always been a human concern. The attempt to provide such an explanation is what philosophers call a worldview. In simple terms, a worldview is an attempt to construct a picture of the whole of reality that can account for every aspect of man's knowledge and experience. Theoretically, there could be any number of worldviews, but in actuality two worldviews have dominated modern thinking. One is called naturalism, the other supernaturalism.

Naturalism makes a modest claim. It claims that all known facts support the view that the whole of reality emerged from and is dependent upon material nature. There is no need to posit the existence of anything beyond the natural realm in order to explain the physical world or, for that matter, humankind itself. Human beings are essentially physico-chemical systems that have their origin in nature and can be studied like the rest of the physical world.

Since naturalists hold that all of reality can be accounted for without appealing to anything outside the time/space material world, they have no need to posit the existence of God as an "explanation" of things. God is an unnecessary hypothesis. Everything can supposedly be explained on other grounds.

The supernaturalists, on the other hand, hold to a more complex view. They affirm that there is more to reality than this material, physical world. Without denying the reality of nature, or the rightful place of the scientific disciplines whose methods are appropriate to their subject matter, Christian supernaturalists affirm their belief in an infinite personal God. The God of the Bible is a spiritual, sentient being who exists apart from the natural order and cannot be known as some natural object. God is the creator of the world who has been redemptively revealed in Jesus Christ.

The God-question is all-important. For if God does not exist there is no basis for talking about any meaning for this world or for ourselves other than that which we choose to give it. Life is then, as Shakespeare's Macbeth said, no more than "a tale told by an idiot, full of sound and fury, signifying nothing." If, on the other hand, God does exist the opposite is true. All of life is full of meaning and value given to it by its creator and redeemer.

Lewis did not find the traditional arguments for God's existence convincing or useful. He had been led to belief in God through two other aspects of experience. One had to do with his sense of moral duty; the other had its roots in "romance" or "joy," his experience of longing for an unknown object—something outside himself that nothing in this world seemed able to satisfy. Lewis found that most people either did not understand or could not relate to the traditional philosophical arguments. But when he talked about these inner experiences of "moral duty" and "longing" he found a common ground that virtually everyone could relate to and identify with. These, he believed, were key clues to the meaning of the universe.

The Moral Law

When naturalists talk about natural laws, they mean things like the law of gravity or laws that govern heredity, physics, or chemistry. Nature is subject to these laws and is not free to disobey them. If you drop an apple, for example, you know it will fall to the ground. The law of gravity determines what it must do; there is no choice. There is another kind of law, however, that is just as real as natural law. Lewis called it the "law of human nature." He was referring, of course, to the rule of right and wrong that we are all *free* to obey or disobey.

One of the common human experiences is the sense of "moral oughtness," the law of right and wrong that is implied in even the most casual things people say. We are forever appealing to some standard of behavior, even in common statements like: "That's my seat, I was there first"—"leave him alone, he isn't doing you any harm"—"Why should you shove in first?"—"Give me a bit of your orange, I gave you a bit of mine"—"Come on, you promised." This experience of "oughtness," Lewis argued, serves to remind us that we are more than physical stuff, that the universe is more than a cosmic machine. It is more like a mind that is conscious, has purpose, and prefers one thing to another. This "something" that is "behind" nature cannot be known through the scientific method, and yet it is implied in all of our statements about decency and fairness. "What interests me about all these remarks," Lewis said, "is that the man who makes them is not merely saying that the other man's behaviour does not happen to please him. He is appealing to some kind of standard of behaviour which he expects the other man to know about."[12]

This sense of moral "oughtness" is not instinct; nor can it be explained away as social convention. On the contrary, it often conflicts with instinct and social convention and judges them when they violate its universal and timeless standard. Lewis was not referring to moral laws (in the plural) or social mores which may differ from one society to another. Moral law(s) may be socially conditioned and may differ from one culture to another in their application, but there must be an absolute and objective moral standard (singular) that stands behind the sense of moral obligation that all persons experience. Otherwise, morality could never rise above personal taste or preference. One might personally abhor Hitler's behavior, for example, but apart from an absolute moral standard there would really be no basis for saying that Hitler was *wrong*. Lewis likened the Moral Law (singular) to what the Chinese called the *Tao*,[13] the sole source of all value judgments.

Lewis agreed with Immanuel Kant that the Moral Law within him was the greatest witness to the existence of an Absolute Lawgiver. The logic of naturalism's ethic is relativism, but one's inner appeal to a moral standard points to its fulfillment in an absolute moral deity who stands behind the flux of nature.

The Quest for Fulfillment

Naturalism, as a worldview, seemed inadequate to Lewis in other respects as well. One of its greatest deficiencies is that it provides no fulfillment for the quest within man for spiritual meaning. It offers no hope that our natural longings and desires can ever be fulfilled. A supernatural worldview does; it says to us that a purposeful creator does not fill us with longings and desires which nothing in this world can satisfy unless there is another world in which these desires can find their fulfillment:

> Creatures are not born with desires unless satisfaction for those desires exist. A baby feels hunger: well, there is such a thing as food. A duckling wants to swim: well, there is such a thing as water. Men feel sexual desire: well, there is such a thing as sex. If I find in myself a desire which no experience in this world can satisfy, the most probable explanation is that I was made for another world. If none of my earthly pleasures satisfy it, that does not prove that the universe is a fraud. Probably earthly pleasures were never meant to satisfy it, but only to arouse it, to suggest the real thing.[14]

Certain human experiences point beyond themselves and serve as indicators that there is "more." They serve to remind us that there are dimensions of reality that are, in fact, responsible for and give meaning to our natural existence. This realm of fulfillment must be in the realm of the supernatural.

One should, of course, remember that Christianity is more than theism. Theists may believe in God, the absolute, or whatever they may choose to call their ultimate reality, and yet not embrace the Christian belief about God. A Christian worldview is more than belief in the supernatural. It is grounded in a historical claim—the claim that in Jesus Christ God became flesh. Through the life, death, and resurrection of Jesus Christ God's purpose was concretely revealed and fulfilled.

This is the one truth that Christians must *act* upon. According to Lewis, there is no middle ground, no basis for patronizing Jesus by calling him a prophet, a teacher, or a good man. He was either who he claimed to be or else he was a deceiver and blasphemer of the worst kind. Lewis reasoned that:

> If you had gone to Budda and asked him, "Are you the son of Bramah?" he would have said, "My son, you are still in the vale of illusion." If you had gone to Socrates and asked, "Are you Zeus?" he would have laughed at you. If you had gone to Mohammad and asked,

"Are you Allah?" he would first have rent his clothes and then cut your head off. . . . The idea of a great moral teacher is out of the question. In my opinion, the only person who can say that sort of thing is either God or a complete lunatic suffering from that form of delusion which undermines the whole mind of man.[15]

God has indeed left his footprints in the sands of time and space. Lewis believed that there is plenty of evidence that we are not alone, that there is more than nature. He regarded the awe of the "numinous," our sense of "moral oughtness," unfulfilled longings and desires, and our unique capacity to reason as evidences of a supernatural presence in the world. None of these can be adequately explained from a naturalistic perspective. But a knowledge of this truth is not enough. One must surrender to the claims of the historical Jesus. The Christian worldview is more than a truth to be grasped; it is a truth that must be surrendered to and lived out as a matter of personal choice. It is analagous to the "dive." The risk is always there that Jesus was not who he claimed to be, but then one will never know without surrendering to the claim.

The Miraculous

The primary reason why naturalists deny miracles is that they assume that there is really nothing outside of nature to interfere with the natural process. The world, they contend, is a self-operating order that can explain itself in terms of objects and events occurring in time and space. Lewis noted that there are other reasons, however, why many modernists reject the miraculous. It is not uncommon to find those who believe in God but who cannot bring themselves to believe that the supernatural would invade the realm of the natural and interfere with its orderly operations. Such an idea, to them, seems childish and unworthy of the supernatural. Religious modernists were particularly prone to deal with the miraculous in this manner. They viewed the supernaturalism of orthodox Christianity as a worldview embedded in an outmoded science that was no longer viable for those living in an enlightened age. Their denial of miracles did not seem as threatening as that of the secular scientist or philosopher because it was usually cloaked in pious phrases. But in reality, Lewis believed, the effects may have been even more

damaging because the religious view erroneously regarded the supernatural elements in the faith as something extraneous to its core truths.

The problem with this watered-down version of Christianity, Lewis
argued, is that it strips it of its true core. A naturalistic interpretation of
Christianity in either a secular or religious form leaves out all that is
specifically Christian.[16] In actuality, Christianity is the story of a great
miracle for it affirms a creator God who stands outside the process of
nature, yet acts within the process as well. God is the God who intervenes
in nature, the One who enters into the process in order to redeem all who
have been lost through sin. The *Grand Miracle* of the Incarnation is the
Truth that illuminates and pulls all of the parts together. It is the central
plot around which everything else in the story revolves. Apart from the
miraculous, there is no Christian message.

Lewis did not believe, however, that the natural and the supernatural
should be viewed as separate and unrelated phenomena. The natural and
the supernatural are necessarily related by reason of the fact that the
source of both is a purposeful creator and redeemer. God does not, in
fact, break His own laws even in the working of miracles. Miracles
simply fulfill God's purpose for nature at a higher level. They introduce
a new factor, a supernatural factor, that had not been expected into the
situation. The new event does not disrupt the harmony of nature; it
becomes interlocked with it. For example, if a billiard ball encounters a
roughness in the cloth of the billiard table, its motion will not follow a
new law; it will simply follow the law that the roughness of the cloth
introduces into the situation. In a similar manner God may introduce new
factors into history or nature any time they serve God's purpose. These
new factors are not like something "added on" or "out of harmony" with
nature. They constitute the new situation—the new self-consistent reality
of the whole. There is no need to question the propriety of miracles on
the grounds that they are out-of-character for God or that they interfere
with the real story of the universe. Those who think that the story of the
universe is the story of atoms, science, economics, and politics have
missed the real plot. They think death and resurrection are mere expedi-
ents inserted to save a religious story at the expense of introducing a
disrupting factor. That perspective, Lewis claimed, is wrong. The
crucifixion and resurrection of Christ are what the story of the universe
has been anticipating. History is really about Christ. Our story and the
world's story are to be understood in light of his story:

They [miracles] are not exceptions (however rarely they occur) nor irrelevancies. They are precisely those chapters in this great story on which the plot turns. Death and Resurrection are what the story is about; and had we but eyes to see it, this has been hinted on every page, met us, in some disguise, at every turn, and even been muttered in conversations between such minor characters (if they are minor characters) as the vegetables.[17]

The Grand Miracle

Lewis called the Incarnation the *Grand Miracle* because it is the missing chapter in the novel of life. It is the event that illuminates and pulls all of the parts together. One does not have to comprehend fully all that is meant by "God becoming man" in order to see that it is the doctrine that illuminates all others. Lewis compared it to the sun whose noonday light we know is there, not because we can clearly see the sun but because it is what allows us to see everything else.[18]

Incarnation is the story of God's descent into nature, into time and space, down into humanity in order to "come up again and bring the whole ruined world up with Him."[19] The divine Incarnation is the pattern for the whole of reality, both natural and supernatural. "The pattern is there in nature," Lewis contended, "because it was first there in God. All instances of it . . . turn out to be but transpositions of the Divine theme into a minor key. . . . The power of the Higher to come down, the power of the greater to include the less. . . . [T]his is the test of greatness and the subtle harmony that pervades the whole order of the universe."[20]

Incarnation is the pattern of all vegetable life—so aptly illustrated in the annual death and resurrection of the corn. It is the pattern of all animal regeneration as well:

There is descent from the full and perfect organisms into the spermatozoon and ovum, and in the dark womb a life at first inferior in kind to that of the species which is being reproduced: then the slow ascent to the perfect embryo, to the living, conscious baby, and finally to the adult.[21]

The pattern continues, Lewis believed, in our moral and emotional life:

The first innocent and spontaneous desires have to submit to the deathlike process of control or total denial: but from that there is a re-ascent to fully formed character in which the strength of the original material all operates but in a new way. Death and Re-birth—go down to go up—it is a key principle.[22]

Christ is the fulfillment of all that is prefigured in these patterns: "He comes down . . . to recapitulate in the womb ancient and pre-human phases of life; down to the very roots and sea-bed of the Nature He has created. But He goes down to come up again and bring the whole ruined world up with Him."[23] He is a "personification of the corn-king" like the mythological Adonis or Osiris, who died and rose again each year.[24] On the divine level Christ personifies the selective, vicarious process we find in nature. He suffers so that others may live:

He [Christ] is the representative "Die-er" of the universe: and for that very reason the Resurrection and the Life. . . . Because the higher can descend into the lower He who from all eternity has been incessantly plunging Himself in the blessed death of self-surrender to the Father can also most fully descend into the horrible and (for us) involuntary death of the body. Because Vicariousness is the very idiom of the reality He has created, His death can become ours. The whole Miracle, far from denying what we already know of reality, writes the comment which makes that crabbed text plain: or rather, proves itself to be the text on which Nature was only the commentary. In science we have been reading only the notes to a poem; in Christianity we find the poem itself.[25]

Anthropologists were disposed simply to treat Christianity as just another nature religion. Christ was another "dying" and "rising" savior common to the pagans who understood virtually everything else in light of nature's recurring pattern of death and new life. The origins and development of Christianity could thus be explained naturally like all other pagan religions. It could, in fact, be seen as a religion that had originated and evolved from pagan mythologies.

Lewis believed that anthropologists were on to something, but that they had reversed the order. Christ was a figure of the sort the anthropologists described. But the phenomenon was there in nature because it was first in God, the creator of nature. He cannot be explained by nature;

it must be the other way around. The Evangelists did not make the connection; they were writing about the reality itself, not about figures and shadows. But it is a truth implied in the Incarnation. The irony of the matter, Lewis noted, is that the truly historical "dying" and "rising" God appeared among a people (the only ones in the whole Mediterranean world) who had no trace of nature religion and seemed to know nothing about it. And yet he was the reality to which all of nature pointed.

Miracles are "fitting" in a world where God is sovereign over nature. They are organically related to one another and to the whole structure of the Christian religion. They are, in fact, an essential part of the Christian message that "He who has come is not merely a king, but *the* king, her [nature's] king and ours."[26]

The "Fitness" of Miracles

It is one thing to believe that miracles are possible; it is another thing to believe that they actually do occur. David Hume, the eighteenth-century skeptic, concluded that a miracle is the most improbable of all events because it is contrary to our experience of the "uniformity of nature." What passes for miracles, Hume believed, can usually be accounted for by human propensity for naivete, superstition, and exaggeration.

Hume's argument could, of course, be challenged by credible witnesses from throughout the biblical and church tradition. But it was also flawed by an internal contradiction that is particularly relevant to Lewis's argument for the "fitness" of miracles. Hume was a strict empiricist who claimed that all knowledge of events in the real world comes through the five senses. Yet, his belief in the "uniformity of nature" could not possibly come from the five senses. In actuality, it came from Hume's innate sense of the "fitness of things." From Hume's perspective, "A universe in which unprecedented and unpredictable events were at every moment flung into nature would not merely be inconvenient to us: it would be profoundly repugnant. . . . It shocks our 'sense of the fitness of things.' "[27]

The point that Lewis wanted to make is that miracles only violate a sense of the "fitness of things" for those like Hume who are biased in their belief that nature is all there is and that it must therefore behave according to fixed natural laws. Miracles do not, on the other hand, violate the "fitness of things" for those who believe in God (i.e. the supernatural). It is really one's worldview that suggests what may or may not be expected. If God exists, we must not only admit the possibility of miracles: we must admit the probability of miracles when such events are in accordance with the "fitness of things" that a sovereign God decrees.

The Christian holds that God is the absolute sovereign who determines what happens in His world. Contrary to what the scientist or philosopher may fear, however, if miracles are permitted—God does not run a capricious and disorderly universe. The God that Christians believe in is the orderly creator. And because God is, the scientist can be assured that the work of science can successfully continue. Because God is the sovereign God who is free to act, on the other hand, the Christian can also continue to pray.

The sense of "fitness" or "unfitness" that one uses as a criterion by which to judge the probability of miracles depends then upon one's worldview. Given this worldview, the Christian can confidently assert that miracles are consistent with both the character of God and the orderliness of nature. Furthermore, Christians can expect miracles that exhibit "fitness" and illumine the total picture of reality. One does not have to believe naively in every alleged miracle, but it would be foolish to reject out-of-hand a necessary part of the story that helps one better understand the whole plot.

Miracles Old and New

Miracles then are never arbitrary interferences with the laws of nature. They should not be thought of as some form of magic or hocus-pocus that cause things to pop in and out of existence. A Christian view of miracles must not be confused with a mind-set for leprechauns or flying saucers. True miracles are not isolated events. Their credibility is tied to their fitness, and their fitness is directly related to the Grand Miracle that illumines God's pattern of action.

Miracles of the Old Creation

Lewis referred to miracles that reproduce processes in nature as miracles of the old creation. The Virgin Birth of Christ, for example, was a miracle of the old creation. What God did in this miraculous conception was perfectly consistent with what God has done, in a different fashion, for every woman who has ever conceived. God is the giver of all life, but on this one occasion God brought life forth without the normal act of generation. The uniqueness of that conception lay in the fact that this time, "He was creating not simply a man but the Man who was to be Himself: was creating Man anew: was beginning, at this divine and human point, the New Creation of all things."[28]

Turning water into wine at the wedding feast in Cana and the miraculous feeding of the multitude were miracles that demonstrated Christ's power to shorten the natural annual process. Instead of allowing water to become wine through the normal processes of nature, God miraculously made it happen in a moment. In the miraculous feeding God made a little to become much instantaneously. Instead of allowing the natural processes of fertility and fecundity to take place, God brought it forth immediately. The instant miracle is what the New Testament evangelists called "signs" and "wonders," but they were no more God's work than that which God is constantly doing through a more natural manner. These kinds of miracles attract our attention because they are not happening according to the processes we have come to expect. A sign, by its very nature, is something that points beyond itself. The miracles of Jesus were signs that pointed to a divine power and presence that could not be reduced to mere natural phenomena. Jesus manifested that presence and power of the supernatural order in a manner that could not be confused with the normal workings of nature, and yet he did so in a manner that did not disrupt the continuity between the natural and the supernatural that one would expect from the creator of nature.

The same can be said for Jesus' miracles of healing. In Palestine Jesus met the sick and healed many of them instantly. But in truth he was only doing more quickly what he does over and over in allowing the slow but recuperative and self-corrective energy of nature to heal our bodies. Miracles of the old creation reveal him to be the sovereign power that lies behind all of the laws and processes of nature. What the pagans attribute to Ceres or Adonis, Genius and Venus, Bacchus and Apollo, Christians attribute to the man from Galilee who died and rose from the dead during the reign of Pontius Pilate.

Miracles of the New Creation

All of Jesus' miracles, however, did not point to what the God of nature had already done through creation. Many of Jesus' miracles were prophetic; they were but a foretaste of a nature that is still in the future. Lewis called those miracles that focus on the order that is to come the miracles of the new creation. Christ is the "firstfruits" of the new order, the first of his kind. His resurrection was the first event of its kind in the whole history of the universe. He had defeated the king of death and become the pioneer, the "firstfruits" of a whole new existence. This new existence was foreshadowed in the raising of Lazarus and Christ's walking on the water. His resurrection anticipated that time when we who are "sons of God" will enter into that "glorious liberty" that is not possible under the old order. He is the pioneer of that which is yet to come.

In the new state of things the process of death will be reversed. Nature herself will have been altered. But this does not mean that the new creation will completely exclude the old order. Heaven will not simply be some kind of mystical experience. It will have some continuity with the old creation that God created and called "good." The two are forever interlocked. Heaven, we are told, is a place of spiritual splendor and ceaseless adoration, but it is also a bodily life. This is what the ascension teaches us, and this is why the ascension is a necessary part of the resurrection story:

> Christian teaching by saying that God made the world and called it good teaches that Nature or environment cannot be irrelevant to spiritual beatitude in general. . . . By teaching the resurrection of the body it teaches that Heaven is not merely a state of the spirit but a state of the body as well: and therefore a state of Nature as a whole.[29]

This is the same truth, in principle, that we know from the Incarnation and from the constitution of our own nature as a union of body and spirit. "To shrink back from all that can be called Nature into negative spirituality," Lewis said, "is as if we ran away from horses instead of learning to ride."[30] The sacraments show us how God can unite the spiritual and the natural and make it a means of grace. Spiritual gifts are offered on conditions that require bodily acts, and spiritual bodies are promised on the condition that we control our earthly bodies.

The Problem of Pain

The one problem common to human experience that has produced more than its share of doubters and skeptics has been the problem of pain and suffering. The fact of pain and suffering does not disprove the existence of God, but it has raised serious questions about whether or not God can be the kind of God that Christians claim. Lewis described the logic of the problem in its classic form:

> If God were good, He would wish to make his creatures perfectly happy, and if God were almighty, He would be able to do what He wished. But the creatures are not happy. Therefore God lacks either goodness, or power, or both.[31]

The problem is, of course, a serious one that cannot be simply ignored. What is at stake is the internal consistency of the Bible itself. The biblical claim is that God is perfect in both goodness and power, but if God is perfect in goodness and power how could God allow pain and suffering, which imply that God is either lacking in power or goodness or both? Christian apologists have to take the problem seriously because they know that truth cannot be established on contradictions and/or known facts of experience. A thinking person is not likely to accept the Bible, or any other revelatory claim, simply because it claims to be true. If one did that, there would be no rational basis for accepting the Christian truth claim over that of others. Christians accept the Bible as true because, when accepted, it illuminates and integrates knowledge and experience better than any other truth claim. The question then is whether or not pain is consistent with what the Bible reveals about the character of God. Or, is there an internal contradiction in the Bible?

In *The Problem of Pain,* Lewis argued that the problem is not what it often seems. Christianity is not a system in which we have to fit in the "awkward" fact of pain. In fact, it does not really propose to solve the problem. On the contrary, Christianity creates the problem of pain by assuring us that God is both omnipotent and loving. The Christian, without resorting to simplistic explanations like dualism or pantheism, holds that the world's miseries are perfectly congruent with its creation and guidance by a good and all-powerful Being. Lewis explained by first distinguishing between natural evil, or evil that results from natural causes, and moral evil which results from moral choices:

Natural Evil

Much of the pain and suffering in the world is obviously not attributable to matters of personal choice. The starvation of innocent children, the ravages of tornadoes and hurricanes, the senseless killing of civilians in wars, mothers dying of cancer—all of these are examples of natural evil. The question, of course, is why an all-powerful and loving God would allow it?

The only answer that Lewis could offer to this perpetual and perplexing question was that nature does not always act benevolently or even-handedly because matter has a fixed nature and obeys constant laws. The natural process is often selective, competitive, and undemocratic. Some things suffer for the good of others: "The cat lives on the mouse. . . . The parasite lives on its 'host': the unborn child on its mother. . . . The bees and the flowers live on one another in a more pleasing manner."[32] Natural processes like these are somewhat analogous to death itself. They are neither good nor evil, though they are the consequence of a natural process that has been *spoiled* by sin. The Apostle Paul said that the whole created order groans in all of its parts and eagerly waits to be redeemed (Rom 8:22).

God, however, has not left the natural order without hope of redemption. The redemption of humanity began with the Incarnation, with God's willingness to descend into self-surrender, to accept pain and death for the good of others. This is also the pattern for nature. Part of the good news of the gospel is that pain and death are not the final word for nature anymore than they are for man. In pain and death there is the promise of resurrection and ascension for humanity, but just as importantly is the "promise of a new heaven and a new earth wherein dwelleth righteousness" (2 Pet 3:13). Christianity does not offer an easy solution or a quick fix for the pain and suffering that is experienced throughout nature. What it does offer is the hope of a new order that has not been spoiled by the effects of sin. That hope is guaranteed by the resurrection of Jesus Christ from the dead.

Moral Evil

If God is all-powerful, why did God not simply create a world in which there could be no pain? Lewis addressed this commonly asked question by first clarifying what omnipotence means. He quickly pointed out that omnipotence does not mean the power to do that which is contradictory or intrinsically impossible. Even God does not violate the divinely established order. We all live in a world with fixed laws. God's choices, like ours, have causal consequences. God could have created us unable to sin, but then we would not have been created free. Or, God could create us free, but then not even divine omnipotence could guarantee that we would not sin.

In order for us to be capable of moral goodness, we must also be capable of moral evil. God created humanity good, but by giving us genuine free choice God also made it possible for us to introduce moral evil into the scheme of things. Freedom of choice implies the existence of a self, an "I," that lives in a spiritual environment where choices can be made between the self and its Creator, between the self and others, between the self and an inexorable world of nature. The essence of our sinfulness lies in the fact that the self inevitably chooses itself against all others and lives a self-centered existence. The result is moral evil.

The world of nature is a neutral field. It is neither good nor evil. It is simply the environment in which our choices are played out. God does not protect us from the possibility of wrong actions, and when we choose wrongly, God does not change the laws of nature to protect us from the consequences of our action. God has not created the kind of world, for instance, in which "a wooden beam becomes soft as grass when it is used as a weapon or [the kind of world in which] the air will refuse to obey me if I attempt to set up sound waves that carry lies or insults."[33] The possibility of suffering simply cannot be excluded in the world that God has created without excluding life itself. The idea that there were other alternatives, Lewis argues, overlooks the Christian claim that the kind of world God created was one freely chosen by an all-wise God. It is not, as some have suggested, the "best of all possible worlds;" it is the only possible one.

It makes no sense, Lewis noted, to argue that it would have been better for God not to have created a world at all than to have created one in which evil is possible. Lewis disposed of that argument with one quick shot of logic. "How should I, if I did not exist, profit by not existing," he asked?[34]

The charge that moral evil undermines belief in divine goodness is also defenseless. The problem, Lewis claimed, is that too many confuse divine goodness with a modern concept of "kindness." It is expected that God will show some kind of senile benevolence. "We want," Lewis said, "not so much a Father in Heaven as a grandfather . . . whose plan for the universe was simply that it might be truly said at the end of each day, 'a good time was had by all.' "[35]

Those who are preoccupied with kindness, Lewis believed, are more interested in avoiding pain than they are in becoming what God intended. Divine love, on the other hand, is more concerned with the perfecting of the beloved than it is in merely making us happy. What we must come to understand is that our sinfulness has turned our character into something that is a horror to God; because God loves us God labors to make us lovable. God's highest purpose is not that we love God, though we were made for that too, but "that we may become objects in which the divine love may rest 'well pleased.' "[36] If human happiness were God's highest purpose for us, it would indeed be difficult to justify human suffering. But the fact is that God is more concerned with our goodness than with our happiness. God will not be satisfied until we have the character of a true son. Sonship entails a certain amount of pain and suffering. We are, as it were, in training. God is striving to make us more like Himself. If, in our sufferings, we come to feel that God loves us too little, the truth is that God loves us too much to leave us in our present condition. Lewis made his point in asking:

> When we fall in love with a woman, do we cease to care whether she is clean or dirty, fair or foul. . . . Does any woman regard it as a sign of love in a man that he neither knows nor cares how she is looking? Love may, indeed, love the beloved when her beauty is lost: but not because it is lost. Love may forgive all infirmities and love still in spite of them: but love cannot cease to will their removal.[37]

It is only when we attach a trivial meaning to the word "love," Lewis noted, that we have difficulty in reconciling a loving God with human suffering. God wants what will truly make us happy, but that cannot be realized in our present condition. The worst thing God could do would be to leave us alone, to allow us to simply follow our self-serving inclinations. But "tribulations cannot cease," Lewis admonished, "until God either sees us remade or sees that our remaking is now hopeless."[38]

Lewis suggested that pain is the megaphone that God uses to rouse a deaf world. As long as things are going well, we find self-surrender very difficult. God whispers to us in our pleasures, but shouts in our pain. It is a terrible instrument, but radical measures are necessary to rouse us out of our illusion of self-sufficiency and show us the real universe we are "up against." In our rebelliousness we experience God as an interruption. We refuse to seek our happiness in God. But when we do come to God as a last resort, when we feel there is "nothing better," God is not too proud to accept us. God's love is not dependent upon our having pure motives. God continually searches us out, and pain is one of the terrible means that is necessary in getting our attention. Lewis's intent was not to suggest that pain is not painful. He simply wanted to reassert what the writer of Hebrews said many centuries ago, that suffering is one of God's means of perfecting us (Heb 2:1). "The real problem," Lewis said, "is not why some humble, pious, believing people suffer, but why some do not."[39]

Christianity should not be construed as a masochistic religion that sees some intrinsic good in suffering. "The redemptive effect of suffering," Lewis emphasized, "lies chiefly in its tendency to reduce the rebel will."[40] All of life is not painful. The Father refreshes us often during our journey, but the ever present reality of pain and suffering serves as a constant reminder that this world is not our home. We were made for something better.

This does not mean that everyone attains the prize. It is possible to lose the game and suffer the ultimate pain of hell. Many find the doctrine of hell intolerable. They would remove it, though it has the full support of Scripture, because it seems repulsive and impugns the goodness of God. Lewis carefully considered all of the major arguments that moderns make against the notion of hell and concluded that it is not an irrational doctrine. Hell, he insisted, is not simply a sentence God imposes upon the sinful person; it is "the mere fact of being what he is." Hell is a fitting place, the only logical place, for those who have, by their own choices, made themselves into hellish creatures. It is the consequence of one's refusal to become what a loving God intended.

Lewis's Personal Experience with Grief

It is one thing to talk about pain and suffering in a detached academic setting. It is another matter when painful experiences invade our personal lives. Abstract arguments used to legitimate suffering suddenly seem totally inadequate when painful experiences come home to us. Lewis recognized this fact early on in his career and warned young apologists that there are times when the cogency of our arguments can only be saved by the transforming presence of Christ. Little did he know at the time how true this would prove to be in his own experience. He spoke about the dangers of putting too much trust in one's own arguments:

> I have found that nothing is more dangerous to one's own faith than the work of an apologist. No doctrine of that faith seems to me so spectral, so unreal as one that I have just successfully defended in a public debate. For a moment, you see, it has seemed to rest on oneself: as a result, when you go away from that debate, it seems no stronger than that weak pillar. That is why we apologists take our lives in our hands and can be saved only by falling back continually from the web of our own arguments, as from our intellectual counters, into the Reality —from Christian apologetics into Christ Himself.[41]

Lewis warned that it is not our experiences, our subjectivity, our ideas that are all-important. If this were true, some of them would break us. There must be some objective truth that we can trust that transcends our experience. It was a truth that Lewis would learn first-hand through the death of his wife.

Most of those who had known C. S. Lewis throughout his adult life were surprised when, after a long career as a confirmed bachelor, he married Helen Joy Davidman. Their marriage did not have the immediate appearance of one that had been "arranged in heaven." Joy was a former atheist, a former communist, and was sixteen years Lewis's junior. She was, however, extremely bright and an engaging conversationalist. At first, it was more "a marriage of minds" and another instance of Lewis's almost limitless capacity to befriend someone he cared for or felt some duty toward. Joy was an American poet, a divorcee with two small children. Lewis's original intention was to marry her, in a civil ceremony, so that she could legally remain in Great Britain and raise her children away from an abusive husband. He had no intention of even consummating the marriage. Soon after their marriage, however, they discovered that Joy had cancer. Her illness drew them closer together, and they were soon very much in love.

Jack insisted upon a religious ceremony and he and Joy enjoyed four intensely happy years of marriage. There was a period of hope when the cancer went into remission, but then it was back again. Joy died during the summer of 1960, and Lewis found himself alone again. But this time it was different. He discovered life without Helen to be virtually unbearable. Her physical and spiritual absence tormented him. He could find no comfort, and for the first time since his conversion he began to experience inner rage and pangs of doubt. He refused to be consoled by well-meaning friends who suggested that their former relationship could be restored in some future life. "Talk to me about the truth of religion and I'll gladly listen," Lewis retorted. "Talk to me about the duty of religion," he said, "and I'll listen submissively. But don't talk to me about the consolations of religion or I shall suspect that you don't understand."[42]

In *A Grief Observed* Lewis talked candidly about his struggle with doubt. After a lifetime of defending the integrity of the Christian faith, he found himself struggling to believe in a benevolent deity. But he did not succumb to doubt.[43] His trust in God's objective reality pulled him through this most difficult time in his life. His enduring conviction was that it is Christ, the object of our faith, that is ultimately important—not our subjectivity, our emotions, or our arguments. God must be trusted for what God is in Himself, not for what happens to us—however joyous or painful it might be. We are not asked to create some kind of subjective meaning out of life's experiences but to humbly acknowledge the objective meaning that God has already revealed through creation and through Christ. Reason, beauty, and morality cannot simply be read out of life's experiences. Neither can hope. They must all be accepted and appropriated on the basis of what God has said about them through God's works of creation and redemption. All we can do is acknowledge God and "give in" to His truth and His demands.

Joy's death made Lewis painfully aware that every attempt to use God as a means to some other end, even the good end of uniting us with those we love, is a "house of cards." The road to joy ran through God, but God cannot be used as a road. The only way Jack could meet Joy again was to learn to love God so much that it didn't really matter. In the meantime, he vowed that he would not become obsessed with her memory or her image. What was important was her independent reality. In that respect, Lewis admitted, Joy and all the dead are like God. Their reality transcends our painful experiences, and that is what we must depend upon to sustain us in our time of trial. Lewis's life did not end in great comfort but neither did it end in skepticism or despair because he learned what every Christian must—that it is the object of our faith, not our experiences, that is all-important:

> My idea of God is not a divine idea. It has to be shattered time after time. He shatters it Himself. He is the great iconoclast. Could we not almost say that this shattering is one of the marks of His presence? The Incarnation is the supreme example. It leaves all previous ideas of the Messiah in ruins. And most are 'offended' by the iconoclasm; and blessed are those who are not. . . . All reality is iconoclastic. The earthly beloved, even in this life, incessantly triumphs over your mere idea of her. And you want her too; you want her with all her resistances, all her faults, all her unexpectedness. That is, in her foursquare and independent reality. . . . Not my idea of God, but God. Not my idea of Helen, but Helen. Yes, and also not my idea of my neighbour, but my neighbour.[44]

There were times of bitter loneliness and pain after Joy's death. There were days when Lewis barely found enough inner strength to face the day ahead, but he remained faithful to the end. He had learned through experience what he already knew in his head: that the Christian cannot live out of his experiences or his circumstances. The only sure foundation is the objective reality of God and His promises.

Notes

[1]Hooper, *God in the Dock*, 98.

[2]Paul L. Holmer, *C. S. Lewis: The Shape of His Faith and Thought* (New York: Harper and Row, 1976) 95.

[3]Walter Hooper, ed., *Christian Reflections* (Grand Rapids MI: Eerdmans Publishing Co., 1967) 154.

[4]Ibid., 157.   [5]Ibid., 153.

[6]C. S. Lewis, *Miracles* (New York: Macmillan Publishing Co., 1960) 134.

[7]Ibid.

[8]Chad Walsh, *C. S. Lewis: Apostle to the Skeptics* (New York: Macmillan Publishing Co., 1949) 46, 47.

[9]Ibid., 47.

[10]Clyde S. Kilby, *The Christian World of C. S. Lewis* (Grand Rapids MI: Eerdmans Publishing Co., 1964) 116.

[11]Ibid., 136.

[12]Lewis, *Mere Christianity*, 17.

[13]Some refer to the *Tao* as Natural Law, others refer to it as Traditional Morality or the First Principle of Practical Reason. At any rate, Lewis argued, "It is not one among a series of possible systems of value. It is the sole source of all value judgments."

[14]Lewis, *Mere Christianity*, 120.

[15]Hooper, *God in the Dock*, 158.

[16]Lewis, *Miracles*, 68-70.

[17]Ibid., 98.   [18]Ibid., 110.   [19]Ibid., 111.

[20]Ibid., 112.   [21]Ibid.   [22]Ibid.

[23]Ibid., 111.   [24]Ibid., 113.   [25]Ibid., 130.

[26]Ibid., 132.   [27]Ibid., 104.   [28]Ibid., 138.

[29]Ibid., 161.   [30]Ibid., 163.

[31]C. S. Lewis, *The Problem of Pain* (New York: Macmillan Publishing Co., 1978) 26.

[32]Lewis, *Miracles*, 118.

[33]Lewis, *The Problem of Pain*, 33.

[34]Ibid., 36.   [35]Ibid., 40.   [36]Ibid., 48.

[37]Ibid., 46.   [38]Ibid., 107.   [39]Ibid., 104.

[40]Ibid., 112.

[41]Hooper, *God in the Dock*, 103.

[42]C. S. Lewis, *A Grief Observed* (New York: Seabury Press, Inc., 1988) 28.

[43]John Beversluis, professor of philosophy at Butler University, wrote a book entitled *C. S. Lewis and the Search for Rational Religion* in which he argued that the death of Lewis's wife left his faith in shreds. Beversluis's argument, however, is groundless. According to Walter Hooper, Beversluis later admitted that he had overstated his case.

[44]Lewis, *A Grief Observed*, 76-78.

3.
In Defense of Permanent Things

T. S. Eliot coined the term "Permanent things" in reference to the enduring standards that in times past constituted the essence of our Western civilization. An impressive number of Anglo-Christians have mourned the loss of these standards and voiced the fear that their loss portends grave consequences for the future of our civilization. G. K. Chesterton, W. H. Auden, Charles Williams, Dorothy Sayers, and J. R. R. Tolkien joined Eliot and C. S. Lewis in a chorus of warning during the first half of this century. Lewis's interest in permanent things was conspicuously present in all of his writings, but his concern for the preservation of the permanent truths and values that had sustained Western civilization was carefully focused in the inaugural address he gave at Cambridge.

Magdalene College at Cambridge, Oxford's old rival, recognized Lewis's important contribution to the field of English literary history and criticism, and in 1955 they honored him with a chair in Medieval and Renaissance literature.[1] In his inaugural lecture Lewis described himself as "A Man of the Old West." He was, no doubt, thinking primarily of his work as a literary critic, but he was also addressing the broader commitment he had to the overarching standards of Western civilization that were quickly disappearing. Lewis's approach to literature was to take it on its own terms. He did not believe that literature should be read from the perspective of a modern person's response. "One thing I know," Lewis said, "I'd give a great deal to hear any ancient Athenian, even a stupid one, talking about Greek tragedy. He would know in his bones so much that we seek in vain."[2] Lewis's objective as a critic was not to be creative, or to add his interpretation, but to read a text as a native.

The "old dinosaur," as he called himself, desired nothing more than to stand before the modern world as that Athenian might stand—as a native who understood and appreciated the old realities. Lewis was very much aware that he was living in a new era, a post-Christian era that was radically different from the Christian and even the pre-Christian paganism of the past. He believed, however, that what separated the Christian from the post-Christian was more radical than that which separated Christians from pagans. "The gap between those who worshiped different gods is not so wide," Lewis argued, "as that between those who worship and those who don't."[3] Both pagans and Christians were at least open to supernatural forces.

The Post-Christian perspective basically discarded the assumption that humans are fallen and in need of redemption. It confesses no belief in timeless values and moral absolutes. Consequently, there is nothing to worship but humanity itself and the works of human hands. The Post-Christian person stands, as it were, as a lonely individual before an impersonal universe that has no purpose or meaning apart from that which he or she creates.

Lewis had no interest in merely idealizing the past. "Our ancestors," he admitted, "were cruel, lecherous, greedy and stupid—like ourselves . . . but was civilization often in serious danger of disappearing? No," he answered, "but now it is."[4] The risk of its moral and spiritual collapse was more imminent because the foundations that had supported our civilization had been eroded. The preservation of Western civilization was actually not Lewis's supreme interest. That was a secondary interest. For civilization to be safe, it must be subject to the permanent truths and values that undergird the Christian worldview. To make civilization supreme is to make it vulnerable.[5] The surest foundation for Western man would be to "seek first the kingdom of God and His righteousness" (Matt 6:33).

The changes that had altered the public mind about permanent things in the past hundred years were disturbing because they represented a move away from the truths and values of the kingdom of God. Any kingdom whose beliefs and values stand in conflict with the kingdom of God should not expect to stand. Augustine argued this point many centuries ago in *The City of God*, and, in principle, Lewis fully agreed. It is indeed frightful to live in a world where "permanent things" have been forsaken in favor of one in which everything is believed to be in a state of flux, where there is nothing more permanent to live for than what one "approves of" and "feels good about."

The Loss of Permanent Truth and Value

Do changeless, permanent things actually exist? Is there anything we can count on to remain constant? This age-old question preoccupied the ancient Greeks and continues to engage serious thinkers today. It is not an insignificant matter. What one believes about the existence of permanent things largely determines what one believes about the nature of truth and value. And what one believes about truth and value determines how one lives one's life. It is more than an abstract speculative question; it is a life question of utmost significance.

Throughout most of Western history the existence of permanent things was assumed; today, it is not. What was once the prevailing conviction among educated Westerners has, in modern times, become a "dead option" for many intellectuals. It has been taken over, Lewis believed, by the twin "myths" of evolutionism and historicism.

Evolutionism

Modern persons, like the ancients, live by their myths. Lewis uses the term "myth" in this instance to refer to a picture of reality that has resulted from the imagination and not from reason. He was convinced that evolutionism has been the great imaginative myth of the nineteenth and twentieth centuries. It was an idea that found widespread expression in Romantic literature and music some time before Darwin's *Origin of the Species* in 1859. The imagination of Westerners had been prepared for evolutionism some time before its appearance in the field of science. When biological evolution established itself as scientific orthodoxy, the concept became even more marketable to other disciplines and soon found acceptance in the popular mind.

Lewis was careful to distinguish the *theory* of evolution, held by biologists, from accepted popular notions about evolutionism or developmentalism. The biologist holds to evolution as a scientific hypothesis on the same grounds as any other hypothesis: that it can account for more facts with fewer assumptions. Whether that hypothesis be true or not, it does not presume to be anything more than a hypothesis and it certainly cannot become a cosmic, metaphysical, or eschatological statement. On the mythical level, on the other hand, that is precisely what evolutionism becomes. As a scientific theory, evolution simply tries to explain changes within organic life on this planet. In the imaginative popular mind, however, it is assumed that changes imply improvement, that things are moving "onwards and upwards." What starts out as a tentative theory becomes a factual statement about progress on a cosmic scale:

Having first turned what was a theory of change into a theory of improvement, it [evolutionism] then makes this a cosmic theory. Not merely terrestial organisms but everything is moving "upwards and onwards." Reason has "evolved" out of instinct, virtue out of complexes, poetry out of erotic howls and grunts, civilization out of savagery, the organic out of inorganic, the solar system out of some sidereal soup or traffic block. And conversely, reason, virtue, art and civilization as we now know them are only the crude or embryonic beginnings of far better things—perhaps Deity itself—in the remote future. For in the Myth, "Evolution" (as the Myth understands it) is the formula of all existence. . . . To those brought up on the Myth nothing seems more normal, more natural, more plausible, than that chaos should turn into order, death into life, ignorance into knowledge. And with this we reach the fullblown Myth. It is one of the most moving and satisfying world dramas which have ever been imagined.[6]

Lewis was himself a romantic. There was much in the Myth that he found enchanting. Though he spoke of the Myth as something to be debunked and buried, he doubted that its popularity with the masses could be dispelled. In the folk imagination, evolutionism is a convenient and plausible explanation of the movement of things on a cosmic scale. Everything is becoming everything else—the later stages always being superior to the earlier ones. It is always a matter of the "developed" evolving from the "undeveloped," never a matter of conforming to some permanent truth or value. Love comes out of lust, virtue out of instinct. In this way one can "debunk" all of the respectable things by passing them off as improvements. On the other hand, disrespectable things never seem as bad as they are because they can be represented as the undeveloped forms of the better things. Vice is only undeveloped virtue, egoism only undeveloped altruism. A little more time and a little more education will take care of it. Things are never really totally different in kind; they are only different in degree. On the moral level then, sin is never quite as bad as it seems, and righteousness never as good. There is no basis for a real qualitative difference between them.

Political parties have a stake in the Myth for they all claim to represent what is positive and good in a changing society. Progressive politics never concentrates on conserving the good; it concentrates on changing things for the better in the future. Evolutionism is also an economic ally of those who manufacture and sell us goods and provide our services. Popular evolutionism suits them fine. Nothing is expected to last, and good workmanship can be minimized. Obselesence is not only natural, it can be planned. The old models will always be superceded. The latest fashions are always superior. Consumerism is the order of the day. Lewis sarcastically noted that in our time "sales resistance [had become] the modern sin against the Holy Ghost."[7]

Convinced that they have mastered nature and become the controllers of their own fates, modern persons are ready to rule the galaxy. Lewis spoke disparagingly of modern humanity's vision for the future: "Eugenics have made certain that only demi-gods will now be born; psycho-analysis that none of them will lose or smirch his divinity: economics that they shall have to hand all that demi-gods require. Man has ascended his throne. Man has become God."[8]

Lewis admitted that he too felt the enchantment of the Myth. The only part of him the Myth did not appeal to, he noted, was his reason. It was on rational grounds that he challenged its validity. The self-contradiction in the Myth is its Achilles' heel. It asks one to accept the reasonableness of the Myth while claiming that reason itself is the product of a mindless process. A materialistic evolutionary account of human thought cannot elevate it above a zoological fact about *homo sapiens*. All that one can talk about, from this perspective, is how the brain works. There is no basis in evolutionism for talking about a non-human universal reality that gives validity to our logic that, of course, includes the logic of the "Myth."

This irrationalism is fatal to the physical sciences, upon which the "Myth" largely rests, because they depend upon the validity of inference. If logical inferences cannot be trusted, then the sciences themselves are groundless. That which is the product of an endless and mindless "becoming" is hardly acceptable as a rational basis for anything— certainly not for science. Lewis explained:

> The real sciences cannot be accepted for a moment unless rational inferences are valid: for every science claims to be a series of inferences from observed facts. . . . Unless you start by believing that reality in the remotest space and the remotest time rigidly obeys the laws of logic, you can have no ground for believing in any astronomy, any biology, any palaeontology, any archaeology. To reach the positions held by the real scientists—which are then taken over by the Myth—you must—in fact, treat reason as an absolute. But at the same

time the Myth asks me to believe that reason is simply the unforeseen and unintended by-product of its endless and aimless becoming. The content of the Myth thus knocks from under me the only ground on which I could possibly believe the Myth to be true.[9]

Lewis argued that we must give up talking about reason as something merely *human*. Reason is not something shut up in our heads, he said. It is something "out there," something permanent outside us that exists as an objective reality. We do not read rationality into an irrational universe; rather, our human knowledge is possible because God created us capable of responding to a rationality that saturates the universe.

If there is an objective truth in the universe that has a supernatural source, and if we have the capacity to know this truth, is it not also reasonable to assume that we live in a universe with absolute and objective values as well? All human accusations, even our accusation that the universe is valueless, implies a standard:

> If a Brute and Blackguard made the world, then he also made our minds. If he made our minds, he also made the standard in them whereby we judge him to be a Brute and Blackguard. And how can we trust a standard which comes from such a brutal and blackguardly source? If we reject him, we ought to reject all his works. But one of his works is this very moral standard by which we reject him. If we accept this standard then we are really implying that he is not a Brute and Blackguard. If we reject it, then we have thrown away the only instrument by which we can condemn him. Heroic anti-theism thus has a contradiction in its centre. You must trust the universe in one respect in order to condemn it in every other.
>
> What happens to our sense of values is, in fact, exactly what happens to our logic. If it is a purely human sense of values—a biological by-product in a particular species with no relevance to reality—then we cannot, having once realized this, continue to use it as the ground for what are meant to be serious criticisms of the nature of things.[10]

The point that Lewis was making, of course, is that neither our minds nor our moral standards are alien to reality. We can reason and we have moral standards because there is an objective truth and an objective standard of morality in the universe. Otherwise, all of our thoughts and all of our moral standards would be worthless. Lewis argued for standards of beauty on the same grounds. "There is no reason why our reaction to a beautiful landscape should not be the response, however humanly blurred and partial, to a something that is really there."[11] Life cannot then be meaningless flux if there are at least these three permanent things—the true, the good, and the beautiful.

Historicism

It is not necessary to say as much about Lewis's criticism of historicism because he simply regarded it as the extension of evolutionary thought into the realm of history. Again, Lewis was careful not to impugn a legitimate discipline. He distinguished the noble discipline of history from the "fatal pseudo-philosophy" he called *historicism*.

Lewis characterized historicism as the tendency on the part of theologians, philosophers, politicians, and others to interpret the historical process on the basis of their own learning or genius—using evolutionism as their principle of interpretation. He was not opposed to finding a "meaning" in history or in some particular historical event through divine revelation, but he had no confidence in our natural ability to read the meaning of the process out of the process itself. The meaning of history had to come from "beyond history."

Those who stare too long at the flux of history tend to see vague patterns, "like pictures in the fire," Lewis noted. But the well-defined plot of history cannot be known through speculative imagination. In the modern world, he believed, there is the tendency to adopt some "grand theory" of history and then religiously follow its path. The pantheistic thought of Hegel and the materialistic promises of Karl Marx are good examples of grand theories that have seemed promising and attractive to masses of people in the past hundred years. Many have followed these theories of history as one would follow a religion, trusting that world history was moving in the direction of improvement for humankind —trusting in them as one would some kind of eschatological hope. The fatal assumption has always been that the "good" would somehow emerge out of the flux of history instead of breaking into history.

Progressivism, or belief in change for the better, is not supported by the well-defined plot of the Christian story that pivots on Creation, the Fall, Redemption, and Judgment. The unchanging truth about humanity that we know from "beyond" history is that we are sinners in need of redemption. No amount of change in human environment or in our accidental qualities can alter that fact about our essence. "Whatever we have been," Lewis believed, "we are still." The only two events that have ever changed humanity's essence are the Fall and Redemption.[12]

The Poison of Subjectivity

Lewis's emphasis upon objective truth and value was not intended to suggest that all subjective desires are suspect or that subjective experiences are foreign to Christianity. There is, Lewis insisted, something within a person that says, "I want God," no less than hunger saying "I want food," or thirst saying, "I want water." Our knowledge of God is more than a matter of raw truth. It is our heart's deepest yearning to know God as one knows a person. We yearn to enjoy God, to experience God's presence.

Subjective feelings and emotions are, in fact, closely connected with our beliefs. They are tandem experiences. It is altogether normal, for example, for a person to feel the emotion of gratitude when that person has been blessed by a benefactor. It would be unreasonable not to feel grateful. Similarly, one would expect to feel anger toward a gross injustice. The lack of it would indicate an insensitivity to the moral order that governs us. The Apostle Paul, for instance, spoke of virtues that the Holy Spirit cultivates in us when we are indwelt by God's power and presence. Virtues like love, joy, and peace have their emotional expression, but these emotions or subjective experiences are tied to an independent objective reality. When appropriate emotions are properly connected with true Christian beliefs, stable virtues and experiences will result. Both are important to each other. Sound theology or proper beliefs shape our emotions, and proper emotions, in turn, help to establish our theology.

Lewis had no difficulty with this kind of subjectivity. It was, in fact, very important to him. One will remember that he regarded unfulfilled desires as indicators from experience that there is a realm of fulfillment beyond this world. The kind of subjectivity that Lewis rejected is the kind that disconnects emotions and desires from the *Tao*, the objective source of all meaning and value.[13] Instead of focusing on the *Tao* and allowing proper emotions and values to follow from the discovery of the object and its meaning, the subjectivist focuses on the emotions themselves and tries to create meaning and value out of his own subjectivity. Lewis illustrated the fallacy from his own experience:

> I myself do not enjoy the society of small children: because I speak from within the *Tao*, I recognize this as a defect in myself—just as a man may have to recognize that he is tone deaf or color blind. And because our approvals and disapprovals are thus recognitions of objective value or responses to an objective order, therefore emotional states can be in harmony with reason (when we feel liking for what ought to be approved) or out of harmony with reason (when we perceive that liking is due but cannot feel it). No emotion is, in itself, a judgment: in that sense all emotions and sentiments are alogical. But they can be reasonable or unreasonable as they conform to Reason or fail to conform. The heart never takes the place of the head: but it can, and should, obey it.[14]

The proper relation between truth and subjectivity is not an insignificant matter. What is at stake in the relation is the doctrine of objective truth and value. To reject it, Lewis reminded us, is to reject the only basis we have for saying that some attitudes are really true while others are false. Similarly, there is no basis for value apart from permanent standards. "The human mind," Lewis noted, "has no more power of inventing a new value than of imagining a new primary color, or, indeed, of creating a new sun and a new sky for it to move in."[15] Once objective value has been given up, there is nothing to take its place but one's "feelings." And they are the feelings that we have been conditioned to have.

The best that one can hope for when *truth* and *objective reality* have been abandoned is the gratification of one's own subjectivity and/or a dependence upon practical results. This has been amply illustrated in virtually every philosophical, artistic, and scientific field of endeavor in the twentieth century. Its political manifestation is embodied in all attempts to disassociate political power from that which is true and right and attach it instead to successful propaganda. This attitude has, of course, not been restricted to any one political party or movement. It has been readily adopted by both wings on the political spectrum. Subjectivism finds its religious expression in those who value religion primarily for its usefulness or because religion helps them "feel better."

Religionists of this sort, Lewis noted, "only want to know if it [religion] will be comforting, or 'inspiring', or socially useful."[16]

Lewis traced the influence of subjectivity on science, education, and ethics in somewhat greater detail. These influences will be noted in the sections that follow.

The Magician's Bargain

Many have heard about the proverbial "magician's bargain." It is the would-be magician's willingness to give up his soul in return for magical power. The fateful end of the bargain is the realization that the conferred power never really belongs to the magician but, in fact, enslaves him. That through which he meant to conquer, in the end, conquers him.

The irony of the "magician's bargain" is nowhere better illustrated than in the field of applied science. Modern technology was meant to represent humanity's ultimate triumph over nature. It was expected that technology would usher in a better and happier life for all. As it turns out, however, our power over nature has really become a means of exercising power over other persons by using nature as an instrument. Lewis alluded to the contraceptive as an example of this paradox:

> As regards contraceptives there is a paradoxical, negative sense in which all possible future generations are the patients or subjects of a power wielded by those already alive. By contraception simply, they are denied existence; by contraception used as a means of selective breeding, they are, without their concurring voice, made to be what one generation, for its own reasons, may choose to prefer."[17]

In the same paradoxical way, he noted, we become the target for our own bombs and the victims of our own propaganda. The final stage comes, however, with our surrender of ourselves:

> The final stage is come when Man by eugenics, by pre-natal conditioning, and by an education and propaganda based on a perfect applied psychology, has obtained full control over himself. Human nature will be the last part of Nature to surrender to Man. The battle will then be won. We shall . . . be henceforth free to make our species whatever we wish it to be. The battle will indeed be won. But who, precisely, will have won it?[18]

Lewis was particularly concerned about the developments he believed were taking place in the field of education. These developments too represented acts of self-surrender. In the old system, he noted, there was the *Tao*, the overarching standard of truth and value to which both student and teacher were expected to conform. There was no liberty to depart from it:

> They [the old teachers] did not cut some men to some pattern they had chosen. They handed on what they had received: they initiated the young neophyte into the mysteries of humanity which over-arched him and them alike. It was but old birds teaching young birds to fly.[19]

When the *Tao* has been surrendered, however, there are no over-arching truths and values. The only values are those of the Conditioners. The conditioned are the victims of whatever artificial tao the Conditioners have chosen. The Conditioners, by necessity, become the Motivators and Managers. Their role is to convince the conditioned that they ought to like what the Conditioners say and that they ought to use the methods the Conditioners suggest in order to achieve the artificial tao. In a classic statement from *The Abolition of Man*, Lewis summarized the profound difference between the old attitude and the new:

> For the wise men of old the cardinal problem had been how to conform the soul to reality, and the solution had been knowledge, self-discipline, and virtue. For magic and applied science alike the problem is how to subdue reality to the wishes of men: the salvation is a technique; and both, in the practice of this technology, are ready to do things hitherto regarded as disgusting and impious.[20]

It is not that persons cannot be happy outside the *Tao*. They can. It does not necessarily mean that they will be evil persons. They may not. The tragedy is that they cease to be persons at all. They become specimens, artifacts. Our attempt to conquer nature, which in the final analysis includes ourselves, results in our own abolition.

Men without Chests

Belief in a realm of objective truth and value does not of itself produce moral character. It is not enough to know the truth; we must live truthfully. It is not enough to know the good; we are to be good. The justification of a virtue does not itself enable one to be virtuous. Virtuous living requires the kind of trained habit that God is graciously willing to nurture us in but that we must be willing to practice. Moral character is more than a sudden impulse or a passing inclination. It is a moral disposition to choose and do what is right, and this disposition is the product of something more than a single factor in a person's life. Developing moral character, Lewis believed, is somewhat analagous to becoming a good tennis player:

> Someone who is not a good tennis player may now and then make a good shot. What you mean by a good player is the man whose eye and muscles and nerves have been so trained by making innumerable good shots that they can now be relied on. They have a certain tone or quality which is there even when he is not playing, just as a mathematician's mind has a certain habit and outlook which is there even when he is not doing mathematics. In the same way a man who perseveres in doing just actions gets in the end a certain quality of character. It is that quality rather than the particular actions which we mean when we talk of "virtue."[21]

Moral character is not so much a matter of our head winning out over our instincts or vice versa, but of both being ruled by what Lewis called the middle element—the "chest." The instincts or impulses that God has given us are not in themselves good or evil. They must be cultivated, through trained habit, into stable sentiments. Without natural instincts a person is mere spirit. Without intellect he or she is mere animal. We were not meant to be ruled entirely by our heads, as the ancient Greeks supposed, or by our stomachs—as many moderns seemingly believe. The Christian view, Lewis believed, is that both should be ruled by the middle element of moral discipline. Persons without moral discipline are like men without chests.

Lewis declared,

> Strickly speaking there are no such things as good and bad impulses. Think of . . . a piano. It has not got two kinds of notes on it, the "right" notes and the "wrong" ones. Every single note is right at one time and wrong at another. The Moral Law is not any one instinct or any set of

instincts: it is something which makes a kind of tune (the tune we call goodness or right conduct) by directing the instincts.[22]

Nature does not deal us all the same hand. Our instincts differ. Some have better raw material than others; some through heredity, others through training and environment. The point is that we must all play, as best we can, the hand that we have been dealt. God does not judge us on the basis of the raw material but on the basis of the choices we make.

The choices we make are either making us into more "heavenly" or more "hellish" creatures. And the more heavenly we become, the better we see our own badness and the need we have for grace. "You can understand the nature of drunkenness," Lewis noted, "when you are sober, not when you are drunk. Good people know about both good and evil: bad people do not know about either."[23]

Lewis's understanding of moral development was not one that disengaged nature from grace. Nor was it one that excluded human will and reason from the Divine initiative. In *The Four Loves* Lewis compared the processes of moral growth to that of a garden:

It is no disparagement to a garden to say that it will not fence and weed itself, nor prune its own fruit trees, nor roll and cut its own lawns. A garden is a good thing but that is not the sort of goodness it has. It will remain a garden, as distinct from a wilderness, only if someone does all these things to it. Its real glory is of quite a different kind. The very fact that it needs constant weeding and pruning bears witness to that glory. It teems with life. It glows with colour and smells like heaven and puts forward at every hour of a summer day beauties which man could never have created and could not even, on his own resources, have imagined. If you want to see the difference between its contribution and the gardener's, put the commonest weed it grows side by side with his hoes, rakes, shears, and packet of weed killer; you have put beauty, energy, fecundity beside dead, sterile things. Just so, our 'decency and common sense' show grey and deathlike beside the geniality of love. And when the garden is in its full glory the gardener's contributions to that glory will still have been in a sense paltry compared with those of nature. Without life springing from the earth, without rain, light and heat descending from the sky, he could do nothing. When he has done all, he has merely encouraged here and discouraged there, powers and beauties that have a different source. But his share, though small, is indispensable and laborious. When God planted a garden He set a man over it and set the man under Himself. When He planted the garden of our nature and caused the flowering, fruiting loves to grow there, He set our will to 'dress' them. Compared with them it is dry and cold. And unless His grace comes down, like the rain and the sunshine, we shall use this tool to little purpose. But its laborious—and largely negative—services are indispensable. If they were needed when the garden was still Paradisal, how much more now when the soil has gone sour and the worst weeds seem to thrive on it best? But heaven forbid we should work in the spirit of prigs and Stoics. While we hack and prune we know very well that what we are hacking and pruning is big with a splendour and vitality which our rational will could never of itself have supplied. To liberate that splendour, to let it become fully what it is trying to be, to have tall trees instead of scrubby tangles, and sweet apples instead of crabs, is part of our purpose.[24]

The problem with modern moral education is that it has capitulated to what persons like rather than what they *ought* to like. Those who stand outside the *Tao* can only regard the "ought" as some kind of subjective feeling. They seek to debunk objective truth and value and then expect to continue on as usual under a full head of "drive" and "creativity." The conditioners, or propagandists, become the man-moulders, and the result is men without chests—men without moral discipline. Lewis noted,

In a sort of ghastly simplicity we remove the organ [objective value] and demand the function. We make men without chests and expect of them virtue and enterprise. We laugh at honour and are shocked to find traitors in our midst. We castrate and bid the geldings be fruitful.[25]

Lewis agreed with Aristotle who said that the "aim of education is to make the pupil like and dislike what he ought." The task is to train one's habits so that appropriate responses will follow, regardless of the actions of others. One must be true to his or her own nature as that nature is defined by the *Tao*. The difference between the old and the new education is that the one was interested in propagation, the other in propaganda. Lewis observed,

Where the old initiated, the new merely "conditions." The old dealt with its pupils as grown birds deal with young birds when they teach them to fly: the new deals with them more as the poultry-keeper deals with young birds—making them thus or thus for purposes of which the birds know nothing.[26]

The new education, with its appeal to "democratic" feelings and values, is undoubtedly more appealing to those who have been conditioned to value individuality so highly. But Lewis doubted that such feelings and values could continue to preserve democracy. He wrote:

> Beauty is not democratic; she reveals herself more to the few than to the many, more to the persistent and disciplined seekers than to the careless. Virtue is not democratic; she is achieved by those who pursue her more hotly than most men. Truth is not democratic; she demands special talents and special industry in those to whom she gives her favours. Political democracy is doomed if it tries to extend its demand for equality into these higher spheres. Ethical, intellectual, or aesthetic democracy is death.[27]

The concept of equality, Lewis believed, has no place in the world of the mind. He was not even sure that it could succeed as a social concept. An approach to education that forsakes the demands of excellence cannot continue to support true democracy. An inferiorly educated nation, he insisted, cannot survive indefinitely for "it can escape destruction only if its rivals and enemies are so obliging as to adopt the same system. A nation of dunces can be safe only in a world of dunces."[28]

A Theology for Monday Morning

Archimedes, the greatest of ancient scientists, was intoxicated with the potential that he saw in the lever and the pulley. He announced that if he had a fixed fulcrum to work with he could move anything. "Give me a place to stand on," he said, "and I will move the world." Archimedes enduring contribution to philosophy was his recognition of the fact that we must all have something permanent to stand upon.

Lewis called himself a dinosaur, but his contemporaries found an uncanny relevance in his affirmation that there is something to stand upon —a realm of permanent things that cannot be conditioned or relativized by the historical, the transitory, the individual. These were the realities that had attracted the Greek mind and sustained the overarching values of Western civilization until modern times.

Lewis never believed, however, that all truth exists in some abstract transhistorical realm. One will recall that it was the concrete demands of the incarnate Jesus that pulled Lewis out of the comforts of abstract theism. After his conversion to Christianity and its incarnational perspective, Lewis was never comfortable with either a Greek or a modern understanding of truth. In the one [the Greek], there was the tendency to remove truth from the concrete conditions of human experience. In the other [the modern], there is the tendency to restrict all truth and value to the relativities of history.

Christianity, on the other hand, claims a standard of truth and goodness from beyond history but asserts that this truth has, in Jesus Christ, entered into history and the realm of human experience. Christian truth is not lost nor distorted by entering into the relativity of time. Christ alone is what gives permanent meaning to the flux of nature and history. This is, of course, the truth of the Incarnation. The Truth that God has given to humanity is the truth of the "Word become flesh."

God's "glory" is a glory that has been revealed under human conditions. If we are to be like God, the glory of the true, the good, and the beautiful must be revealed in our flesh and in our dealings with our neighbor. "God is made visible to us," John Wesley said, "in our neighbor." God never meant for us to become so earthly minded as to possess no heavenly wisdom, but neither did God intend for us to become so heavenly minded as to be no earthly good. The glory that we presently share with Christ is a glory that feels the weight of this world's pain and suffering.

We do not become more effective in this world by ceasing to think of the other world. On the contrary, we find both earthly and heavenly meaning when we begin with the heavenly perspective. The sense of eternity in what we do in the here-and-now is what gives perspective and value to the earthly task. Lewis urged that we must never forget the importance of what we have been called to do now nor allow the mundaneness of everyday life to diminish the sacredness of ordinary tasks and relationships.

In his well-known essay entitled "The Weight of Glory" Lewis movingly reminds us of the future glory we anticipate, but he concludes by exhorting us to remember that:

The cross comes before the crown and tomorrow is a Monday morning. . . . It may be possible for each to think too much of his own potential glory hereafter; it is hardly possible for him to think too often or too deeply about that of his neighbor. The load, or weight, or burden of my neighbor's glory should be laid on my back. . . . It is a serious thing to remember that the dullest and most uninteresting person you can talk to may one day be a creature which . . . you would be strongly tempted to worship, or else a horror and a corruption such as you now meet only in a nightmare. All day long we are, in some degree, helping each other to one or other of these destinations. It is in the light of these overwhelming possibilities . . . that we should conduct all our dealings with one another, all friendships, all loves, all play, all politics. There are no *ordinary* people. You have never talked to a mere mortal. . . . [I]t is immortals whom we joke with, work with, marry, snub, and exploit—immortal horrors or everlasting splendors. This does not mean that we are to be perpetually solemn. We must play. But our merriment must be of that kind (and it is, in fact, the merriest kind) which exists between people who have, from the outset, taken each other seriously—no flippancy, no superiority, no presumption. . . . Next to the Blessed Sacrament itself, your neighbor is the holiest object presented to your senses. If he is your Christian neighbor, he is holy in almost the same way, for in him also Christ *vere latitat*—the glorifier and the glorified, Glory Himself, is truly hidden.[29]

It is people, our neighbors whom we meet daily, who are permanent. Our highest calling in life is to help them reach that future glory for which they were created. Most of them will not find it in the lecture hall or even through the pulpit. Our Monday-morning theology, our love, is more likely to lead them to faith than our expositions or our arguments. The best service we can render to the skeptics and the half-convinced is to help them find the company of those who care. In the company of those who care they can more clearly see the truth for themselves.

Notes

[1]It is common knowledge that Lewis was passed over for a professorship at Oxford because of his Christian books. Many of his colleagues who did not share his faith were critical of his spending so much time on writings outside of his

academic specialty. Even some of his friends expressed disapproval with what they considered his "evangelistic" style.

[2]C. S. Lewis, "The Great Divide," *Christian History,* ed. Mark H. Tuttle (Worchester PA: Christian History Institute, 1985) 4/3:32.

[3]Ibid.

[4]Peter Kreeft, "Western Civilization at the Crossroads," *Christian History,* ed. Mark H. Tuttle (Worchester PA: Christian History Institute, 1985) 4/3:26.

[5]Ibid., 25.

[6]Hooper, *Christian Reflections,* 86.

[7]Ibid., 92.   [8]Ibid., 88.   [9]Ibid., 89.

[10]Ibid., 66, 67.   [11]Ibid., 71.

[12]Kreeft, "Western Civilization at the Crossroads," 26.

[13]Lewis used the Chinese concept of the *Tao* to refer to the reality beyond all predicates, that which provides the basis for the doctrine of objective value—regardless of its form (Platonic, Aristotelian, Stoic, Oriental, or Christian). He rejected the notion of legitimate emotions unrelated to the *Tao* itself.

[14]C. S. Lewis, *The Abolition of Man* (New York: Macmillan Publishing Co., 1973) 29, 30.

[15]Ibid., 56, 57.

[16]Walter Hooper, ed., *Present Concerns: Essays by C. S. Lewis* (New York: Harcourt, Brace, Jovanovich, Publishers, 1986) 65.

[17]Lewis, *The Abolition of Man,* 68.

[18]Ibid., 72.   [19]Ibid., 74.   [20]Ibid., 88.

[21]Lewis, *Mere Christianity,* 77.

[22]Ibid., 23.   [23]Ibid., 87.

[24]C. S. Lewis, *The Four Loves* (New York: Harcourt, Brace, Jovanovich, Publishers, 1960) 163-65.

[25]Lewis, *The Abolition of Man,* 35.

[26]Ibid., 33.

[27]Walter Hooper, *Present Concerns,* 34.

[28]Ibid., 33.

[29]Walter Hooper, ed., *The Weight of Glory and Other Essays* (New York: Macmillan Publishing Co., 1965) 18, 19.

Selected Bibliography

The sources listed are from American rather than British editions. They are not necessarily listed in alphabetical order.

Personal and Autobiographical

Surprised By Joy: The Shape of My Early Life. New York: Harcourt, Brace, Jovanovich, 1966.
A Grief Observed. New York: Bantam, 1976.
Letters, W. H. Lewis, ed. New York: Harcourt, Brace, Jovanovich, 1966.
Letters to an American Lady. Grand Rapids: Eerdmans, 1967.

Religious and Philosophical Works

Mere Christianity. New York: Macmillan, 1978.
Miracles: A Preliminary Study. New York: Macmillan, 1978.
The Problem of Pain. New York: Macmillan, 1978.
The Abolition of Man. New York: Macmillan, 1978.
The Screwtape Letters. New York: Macmillan, 1982.
The Four Loves. New York: Harcourt, Brace, Jovanovich, 1971.
Letters to Malcolm: Chiefly on Prayer. New York: Harcourt, Brace, Jovanovich, 1973.
Reflections on the Psalms. New York: Walker and Co., 1985.

Collections of Essays

The Weight of Glory and Other Addresses. New York: Macmillan, 1980.
God in the Dock. Grand Rapids MI: Eerdmans, 1970.
Christian Reflections. Grand Rapids MI: Eerdmans, 1968.
The World's Last Night and Other Essays. New York: Harcourt, Brace, Jovanovich, 1973.
Present Concerns. New York: Harcourt, Brace, Jovanovich, 1975.
Of Other Worlds: Essays and Stories. New York: Harcourt, Brace, Jovanovich, 1975.

Fiction

Till We Have Faces: A Myth Retold. New York: Harcourt, Brace, Jovanovich, 1980.

The Great Divorce. New York: Macmillan, 1978.

The Space Trilogy, 3 vols., including *Out of the Silent Planet, Perelandra,* and *That Hideous Strength.* New York: Macmillan, 1986.

The Pilgrim's Regress: An Allegorical Apology for Christianity, Reason, and Romanticism. New York: Bantam, 1981.

The Chronicles of Narnia, 7 vols., including *The Lion, the Witch and the Wardrobe, Prince Caspian, The Voyage of the "Dawn Treader," The Silver Chair, The Horse and His Boy, The Magician's Nephew,* and *The Last Battle.* New York: Macmillan, 1986.

Poetry

Poems. New York: Harcourt, Brace, Jovanovich, 1977.

Narrative Poems. New York: Harcourt, Brace, Jovanovich, 1979.

Literary History and Criticism

The Discarded Image: An Introduction to Medieval and Renaissance Literature. Cambridge: Cambridge University Press, 1964.

A Preface to "Paradise Lost." New York: Oxford University Press, 1942.

The Allegory of Love: A Study in Medieval Tradition. New York: Oxford University Press, 1936.

An Experiment in Criticism. New York: Cambridge University Press, 1961.

Studies in Words. Cambridge: Cambridge University Press, 1960.

English Literature in the Sixteenth Century, Excluding Drama (Volume 3 of *The Oxford History of English Literature*). Oxford: Clarendon Press, 1954.

On Stories and Other Essays on Literature. New York: Harcourt, Brace, Jovanovich, 1982.

Selected Secondary Sources

Beversluis, John. *C. S. Lewis and the Search for Rational Religion.* Grand Rapids MI: Eerdmans, 1985.

Carpenter, Humphrey. *The Inklings: C. S. Lewis, J. R. R. Tolkien, Charles Williams and their Friends.* Boston: Houghton Mifflin, 1979.

Como, James T. *C. S. Lewis at the Breakfast Table and Other Reminiscences.* New York: Macmillan, 1979.

Christopher, Joe R. *C. S. Lewis: An Annotated Checklist.* Kent OH: Kent State University Press, 1964.

Dorsett, Lyle W. *And God Came in: The Extraordinary Life of Joy Davidman, Her Life and Marriage to C. S. Lewis.* New York: Macmillan, 1983.

Green, Roger Lancelyn. *C. S. Lewis, A Biography.* New York: Harcourt, Brace, Jovanovich, 1974.

Kreeft, Peter. *C. S. Lewis: A Critical Essay.* Front Royal VA: Christendom College Press, 1988.

Schakel, Peter J. *Reason and Imagination in C. S. Lewis.* Grand Rapids MI: Eerdmans, 1984.

Ford, Paul. *Companion to Narnia.* San Francisco CA: Harper and Row, 1980.

Holmer, Paul L. *C. S. Lewis: The Shape of His Faith and Thought.* New York: Harper and Row, 1976.

Walsh, Chad. *C. S. Lewis: Apostle to the Skeptics.* New York: Macmillan, 1949.

Purtill, Richard J. *C. S. Lewis' Case for the Christian Faith.* Grand Rapids MI: Eerdmans, 1964.

Kilby, Clyde. *The Christian World of C. S. Lewis.* Grand Rapids MI: Eerdmans, 1964.

Kilby, Clyde. *C. S. Lewis: Images of His World.* Grand Rapids MI: Eerdmans, 1973.

Schakel, Peter J., ed. *The Longing for a Form: Essays on the Fiction of C. S. Lewis.* Kent OH: Kent State University Press,

Part Two: Edward John Carnell

Introduction

4. The Intellectual Odyssey of Edward John Carnell

   A. The Journey
   B. The Old Evangelicalism
   C. The Rise of Fundamentalism
   D. Orthodoxy Gone Cultic
   E. The High Cost of Courage
   F. The Carnell Legacy

5. A Coherent and Relevant Faith

   A. The Gospel and Culture
   B. A Gospel for the Whole Person
   C. A Reasonable Faith
     1. Faith: A Legitimate Assumption
     2. Systematic Consistency: The Test for Truth
   D. A Wise Choice
     1. Materialism and Pleasure: The Values of a
        Sensate Culture
     2. Scientific Positivism: Worshiping a Method
     3. Humanism: A Devotion to Man
     4. Theism: Commitment to God
   E. A Satisfied Heart

Selected Bibliography

Introduction

Michelangelo's famous "Pieta," which graces the entrance to St. Peter's Cathedral in Rome, was undoubtedly the work that established his reputation as the greatest of renaissance sculptors. But it was not the work that presented Michelangelo with his greatest challenge. Having completed the "Pieta," he returned to Florence where he discovered a hugh block of marble in the courtyard of the cathedral from which an earlier sculptor had attempted to carve a statue. The earlier sculptor had, however, only succeeded in disfiguring it. Other sculptors who had considered using the valuable block decided against it out of fear of risking the humiliation of further failure. Michelangelo accepted the challenge, and from the disfigured block he carved his famous statue of "David," which became the symbol of the city of Florence.

His project took two years, and when it was finished Michelangelo's "David" stood fifteen feet high and became known as "The Giant." Unlike Donatello's "David," which depicted David as a puny boyish figure in a shepherd's hat, Michelangelo's "David" was a youthful warrior whose face reflected courage and whose body denoted physical beauty and strength. The long-limbed youth was still awkward. He had not yet attained full harmonious development, but Michelangelo had artfully depicted David's potential for greatness. The statue was meant to represent the youthful David at the moment when he says to Goliath, "I have come unto thee in the name of the Lord of Hosts." Michelangelo's "David" became the pride of the citizens of Florence and came to symbolize the spirit of the Italian Renaissance. It extolled the glory of man and the rebirth of classical learning.

In the post World War II era a renaissance of another kind began to take form in America. This one was religious in nature. Its aim was to restore the power and vision of Protestant orthodoxy through a revival of theological scholarship. In this way the leaders of the movement felt that they could bring greater glory to God.

This movement, too, had its symbols. A young evangelical scholar named Edward John Carnell stood proudly as one of the "Davids" of this religious renaissance. He was not a natural born leader. He was socially awkward and ill-at-ease in administrative roles, but Carnell stood tall and squarely in the forefront of a newly emerging brain trust that hoped to restore intellectual respectability to conservative theology.

The evangelical movement had its roots in American fundamentalism. But few of the newly emerging evangelicals were happy about wearing the fundamentalist label. There were simply too many negatives to be overcome. The fundamentalist movement had served as a rallying point for a few gifted and many not-so-gifted conservatives who had rushed to do battle with modernists in the aftermath of the controversy over evolution and biblical criticism. Many fundamentalists were sincere and well-intentioned but could be likened to the Florentine sculptor of Michelangelo's day who had only succeeded in disfiguring his work. They may have been right in their affirmation of the fundamentals of the faith, but they had, in the minds of many evangelicals of the time, distorted the classical Christian message through cultic ideological thinking.

Evangelicals proudly wore the conservative label because they valiantly held to and defended the historic doctrines of the Christian faith. But they tended to avoid the "fundamentalist" tag because it had come to represent truth in the service of a cause with which they could no longer identify. They regarded themselves as "evangelicals" because they were fully committed to the gospel of grace that is revealed in Jesus Christ, but they rejected the notion that "evangelical" represented some ideological party within the larger community of faith. Their commitment was to the classical theological tradition with its affirmation of a supernatural worldview and the historical trustworthiness of the biblical record. They proudly identified with the fundamentalist's stated belief in the Virgin Birth of Christ, his miracles, his deity and bodily resurrection, his substitutionary atonement for sin, and his second coming. Their differences were not over doctrine, except perhaps for eschatology, but over matters relating to attitude and behavior that had cost fundamentalists their credibility. Outspoken and misguided fundamentalists had exhibited such extreme intolerance, separatism, anti-intellectualism, and pharisaism that most non-conservatives concluded that they no longer deserved to be taken seriously. The infamous Scopes "monkey trial" in Dayton, Tennessee, in 1925 came to symbolize a movement that had betrayed its own serious beginnings by turning itself into a laughing stock.

Carnell was among those evangelical theologians who were conservative in theology but unhappy about being called "fundamentalist." He wanted to see the movement purged of its "cultic" elements and its intellectual respectability and integrity restored. The model he held up for emulation was the Reformed tradition, which he regarded as classical orthodoxy. He described classical orthodoxy as "that branch of Christendom which limits the ground of religious authority to the Bible."[1] What was needed, he believed, was an atmospheric change in attitude among Christian conservatives. Before the "David" of evangelicalism could successfully meet the "Goliath" of modernism "in the name of the Lord of Hosts," Carnell believed, it would first have to reform itself.

Carnell's vision for the evangelical movement in general, and for Fuller Theological Seminary in particular, was publicly articulated on 17 May 1955 when he stood, like a youthful David, before the faculty, students, and friends of the newly formed seminary to give his inaugural address. What he said that day set the agenda and the tone for an entire religious movement. It delineated an attitudinal difference between the new evangelicals and their hard-line fundamentalist brethren—a cleavage that had begun to appear about a decade earlier.

In his inaugural address Carnell called for a seminary marked by an atmosphere of love, tolerance, forgiveness, and academic freedom in which students and professors alike could pursue their studies.[2] He made no attempt to appease the seminary's fundamentalist supporters by using expected jargon or by making explicit reference to the historic doctrines of the church, though he had an unmistakable respect for and devotion to the theological distinctives that inhered in the seminary. He believed that a seminary that was truly centered in the word of God would provide the kind of intellectual and spiritual support that evangelicalism desperately needed. Carnell's dream was to see classical orthodoxy restored to its rightful place in the American religious tradition. To that end he devoted his learning and his life.

Notes

[1]Edward John Carnell, *The Case for Orthodox Theology* (Philadelphia PA: Westminster Press, 1959) 13.

[2]Edward John Carnell, "The Glory of a Theological Seminary," Pasadena CA: Fuller Theological Seminary Alumni Association.

4.
The Intellectual Odyssey
of Edward John Carnell

Theology, like good fiction, is always biographical. A theologian's intellectual commitments are always tied to the flesh and blood experiences out of which they arise. They can never be disembodied from real life experiences without robbing them of their vitality and form. What is most important and most interesting about intellectual pilgrimages are the twists and turns, the key events that shape the theologian's life and thought and give direction and meaning to his or her journey.

This brief introduction does not attempt to recount all of the biographical facts about Edward John Carnell but to recall some of the "flesh and blood" episodes in his life that will enable those not familiar with Carnell's story to understand better and appreciate his outstanding contribution to Christian apologetics in the twentieth century.

The Journey

Edward John Carnell's journey began in Antigo, Wisconsin, on 28 June 1919, the same day that World War I ended with the signing of the Treaty of Versailles. Edward was the third of four children born to Herbert and Fannie Carnell, the local pastor of Antigo's First Baptist Church. Herbert's roots went back to England where he had been born the thirteenth of fifteen children. In 1907, at the age of eighteen, he seized the chance for better economic opportunity in America and sailed from Southampton to Ellis Island where he was processed as an immigrant. He then boarded a train for Illinois to rejoin a brother. His original dream had been to better his economic life in America, but he soon found himself drawn toward a different future than he had envisioned.

Herbert's response to a sense of calling he felt upon his life was to enroll in the two-year pastor's course at Moody Bible Institute in Chicago to prepare for Christian ministry. It was there that he was introduced to American fundamentalism and to Fannie Carstens, whom he married. Both relationships were to endure. Until their retirement in 1962, Herbert and Fannie Carnell spent the better part of their lives in small fundamentalist Baptist pastorates in the American Midwest.

Times were hard in the pastorate during the 1920s, 1930s, and 1940s. More often than not the churches the Carnell's pastored were small, and the salary was always meagre. For a short while during the late 1920s Herbert left the ministry for secular employment, but reentered the ministry when the onset of the Great Depression cost him his job. Life in the Carnell household was somewhat rigid and strict, as it was in most Baptist parsonages of the time, but pastor Carnell was a moderate by fundamentalist standards. The Carnell children sometimes found their environment difficult, particularly during their teens, but it was never an intolerable situation.

Young Edward's growing up years were rather normal and uneventful. His high school grades were average, and his social experiences comparable to other teens living in a similar environment. But by late adolescence there were clear indications that he was a bright and moody young man who would one day have to work through some personal conflicts.

Those who knew him best during his formative years remember Edward's early struggle to discover his own sense of identity. He saw the good and admirable traits that characterized many fundamentalists with whom he associated, but he also witnessed and experienced the legalisms and distasteful attitudes that characterized so many others. He was determined to chart his own course. But shedding stereotyped behaviors, ideological thought patterns, and fundamentalist attitudes without appearing rebellious was no simple task.

The opportune time for young Carnell to begin working through his identity crisis and begin realizing his own personal goals came when he entered Wheaton College. The college at that time had a reputation for being one of the best Christian liberal arts colleges in the country. Carnell's high school grades had not been that promising, but the quality of his academic performance began to improve significantly once he found his proper niche in the philosophy major at Wheaton. Carnell had to work long hours in the college dining room in order to pay his tuition, but he always managed to find time for his philosophy assignments. Gordon Clark became Carnell's philosophy mentor at Wheaton and exerted a lasting influence upon his young student. Clark was a committed Calvinist with a strong interest in apologetics. He took a special interest in Carnell and seemed to enjoy mentoring him in the finer points of his discipline. In later years Carnell had minor intellectual disagreements with his old teacher, but he never forgot the major impact that Gordon Clark had made upon his thought life.

After taking his B.A. in philosophy from Wheaton, Carnell entered Westminster Theological Seminary in Philadelphia for graduate study. Westminster had been founded in 1929 by John Greshem Machen and other separatists from Princeton Seminary. The stated rationale for its existence was its commitment to the word of God and the Westminster Standards that the seminary's founders claimed had been forsaken at Princeton. Its mission was to preserve the theological heritage of the old Princeton and to equip young ministers to meet the challenges of the modern world from the perspective of the Reformed dogmatism of men like Archibald Alexander, John Hodge, and Benjamin Warfield. With the outstanding exception of Gordon Clark, Wheaton's faculty had been basically Arminian, but Westminster was a bastion of Calvinism. Carnell studied systematic theology under John Murray and apologetics under Cornelius Van Til—both staunch Calvinists. Despite some personal disagreements with Van Til's apologetic method, Carnell distinguished himself in Van Til's classes and won the prize that was awarded to the outstanding student in apologetics.

Carnell enjoyed the academic challenge at Westminster but profited from his matriculation there for personal reasons as well. During his last term he married Shirley Rowe, a school teacher from Wisconsin, whom he had met earlier on the Wheaton campus. He took his Th.B and Th.M degrees at Westminster with distinction and shortly thereafter was ordained to the Baptist ministry. He and Shirley were now ready to embark on Edward's dream—to work toward the Ph.D. in history and philosophy of religion at Harvard Divinity School. Harvard was a center of liberalism, an unlikely place for young men from a fundamentalist background, but Carnell was anxious to prove that he deserved to be at this prestigious university. The fall of 1944 found Edward and Shirley settled in Cambridge, just a few short blocks from the Divinity School—ready for the challenges of a Harvard education.

Students at the Harvard Divinity School were taught from a naturalistic, historicist, critical perspective that ordinarily would have been inimical to any fundamentalist. It so happened, however, that there were a number of outstanding graduate students from fundamentalist backgrounds at Harvard during this era who were anxious to face the intellectual challenges that were posed by the critical methods in their disciplines. Most of these young fundamentalist intellectuals were destined to become future leaders in the newly rising evangelical movement. Among them were Merrill Tenney, Kenneth Kantzer, John Gerstner, Harold Kuhn, Paul Jewett, George Eldon Ladd, Samuel Schultz, and Glenn Barker. There were inevitable ideological conflicts between these conservative students and the liberal Harvard faculty, but, in general, the faculty at Harvard was liberal enough and gracious enough to tolerate differences so long as students were committed to responsible scholarship. This era of so-called "Fundamentalism-on-the-Charles" was one that demanded unprecedented commitment to scholarship and self-examination on the part of the young evangelicals. Intellectual commitments that would shape and support the newly rising evangelical movement were being forged on an anvil of hard work and critical thinking in the ultra-liberal environment of Harvard University. The bygone era of easy answers, often derived from a narrow dogmatism, no longer seemed as satisfying to the young fundamentalists as they had once been. Carnell went through periods of personal intellectual struggle and admitted that there were times when his "old sack of stock answers" seemed empty.

Carnell had modest financial assistance from a scholarship, but it was not nearly enough. When the opportunity came for him to become the interim pastor of the First Baptist Church in nearby Marblehead, Massachusetts, he and Shirley gladly accepted. He also began to do some part-time teaching at Gordon College. It was during this time that Carnell recognized that teaching, not pastoring, was his real gift and calling. He enjoyed the classroom immensely, and his students consistently lauded the quality and resourcefulness of his teaching.

Two things of particular note happened to Carnell while he was still a graduate student at Harvard that would impact his future influence in the evangelical community. He somehow found time to work out a comprehensive rationalist perspective on apologetics and submitted the manuscript to the Eerdman's Publishing Company in response to an Evangelical Book Award contest they were sponsoring. Some fifty manuscripts had been submitted, but Carnell's won the prize. The prize was $5,000—an enormous sum in those days—but more importantly, the raving reviews from evangelicals brought wide-spread attention to the young Harward theologian. Evangelicals from across the country were convinced that they had seen a bright new star in the east.

The other development of note was Carnell's entrance into the Ph.D. program in philosophy at nearby Boston University while he was still a Th.D. candidate at Harvard. Carnell was anxious to study under the personalist philosopher E. S. Brightman and to delve more deeply into the existentialist philosophy of Søren Kierkegaard. This overlapping of doctoral programs did not set well with the Harvard faculty, but he was able to finish both programs as planned. In June of 1948 Carnell finished the Th.D. from Harvard with a dissertation on Reinhold Niebuhr that would later be published under the title *The Theology of Reinhold Niebuhr* (1950). Shortly thereafter he finished the Ph.D at Boston with a dissertation on Søren Kierkegaard that would be published under the title *The Burden of Søren Kierkegaard* (1965). The subjects of these two dissertations exercised a considerable influence on Carnell's later thought and writings.

Carnell's prize-winning volume on apologetics while he was at Harvard was entitled *Introduction to Christian Apologetics* (1948). This was later followed by other works on apologetics: *A Philosophy of the Christian Religion* (1952), *Christian Commitment* (1957), and *The Kingdom of Love and the Pride of Life* (1960). All were creative attempts to speak relevantly to thinking persons who were looking for a faith they could embrace with the consent of all their faculties. Carnell considered *Christian Commitment* his best work, but it turned out to be his biggest disappointment. It never received the attention he felt it deserved.

At the request of the Westminster Press, Carnell authored one of a series of three books intended to provide contemporary students of theology with a clear statement of the three prominent theological positions of the time. Carnell's work was entitled *The Case for Orthodoxy* (1960) and represented the conservative Reformed tradition. The other two in the series were *The Case for Theology in Liberal Perspective* by L. Harold DeWolf and *The Case for a New Reformation Theology* (a Neo-Orthodox perspective) by William Hordern. In his volume Carnell went beyond a mere articulation of the conservative position. He used the occasion to clear the air about the distinction between historic Reformed theology and modern fundamentalism. He ended by castigating fundamentalists for their "cultic" attitudes and practices. It was a bold but costly venture on Carnell's part. His critique of fundamentalism, which Carnell feared many would identify with conservative classical theology, created a breech between himself and fundamentalists that would never be healed.

Most of Carnell's writings referred to here were published after 1948 when Carnell moved west to the newly established Fuller Theological Seminary in Pasadena, California. He remained there until his death in 1967—serving as the president of the seminary for five years and later devoting full time to the classroom as professor of ethics and philosophy of religion. Carnell died, under mysterious circumstances, at the relatively young age of forty-seven. But during these few eventful years Carnell became a seminal figure, a pacesetter in shaping the thought and vision of what has been called "the evangelical renaissance" of the twentieth century.

The Old Evangelicalism

Kenneth Scott Latourette, the well-known Yale church historian, called the nineteenth century the "Great Century" in church history because of the church's unprecedented growth and vitality during this period. It was a period of missionary expansion throughout the world and particularly in America. In 1800, Latourette noted, only 6.9 percent of the American population had formal membership in some religious body, but by 1910 that figure had increased six-fold to 43.5 percent.[1]

Many currents in American history contributed to the growth. There was the expansion of the American frontier, the winning of the immigrants, the spread of Christianity among Indians and Blacks, and the evangelization of the burgeoning cities. Through the phenomenon of revivalism evangelical doctrines were preached, taught, and established as the unofficial creeds of the nation. George Marsden, a prominent religious historian, observed that the evangelical influences penetraded the country's institutions of higher learning, the popular culture, and the highest seats of government. American schools and colleges taught broadly evangelical doctrines, most universities required chapel attendance, and evangelical piety was expected, though not required, in the White House.[2] The mainstream of religious life in America during the nineteenth century was clearly located within the broad framework of evangelical Protestantism.

Evangelical piety was generally carried forward through revivals, camp meetings, missionary societies, Sunday Schools, youth movements, and educational institutions. Its leaders, for the most part, were common men and women who spoke the language of the frontiersman and the new urbanites. Famous preachers like Charles G. Finney and Dwight L. Moody were particularly effective in communicating the evangelical message and winning others to Christ and the church, but laity were also prominently involved in teaching and preaching, in leading lay organizations, and in personal soul-winning. In general there was not nearly as much interest in a professional clergy, theological subleties, or in Christianizing the social order as there was in basic Bible knowledge and practical Christian living. The old evangelicalism was, without doubt, marked by its emphasis upon personal piety and practical Christian living.

This did not mean, however, that evangelical piety was theologically amorphous. It had a fairly well-defined doctrinal content that was essentially the same as that which would later be delineated by fundamentalists: an affirmation of the supernatural origins of Christianity and the authority of Scripture from which they took their belief in the virgin birth and deity of Christ, his miracles and bodily resurrection, substitutionary atonement for sin, and his second coming. Evangelical doctrine was premised on the touchstone beliefs that all persons are sinners, that salvation from eternal damnation is possible only through Christ's atoning work on the cross, and that the primary purpose of the church is to win every lost person to Christ that it possibly can.

If the nineteenth century was the "Great Century" for religious growth and vitality in America, it was also, in the words of Sydney Ahlstrom, an "ordeal of faith."[3] Virtually everything that evangelical Protestantism stood for began to be challenged by philosophy, science, and the forces of liberalism during the last quarter of the century. Particularly disturbing, from the perspective of evangelicals, was the basic denial of Christianity's supernatural origins and the historical trustworthiness of the Bible.

Theological liberalism was grounded in the Ritschlian theology that dominated Protestant thought in Germany from 1875 to World War I and in America from the turn of the century until as late as the 1930s. Indebted to the critical idealism of Immanuel Kant, Ritschlianism precipitated an era of metaphysical agnosticism and a resultant surge of historical positivism. It was a time of emphasis on the empirical and the historical, and there followed an unprecedented openness to the conclusions of science and the application of historical-critical research to the biblical texts and the history of dogma. Ritschlian liberalism, with its skepticism toward metaphysics, its rejection of traditional dogma and natural theology, and its concentration on the historical Jesus with his ethical teachings and proclamation of the kingdom of God, seemed to be the perfect expression of liberal Protestantism.[4]

In America the liberal influence was filtered through the particular thinking of men like Horace Bushnell, William Newton Clarke, Borden Parker Bowne, Washington Gladden, and Walter Rauschenbusch. The result of the liberal influence was a greater emphasis in publications, in seminaries, and pulpits on such themes as moral education, the humanity of Jesus, the goodness of man, the inevitable progress of mankind, and the need to bring all of society into conformity with the ethical teachings of Jesus and the kingdom of God. The "liberal spirit" was expected to liberate religion from obscurantism and creedal traditions that purportedly bound person's minds to outdated worldviews and doctrines. Liberals, in general, saw their movement as a logical extension of the Enlightenment, carrying Protestant churches forward into the progress of modern science and philosophy.

Evangelical conservatives, however, saw the liberal movement in an entirely different light. What liberals called intellectual and social progress, conservatives regarded as something so entirely different from Christianity as to belong in a distinct category. Conservatives were particularly disturbed by the liberals' endorsement of Darwinian evolution, their acceptance of the new geology with its new conceptions of time and process, and the new questions that were being raised about the historical accuracy of the Bible, the history of doctrine, and the uniqueness of the Christian religion. The naturalistic and historicist assumptions that liberals embraced colored everything differently from how evangelicals had historically believed and practiced the Christian religion.

Controversies over evolution and the application of higher criticism to the Scriptures soon created highly emotional rifts between those who espoused the new "scientific" approach and those who viewed themselves as the defenders of the historic Christian message. Battlegrounds were drawn, and verbal clashes began to be heard across the country in seminaries, pulpits, and the presses. Many of the evangelical conservatives, who would later be known as "fundamentalists," saw the struggle as a kind of "holy war" into which they had been called to root out the forces of modernism. Heresy trials, seminary battles, and campaigns to gain doctrinal control in America's major denominations soon followed. The enduring symbol of the conflict turned out to be the infamous Scopes "monkey trial," which took place in Dayton, Tennessee, in 1925.[5]

In time the liberalizing trend won out as liberals gained control of the major seminaries, publications, and public opinion. Liberals were temperamentally suited for the inevitable social changes and could make intellectual adjustments more easily than their conservative counterparts. Many outspoken leaders in the fundamentalist movement inadvertently helped the liberal cause by exhibiting such distasteful attitudes and lack of discretion that they seemed to confirm the liberal charge that they were outdated obscurantists.

Theological liberalism, however, should not be stereotyped. All liberals did not come to the same conclusions or follow the same agenda. More moderate liberals were generally committed to biblical and historical criticism, but they sensed the need to maintain continuity with the historic evangelical faith. As Kenneth Cauthen put it in *The Impact of American Religious Liberalism,* these evangelical liberals were "serious Christians who were searching for a theology that could be believed by intelligent moderns."[6] They accepted the core of the historic Christian faith as normative. The problem, from a conservative point of view, was that by the time liberals had applied their historicist and naturalistic assumptions to the Christian tradition precious little was left in the core to be believed and practiced. In general, this moderate wing of liberalism generally turned out to be anti-creedal, arminian, moralistic, nonsacramental, and substantively weak in their support of traditional evangelical doctrines.

Modernistic liberals, on the other hand, had an even more tenuous connection with traditional Christianity. Their thinking was so shaped by presuppositions and values derived from modern science, philosophy, psychology, and social thought that virtually nothing was left that was uniquely Christian. It was, in fact, not even Christocentric, nor did it affirm the absoluteness of the Christian faith. These liberals, Cauthen says, were more interested in being "intelligent moderns" than they were in being "serious Christians." It no longer seemed viable to modernists to deduce theological conclusions from the Scriptures. Scientific explanations for the origin of man, the development of the universe, and human behavior had rendered theological explanations obsolete.

Traditional evangelicals found the modernist trends totally unacceptable and intolerable. More was at stake than trivial doctrinal differences or attitudes toward modern culture. Christianity itself was on trial. Liberalism represented the dissolution of the historic Christian faith. For evangelicals the mandate was clear: the faith had to be defended at all costs.

The Rise of Fundamentalism

Fundamentalists were a diverse lot, and they too should not be stereotyped. There is no general agreement as to what the term "fundamentalist" actually means, but if we describe them in very general terms, as we must, we could say with a fair degree of accuracy that they were a broad coalition of antimodernists whose roots can be traced to such diverse sources as D. L. Moody's revivalism, American commonsense philosophy, and the Keswick holiness movement. Historians have noted the particular importance of the Bible schools, magazines, missions, and conferences founded by Moody, Adoniram J. Gordon, Cyrus I. Scofield, and Reuben A. Torrey during the 1880s and 1890s as major influences upon the movement.

In its makeup the movement was an interdenominational mix predominantly composed of the Reformed wing in American evangelicalism. Baptists, Presbyterians, and Congregationalists were particularly well represented in the movement. Their theological commitments were usually calvinistic, conservative, and millenarian. Major doctrinal emphases included dispensationalism, the inerrancy of Scripture, personal purity, and the need to evangelize the world. It could be noted, however, that the three latter emphases flowed quite naturally from the fundamentalist's dispensationalist hermeneutic.[7]

Dispensationalism was a peculiar version of premillennialism, the view that Christ will physically return to the earth to establish a kingdom that he will rule over for one thousand years. Dispensationalism divided the world's history into different periods of time leading up to the millennial reign of Christ. The fundamentalist believed that the sixth period just prior to Christ's return, the present "church age," would be marked by apostasy in the churches and a general disregard for truth and moral standards. This dispensationalist scheme of things seemed to explain the rise of modernism and served to legitimate the fundamentalist's own place as a cultural outsider in an ungodly society. More passive fundamentalists were content to accept their perceived dilemma until the coming of Christ when all would be made right by divine intervention. From their perspective, the second coming of Christ was the only hope for society. This view seemed even more credible to many after World War I when hopes had been dashed that the world could be bettered by politics or education. More militant fundamentalists, on the other hand, felt that it was their Christian duty to rise to the challenge and drive the modernists from the pulpits, the presses, and the seminaries.

The Bible was all-important to the fundamentalists because it was their acknowledged source of authority for all that they believed and practiced. Their interpretation of the Bible depended on an errorless and usually a literalistic account of the details of Scripture. This included a literalistic understanding of the *Genesis* account of creation and the flood, of the various accounts of miracles throughout the Bible, and specific prophetic predictions concerning the coming of the Messiah and the events surrounding the end time. Unlike theological liberalism, the tenets of fundamentalism were premised upon an inerrant text.

Given their understanding of history and the nature of things to come, fundamentalists reasoned that faithfulness to God demanded separation from the values and loyalties of this world. On a personal level this usually meant rigid moral codes. Constituents were constantly reminded of such evils as dancing, social drinking, card-playing, theatre attendance, and sexual perversions of every sort.

In the face of deteriorating spiritual conditions within the denominations, fundamentalists often had to make difficult decisions regarding the question of whether or not to separate from churches and seminaries controlled by liberal majorities. Could such churches and seminaries be reformed from within or were they hopelessly apostate? Some fundamentalists seemed to be temperamentally suited for separatism, but others consented to it only as a last resort. J. Greshem Machen, the highly respected New Testament scholar from Princeton, provided the case in point for the latter position. He disapproved of schism in the church in principle, but finally agreed that separatism was sometimes necessary on the grounds that liberalism did not represent historic Christianity.

Virtually all Bible-believing fundamentalists took seriously the "Great Commission" to evangelize the world. The archtypical fundamentalist in this regard was Charles Fuller, radio evangelist for "The Old Fashioned

Revival Hour." His heart burned for evangelism, and this passion prompted him to pour his moral and financial support into the founding of Fuller Theological Seminary for the express purpose of training young men for Christian ministry. Fuller was more practical than ideological in his approach to the fundamentals of the faith. For him, the fundamentals of the faith always translated into the practical message of human sinfulness and the atoning work of Christ. His way of fighting the modernists was to preach a simple but effective gospel message. In his disarmingly simple style Charles Fuller became a household name across America, preaching the gospel to millions over the air waves.

Fundamentalist leaders like Charles Fuller, J. Greshem Machen, Wilbur Smith, J. Oliver Buswell, Carl McIntire, Bob Jones, Sr., and John R. Rice were a disparate group of men. What they had in common were various combinations of the commitments and ideologies that we have mentioned. What led them and their movement to the edge of dissolution was extremism and distasteful attitudes. What started out as an attempt to save Protestant orthodoxy from modernism eventually deteriorated into a cultic aberration. By the end of World War II the fundamentalist image seemed irredeemably tarnished. George Marsden described the popular perception:

> The mention of fundamentalism sparked memories of Billy Sunday's antics, of William Jennings Bryan looking foolish at Dayton, Tennessee, of the rumors of scandal that had surrounded the enticing Aimee Semple McPherson, or of the vivid depictions of the chicanery of America's best-known fictional evangelist, Elmer Gantry. The cultured elite saw current fundamentalist evangelists as the denizens of tent meetings on the edge of town, hucksters of the air waves, or the impresarios at high-pressured youth rallies, corrupting the young and exploiting the impressionable.[8]

Orthodoxy Gone Cultic

It is difficult, if not impossible, to say exactly when large segments of the old fundamentalism converted to the "new evangelicalism." The conversion was definitely more like a process than a crisis experience. It is a foregone conclusion, however, that virtually all of those who became leaders in the new evangelicalism during the 1940s had been fundamentalists in the 1930s. The distinction between "fundamentalist" and "evangelical" was not clearly drawn until the late 1940s when leaders in the newly emerging movement began making such distinctions. Harold Ockenga used the term "new evangelicalism" in connection with Fuller Theological Seminary (founded in 1947), which he, and others, regarded as an integral part of a new reform movement within fundamentalism. Allusions to the new evangelicals also began appearing about the same time in the writings of Carl F. H. Henry. There were specific references in Henry's manifesto, *The Uneasy Conscience of Modern Fundamentalism* (1947) and in a series of articles Henry published on "The Vision of the New Evangelicalism" (1948).

The establishment of the National Association of Evangelicals in 1942 had itself been an implicit criticism of fundamentalism. It was, in effect, the first major reform in an attempt to overcome the "come-outism" mentality of fundamentalists by bringing together the broadest possible coalition of conservative evangelicals. Ockenga, the first president of the association, shared his vision for the NAE when he told the first assembly that they were "the vanguard of a movement." He went on to say that "the division is no longer between the denominations . . . but between those who believe in Christ and the Bible, and those who reject Christ—the Christ of the cross and the Bible."[9] The redrawn battle plan was clearly in reference to the liberals in general and, more precisely, those belonging to the counterpart of the NAE—the Federal Council of Churches (founded in 1908). What Ockenga was calling for was a ceasefire to the infighting among the fundamentalists themselves.

Carl F. H. Henry's *Remaking the Modern Mind* (1946) and *The Uneasy Conscience of Modern Fundamentalism* (1947) were as much constructive critiques of fundamentalism as they were negative criticisms of the drift of modern culture. The first publication was a post-war reminder that the events of the first half-century had demonstrated the inadequacy of the modern philosophical mind. In the face of humanism's and naturalism's failure, Henry urged the new evangelicals to help effect a reformation in thought that would again point Western culture in the direction of Christian theism. The challenging opportunity facing the evangelical community, Henry believed, was that of helping to shape a new world and life view for the forthcoming generation. Henry believed that the great biblical truths espoused by fundamentalists must be the foundation of the remade mind of Western culture. The failure of fundamentalism had been its inability to apply these truths to the social, political, and economic problems confronting the modern world.

This failure, Henry argued, constituted the "uneasy conscience" of fundamentalism. It had a worldview but lacked a life view. Fundamentalists had lost their social passion. That vision had to be rediscovered. The despair over the present world order that had accompanied their dispensationalist understanding of history had caused fundamentalists to narrow their message to the "faithful remnant." What fundamentalism lacked was a world-changing message for a world that stood in desperate need of a transforming gospel. To use the familiar categories of H. Richard Niebuhr, fundamentalism had abandoned the mainstream Christian stance of "Christ the transformer of culture" for the more sectarian mentality of "Christ against culture."[10]

The post-millenialist perspective of modernism placed an undue amount of emphasis upon the role of human effort in establishing an earthly kingdom of God. The fundamentalist's pre-millenialist interpretation of history, by contrast, insisted that the kingdom of God could only be initiated by Christ's return. The work of the kingdom lay entirely outside the realm of human effort and achievement. In contrast to both, Henry encouraged a return to the Augustinian conception of the two cities, the temporal and the eternal that exist concurrently in history. The kingdom is not to be identified with either a *then* or a *now* mentality. It is *both*—now and then. Christians' thought life and behavior must reflect the fact that they are both pilgrims and ambassadors. They must do all that they can to evangelize the world for Christ in anticipation of his return, but they must also seek to shape as much of this world after the likeness of their heavenly homeland as possible. Henry's re-discovery of the Augustinian conception of history was instrumental in moving evangelicals away from the dispensationalism of fundamentalism and the almost total negativism toward culture that had come to be associated with it. George Eldon Ladd, a rising evangelical New Testament scholar, would later move evangelicals further in the direction of a both/and interpretation of history with his *Jesus and the Kingdom: The Eschatology of Biblical Realism.*

There was also a noticeable negativism in the fundamentalist's attitude toward philosophy that was particularly evident in the way fundamentalists had approached apologetics. J. Greshem Machen had been the early intellectual leader in the fundamentalist movement and had admirably defended orthodox doctrines against liberal attack.[11] But he had not moved beyond the refuting and rebutting of arguments into the realm of positive apologetics. Gordon Clark and Cornelius Van Til were also typically fundamentalist in this regard. They differed from each other in their approach to apologetics, but both were fundamentally negative in their attitude toward modern thought and offered little, if any, basis for establishing common ground with the thought life of modern persons. Neither held out any hope of forging a new "mind" on the anvil of Christian premises.

Cornelius Van Til would not admit to any truth in unbelievers. His apologetical method was designed to negate all truth in the unbelievers and their worldview so that the truth of Christianity could stand in absolute contrast. His fear was that if one admits to levels of truth in unbelievers the absolute claims of Christianity would be endangered. If the absolute truth of Christianity is lost, Van Til reasoned, then Christianity can only claim to be "better" than or "preferable" to other truth claims. The gist of Van Til's argument was that the gospel does not appeal to the best that is in culture but sets itself against culture as one would an irreconcilable enemy.[12]

Gordon Clark's method has been described as deductive presuppositionalism. He began by presupposing the existence of the God who is revealed in Scripture and then proceeded to deduce everything else from that, much as one would deduce theorems from a geometrical axiom. Clark believed that Scripture is the only reliable source of true knowledge. Consequently, one's epistemology, educational theory, economic and political theory, and all other elements of thought must be deduced from the Scriptures. Clark's dogmatism was inherently incompatible with all other systems that depended upon the attainment of knowledge outside of the Bible. He did not believe that persons could reason their way to God, but they could apply the law of noncontradiction to other worldviews in order to demonstrate their logical inconsistency. The falsity of all non-Christian theories can be established, Clark believed, if it is pursued long enough. A *reductio ad absurdum* would be the test. Christianity is worthy of a rational persons's choice, Clark argued, because it is more rationally consistent. God has given persons the capacity for reason so that they can rest in the truthfulness of God's Word.[13]

Clark and Van Til were widely appreciated throughout the evangelical community for their defense of Christianity's absolute truth claims, but in the view of new evangelicals like Henry, Harold Ockenga, and Carnell the fundamentalist attitude toward culture was inconsistent with the total scope of biblical revelation and was fated to end in intellectual stagnation. Carnell was more vocal in his denunciation of the negativism:

> When orthodoxy says that the Bible is the only rule of faith and practice, the fundamentalist promptly concludes that everything worth knowing is in the Bible. The result is a withdrawal from the dialogue of man as man. Nothing can be learned from general wisdom, says the fundamentalist, for the natural man is wrong in starting point, method, and conclusion. When the natural man says 'this is a rose,' he means, 'This is a not-made-by-the-triune-God rose.' Everything he says is blasphemy.

It is *non-sequitur* reasoning of this sort that places fundamentalism at the extreme right in the theological spectrum. Classical orthodoxy says that God is revealed in general as well as in special revelation. The Bible completes the witness of God in nature; it does not negate it.[14]

It was precisely this kind of negative reasoning, Carnell believed, that allowed fundamentalists to lower their educational standards, substitute piety for scholarship, eschew all evidences they perceived to be damaging to the faith, and criticize translations of the Bible with which they were unfamiliar.

Carnell further maintained that this kind of negative thinking had also manifested itself in a negative ethic that prompted a quest for status within the cult. He scorned the legalism and hypocrisy he associated with the fundamentalist ethic:

> Whereas Christ was virtuous because he loved God with all his heart and his neighbor as himself, the fundamentalist is virtuous because he does not smoke, dance, or play cards. . . . Fundamentalists, it so happens, are afraid of one another. If a fundamentalist is seen entering a theater, he may be tattled on by a fellow fundamentalist. In this event the guilty party would 'lose his testimony,' i.e., his status in the cult would be threatened. . . . Separation promotes status in the cult; unity through love does not.[15]

The breech that developed between Carnell and hard-core fundamentalists began rather innocently. The occasion was Carnell's inaugural address as the first full-time president of Fuller Theological Seminary. From an outsider's point of view the address was not controversial. On the contrary, Carnell's positive comments and the vision he shared for the seminary were well-received and welcomed as a breath of fresh air. What could be controversial about the president of a Christian seminary calling for an atmosphere of love, tolerance, forgiveness, and academic freedom in which Fuller students and professors alike could follow their academic pursuits? These principles were surely inherent in the idea of a Christian seminary that centered itself in the Word of God. But to hard-line fundamentalists whose ears had long been attuned to other kinds of rhetoric it all sounded like an acquiescence to liberalizing trends. There was particular concern over the fact that Carnell had not explicitly mentioned the seminary's commitment to the inerrancy of Scripture. Carnell's inaugural address had inadvertently driven the first wedge between himself and old-line fundamentalism. Resident fundamentalists at Fuller like Wilbur Smith and Charles Woodbridge and outside leaders in the movement like John R. Rice, Carl McIntyre, and Bob Jones, Sr. never really trusted Carnell after that.

If the first wedge was unintentional, the second one was definitely deliberate. The publication of *The Case for Orthodox Theology* (1960), some five years later, was a deliberate attack on the fundamentalist mentality. The work was supposed to be a statement of what orthodoxy affirms. Carnell did that, but he also used the opportunity to disassociate Reformed orthodoxy from fundamentalism.

The manner in which Carnell attacked fundamentalism was not unlike Flannery O'Connor's use of the grotesque in her fiction. In a work on literary criticism O'Connor explained that those who see by the light of their Christian faith "have the sharpest eyes for the grotesque, for the perverse, and for the unacceptable." The problem, she noted, is that distortions that are repugnant to the eyes of faith may seem quite natural to those who are used to seeing them. In order to get his vision across to a hostile audience the Christian writer may have to resort to a more violent means. "For those who don't hear very well," O'Connor said, "you may have to shout. For those who can't see very well you may have to draw grotesque and startling figures."[16] Carnell obviously felt this same way about the fundamentalists. The time had come to speak in unmistakable language.

"Fundamentalism," Carnell declared, "is orthodoxy gone cultic." Theologically, Carnell judged fundamentalism to be basically sound and orthodox. But in many of its attitudes and practices it had become cultic. He was particularly critical of its ideological thinking, its censorious spirit, and the tendency of fundamentalists to separate from the life of the church at the first signs of heresy.[17] Fundamentalists were particularly perturbed that Carnell dared to criticize Machen, the intellectual hero of the movement, for separating from the Presbyterian church.

Carnell had, in the words of Flannery O'Connor, "shouted loudly" and "drawn large and startling figures." It was not an easy nor a pleasant experience for Carnell, particularly when some of his closest friends and supporters suggested that his tone had been too harsh. But Carnell was convinced that the time had come to use shock, to portray the real grotesqueness of the movement. A definitive break from fundamentalism was overdue. "The uncommitted university student," Carnell argued, "must be assured that biblical Christianity is not necessarily associated with 'the intellectual dishonesty and the ethical hypocrisy of fundamentalism.' Without courage to speak out," he told Ockenga, " 'sick and desperate' orthodoxy will lose to either Rome or Neo-orthodoxy by default.' "[18]

The High Cost of Courage

Karl Barth's much-heralded visit to the United States in 1962 turned out to be an unfortunate happening for Carnell. He was chosen from the evangelical community, along with outstanding theologians from other traditions like Jerald Brauer, Hans Frei, Jaroslav Pelikan, and Schubert Ogden, to submit questions to Barth during his guest appearance at the University of Chicago. Carnell chose to ask Barth questions concerning the inerrancy of Scripture—a subject of perennial interest in the evangelical community.

Carnell's performance on this occasion, however, was less than satisfying to many of his critics—particularly to those who regarded the inerrancy of Scripture as the linchpin doctrine of conservative Christianity. The conservative critics claimed that Carnell had allowed Barth to soft-pedal evangelicalism's cardinal doctrine. Why had he not pushed

Barth more on his view that the Bible "contains errors in its time-bound human form"? Once again Carnell found himself in the position of having to defend himself and his views to his own colleagues and friends. In particular, he found himself further alienated from his old friend and mentor Gordon Clark who had been present at the meeting in Chicago.

Carnell was already paying a high price for his criticism of fundamentalists in *The Case for Orthodox Theology.* Now he was being criticized by many of his close friends and colleagues for being too passive on the crucial issue of Scripture. The harsh criticism and sense of alienation that Carnell felt only added to internalized tensions that had been accumulating for a lifetime.

It was a well-known fact that Carnell had not been physically well for a number of years. He had suffered from insomnia since his youth and had frequent bouts with depression. He was ill at ease in most social situations and never enjoyed the public role he had been asked to fill as a seminary president. He had the temperament of a scholar and writer but constantly experienced the frustration of not having adequate time for teaching or writing. Carnell had been under the care of a psychiatrist during much of the time he had lived in California and had received numerous shock treatments in an effort to bring him out of periods of deep depression. A complete psychological breakdown seemed inevitable.

A more fateful end than expected, however, came in the spring of 1967. Carnell was found dead in his hotel room in Oakland, California, where he was attending an ecumenical workshop sponsored by the Roman Catholic church. The cornoner's report said that he had died from a moderate overdose of sleeping pills, though it was impossible to determine whether the overdose had been an accident or deliberate.

The Carnell Legacy

Despite the controversies that surrounded his life and his death, Edward John Carnell left behind a remarkable legacy. He had helped thousands of evangelicals to work through any feelings of inferiority they might have had about the reasonableness of their faith, and he had played a key role in the founding of an outstanding seminary through which the evangelical faith and vision could be expressed. Readers, students, and colleagues from every walk of life spoke of their indebtedness to this seminal scholar and educator who had helped make their faith intellectually defensible and culturally relevant.

When Carnell's portrait was officially unveiled at the seminary in 1969, several of his friends and former students had the opportunity to speak about his contribution to the evangelical community and his personal influence upon their lives. David Hubbard, president of Fuller Theological Seminary, spoke of his life-long contribution to the evangelical community:

> Edward John Carnell set a bright example for us in three areas: scholarship, educational outlook, and churchmanship. His fertile mind and ready pen blazed fresh theological trails as he sought to defend and proclaim the Christian faith as a world and life view. His painstaking grasp of the details of his field, coupled with his penetrating insight into the crucial questions, are hallmarks of the finest kind of scholarship. During his years as president, Fuller seminary made such remarkable advances in curriculum, faculty appointments, library holdings, and financial stability that full accreditation was achieved. As much as any man, he shaped the seminary's character. His love for the church was seen both in his distaste for divisiveness and in his drive to point out and correct her foibles. A legion of evangelicals around the world owe to him their love of the faith and their loyalty to the church.[19]

Paul Jewett, a life-long friend and colleague, spoke affectionately of their friendship:

> While most people knew Edward John Carnell as a scholar and teacher, I knew him as an unfailing friend. I shall not soon forget our many discussions in philosophy and theology during our student days together in college, seminary, and graduate school as well as during our years of teaching together; but most of all I shall cherish the memory of his kindness, too personal to be elaborated, too genuine to be left to the oblivion of silence.[20]

James P. Morgan, a former student, spoke for the many students who went to Fuller for the opportunity to sit under Carnell's teaching:

> As an undergraduate I heard Dr. Carnell speak but once, and on the strength of that one encounter I came to Fuller seminary. He made it possible for many of us to believe in a future for evangelical theology.

In our moments of doubt and frustration he would speak, and faith in that future would be possible again. He set the theological standard for all of us; whether we agreed or disagreed with his point of view, he was the man by whom we measured our thinking. Again and again in the parish ministry, situations would evoke memory of a theme, an insight, an illustration, and our indebtedness to Dr. Carnell became apparent. His shadow lies long over the lives of all of us who were granted the privilege of sitting in his classroom.[21]

Carnell's effectiveness as a classroom teacher was reflected in the results of a questionnaire in 1985 that was sent to Fuller alumni from each of three eras: 1950–1952 (the first classes); 1957–1959 (the Carnell era); and 1965–1967 (the early Hubbard era). One of the questions alumni were asked was, "While you were at Fuller, which professors had the greatest impact on you?" Carnell was the top finisher for all three eras (decisively in the first two).[22] The results of the questionnaire are even more impressive when one remembers that many of the finest evangelical scholars in the world were teaching at Fuller during these eras—including the likes of Wilbur Smith, George Eldon Ladd, Everett F. Harrison, Carl F. H. Henry (before becoming the editor of *Christianity Today*), Paul Jewett, and William LaSor.

His most far-reaching influence, however, was undoubtedly upon his readers. Through his major writings Carnell was able to reassure thousands of evangelical readers that Christianity offers a world and life view that can satisfy the whole of our faculties. It is to this aspect of the Carnell legacy that we now turn our attention.

Notes

[1] Kenneth Scott Latourette, *A History of Christianity: Reformation to the Present* (New York: Harper and Row, 1975) 2:1230.

[2] George M. Marsden, *Reforming Fundamentalism* (Grand Rapids MI: Eerdman's Publishing Co., 1987) 4.

[3] Sydney E. Ahlstrom, *A Religious History of the American People* (Garden City NJ: Image Books, 1975) 2:224.

[4] See James Livingston's *Modern Christian Thought* (New York: MacMillan Co., 1971) 245-68 for an excellent succinct treatment of the Liberal Movement.

[5] There are many well-known works on the Fundamentalist Movement that provide scholarly insight into the movement. I particularly recommend Norman

F. Furniss, *The Fundamentalist Controversy, 1918–1931* (New Haven CT: Yale University Press, 1954), and George M. Marsden, *Fundamentalism and American Culture: The Shaping of Twentieth Century Evangelicalism, 1870–1925* (New York: Oxford University Press, 1980).

[6]Kenneth Cauthen, *The Impact of American Religious Liberalism* (New York: Harper and Row, 1962) 27.

[7]Marsden argues this point in his writings on fundamentalism.

[8]Marsden, *Reforming Fundamentalism*, 13.

[9]Ibid., 49.

[10]H. Richard Niebuhr, *Christ and Culture* (New York: Harper and Row, 1956).

[11]See Machen's *Christianity and Liberalism* (New York: MacMillan Co., 1923), *The Origin of Paul's Religion* (Grand Rapids MI: Eerdmans Publishing Co., 1925), and *The Virgin Birth of Christ* (Grand Rapids MI: Baker Book House, 1930).

[12]See Cornelius Van Til's *Defense of the Faith* (Phillipsburg NJ: Presbyterian and Reformed Publishing Co., 1980).

[13]See Gordon Clark's *Christian View of Men and Things* (Grand Rapids MI: Eerdmans Publishing Co., 1952) and *Three Types of Religious Philosophy* (Nutley NJ: Craig Press, 1973).

[14]Edward John Carnell, *The Case For Orthodox Theology* (Philadelphia PA: Westminister Press, 1959) 119.

[15]Ibid., 121.

[16]Flannery O'Connor, *Mystery and Manners* (New York: Farrar, Straux, and Giroux, 1969) 33,34.

[17]Carnell, *The Case For Orthodox Theology,* 113-25.

[18]Marsden, *Reforming Fundamentalism,* 188.

[19]Edward John Carnell, "The Glory of a Theological Seminary," Pasadena CA: Fuller Theological Seminary Alumni Association, n. d.

[20]Ibid.   [21]Ibid.

[22]Marsden, *Reforming Fundamentalism,* 301.

5.
A Coherent and Relevant Faith

Edward John Carnell's primary objective as a Christian apologist was to convince his readers that Christianity is both true and relevant to human need. The Christian faith deserves a rational person's choice, he argued, because it provides the most coherent picture of the world and human experience. It is relevant, on the other hand, because it addresses the full range of one's existential, moral, and spiritual needs. What modern persons needed most, Carnell believed, was to be convinced that the Christian faith addresses them in the totality of their being and that it makes contact with them in all points where they are in touch with truth.

The Gospel and Culture

Far more people in the twentieth century are interested in the concrete realities of living than they are in abstract ideas, speculative worldviews, or impersonal methods. Theologies that fail to speak to human need are easily dismissed as arid, authoritarian, and irrelevant. As Alan Richardson, a contemporary apologist, noted: "Today people are more interested in living than in theories; they will see truth in its impact upon the world of real life long before they will recognize it in the writings of the academics or even in the expositions of the preachers."[1]

Carnell was well aware of the risk theologians take when they allow human questions and life situations to set the agenda for theology. He knew how easy is was inadvertently to mistake the word of man for the word of God, thereby distorting the truth of the gospel message and jeopardizing the truth about a person's true humanity. He was fully committed by tradition and conviction to a word-centered theology. Carnell's reformed tradition had rooted him in a God-centered theology and the conviction that a Christian theologian must be committed to the faithful transmission of the revealed word of truth. He did not draw the false conclusion, however, that a commitment to the objective truth and authority of the Bible was at odds with a gospel that was oriented to its hearers. The same word of God that is true is also relevant to human need. If theologians are to communicate the Christian message to modern men and women effectively, they must be willing to address gospel answers to real life questions.

In this regard, Carnell was in essential agreement with Paul Tillich who suggested that the church must be a listening body that is deeply concerned about the world's questions and problems. If the gospel is to be relevant to human need, the church must show a genuine interest in correlating gospel answers with questions that the natural man asks about himself and his world. The most effective apologists, he believed, have been those who have made contact between the gospel and culture. Fundamentalists had been adept at refuting and rebutting arguments against the faith, but they had not demonstrated sufficient interest in providing positive reasons for modern persons to believe the gospel. Their negative attitude toward culture seemed always to place them on the defensive side of the issues. Carnell believed that it was time for evangelicals to play offense. His apologetic aim was to make contact with the modern mind at those points of greatest apologetic significance, but there would be no equivocation regarding the truthfulness or the uniqueness of the Christian message.

One of the reasons that fundamentalists had been so negative toward culture was that they failed to see any truth outside the language of biblical categories. The often drawn conclusion that "everything worth knowing is in the Bible" had the dreadful effect of separating the gospel from the questions the natural man asks about himself and the world. As a result, fundamentalists had cut themselves off from communication with those they should have been concerned to help. They found themselves, in effect, preaching to the choir. What was particularly lacking from the perspective of serious inquirors were gospel answers that satisfactorily dealt with contemporary issues and questions. Was it any wonder that so many questioned the relevance of the Christian faith and regarded the Bible as a dated book?

Carnell insisted, even to his fundamentalist mentors, that evangelicals must be deeply concerned about the issue of relevance. There may be little, if any, "common ground" between the Christian and the non-Christian on the level of systems, Carnell argued, "because Christianity qua system waits for every truth upon God while non-Christianity qua system waits for every truth upon non-God."[2] But on the level of persons there is a vital point of connection. That connection lies in the fact that every person has been created in the image of God. The Creator does not violate by special revelation the bond between time and eternity that He has established.

If we are to get on with our vocation as Christians, Carnell believed, we must accept the risks of building points of contact. Truth is advanced by open dialogue, not by silence. Christians must be willing to make contact between Christian revelation and truths which non-Christians have discovered about nature and life. Christianity's best defense, Carnell asserted, lies not in its repudiation of all truth outside the Bible but in its cogent demonstration to modern persons of "how the gospel answers questions which the natural man, in his search for meaning, has already raised about himself and the world."[3] Through Christian revelation the Christian can complete what is valid in the wisdom of the ages. "May the sad day never come," Carnell pleaded, "when Christians no longer look for truth in Pericles' Funeral Oration or Mill's 'Essay on Liberty.' "[4] The task of the apologist is to remove any props that may be supporting doubt and unbelief. That can best be done by establishing points of contact and demonstrating that the claims of Christ are continuous with truth, not by denying all truth outside the familiar categories of the Bible. Once apologetics has shown that the claims of Christ are continuous with truth, it has done all that it can do. The rest must be left to the proclaiming ministry of the church and the convincing work of the Holy Spirit.

A Gospel for the Whole Person

Carnell was committed to the conviction that the gospel is relevant to *every* person and to the ancillary claim that it can satisfy the basic needs of the *whole* person. His first major work, *An Introduction to Christian Apologetics* (1948), was devoted to demonstrating the reasonableness of biblical Christianity. In this work he appealed primarily to the rational person's need for a coherent view of the whole of reality. He argued that Christianity can explain the facts of nature and human existence more coherently than any alternative worldview. Carnell believed that it was important to dispel the notion that there is something inherently irrational about modern persons believing in the God of the Scriptures or in the conservative interpretation of the Christian faith. Twentieth-century doubters need to be reassured that Christianity's supernatural worldview is still cogent, intellectually respectable, and worthy of being taken seriously.

Carnell recognized, however, that the climate of opinion generated by existentialism and Neo-Orthodoxy in the post-World-War-II era was more non-rational in character and posed a different kind of challenge. Sensing the shift in the intellectual climate, he devoted most of his subsequent writings to a more subjectively based apologetic. He made the initial transition in *A Philosophy of the Christian Religion* (1952) by appealing to axiology. Carnell challenged his readers to commit to a value option that goes beyond the immediacies of life and a restricted "knowledge by inference" to a more personal and heart-satisfying value of fellowship with God by means of a "knowledge by acquaintance."

The more existential and subjective emphasis revealed how heavily Carnell had been influenced by Kierkegaard's method of asking questions from the standpoint of inwardness. He placed an even greater emphasis on the existential and introspective approach in his two final works, *Christian Commitment* (1957) and *The Kingdom of Love and the Pride of Life* (1960). The strength of this later work, in addition to broadening Carnell's apologetical perspective, was a much needed elaboration on the centrality of love and the meaning of true Christian commitment—themes that Carnell felt had been too narrowly conceived in conservative circles. The real obstacle to "being a Christian," Carnell stressed, is not so much a lack of knowledge as it is the failure to act on the knowledge one already has. Reason and knowledge are important but they are never enough. There is something infinitely higher and more important than simply knowing *about* God. Humanity's "highest good" is to enjoy God's fellowship through "knowledge by acquaintance." But there are no epistemological shortcuts or magical solutions. Fellowship with God is grounded in love and commitment. In the spirit of a modern prophet Carnell challenged his readers to accept the gospel on its own life-demanding terms.

In addressing the gospel to more subjectively based concerns, however, Carnell never capitulated to the view that faith could somehow be bifurcated from reason.[5] The Christian faith, he argued, knows no separation of true subjective experience from the ordinary canons of reason. Any form of fideism that seeks to insulate Christian faith from the test of reason and logic does it a disservice. Christianity has nothing to lose and everything to gain by opening itself up to the canons of reason. The heart-satisfying experiences of the Christian life need never be construed as being incompatible with a rational faith. Christianitiy is not an irrational leap into a dark abyss but a faith that a truly rational person will find unreasonable not to trust.

A Reasonable Faith

Carnell's conviction that the Christian faith is rationally sound was not based upon abstract reasoning. It had much more to do with the practical concrete realities of human nature and destiny. Human potential for both greatness and tragedy stem from human nature, from what a person is—a created and finite being in both body and spirit. Because a person is a self-transcending spirit, one cannot simply accept the finite limitations of the physical body and the decaying universe in which one lives. As Carnell put it, a person must be able to relate his "insatiable desire for self-preservation to the realities of a death-doomed body and an impersonal universe."[6] The annals of human history attest to the fact that the human spirit has always sought for redemption and immortality in one form or another. The hope of redemption and immortality are essential to the peace of mind that is the very essence of human happiness. No religion or worldview would be reasonable to a spiritual creature that could not provide some practical solution for the "soul-sorrow" that is inherent in the human condition. As Carnell put it:

> Because man is both body and soul, he is a creature which is subject to perennial frustration and fear. The soul, limited in its soarings only by the law of contradiction, dreams of those reposes of bliss and happiness which it should like to enjoy, only to be crushed to earth at the end of its venture because it is united to a frail body which cannot support these dreams and ideals which the soul sets before itself. In addition to this problem of soul and body, man struggles to relate himself, a personal being, to an ostensibly impersonal universe. The more man meditates upon the incompatibilities which exist between what he might be and what he actually is, the more sorrowful his soul becomes. Man wants life, but he is offered death; he wants peace, but strife and friction are his lot.[7]

In addition to this so-called "practical" problem, Carnell noted that humanity also faces a "theoretical" problem. It is the problem of meaning, or more precisely, what philosophers have called the problem of the one-within-the-many. How can we make sense out of the universe that we live in? Is there any *one* thing or being that can account for the *many* particulars that make up the universe? Or, to put it differently, is there any logical or teleological connection between the particulars that constitute the time-space universe? If not, then the universe must simply be a meaningless hodge-podge of chance from which we can derive no meaning or discern no direction for our lives? In which case, Shakespeare's MacBeth would be right. Life would indeed be "a tale told by an idiot, full of sound and fury, signifying nothing."

The constructive task of philosophy, Carnell noted, is to work out a world and life view, to work toward a rational explanation for the whole course of reality. Human intellect cannot be satisfied with the plurality of the "many" without some unifying principle of meaning to which one can relate the meaning of his life. One's worldview then should be able to answer adequately the theoretical problem of meaning as well as the practical problem of hope for life beyond the grave.

Rationality may have to do with "proofs" and "arguments," but it also has to do with meanings. Christianity has more to offer in this regard, Carnell believed, than any other worldview. What makes Christianity convincing is that it provides a system of meanings that make sense out of all of life's major problems. In short, it provides answers to life's "big questions" in a way that is epistemically sound.

Carnell admitted that there are other alternatives. There are those who choose to believe that life has no meaning. They simply learn to live with their emptiness and despair or else end it all through suicide. Then there are those who choose to believe but do so on non-rational grounds—following Pascal's well-worn argument that "the heart has its reasons which reason knows nothing about." Others simply try to ignore the problem altogether.

Carnell noted that large numbers of Christians are non-apologetic types. Their faith seemingly needs no rational underpinning. They either seem to grasp the truth of Christianity intuitively or simply exercize the will-to-believe. But there are more rational souls, he believed, whose faith needs the support of reason. The beauty of the matter, Carnell contended, is that while rational evidence is not required, it is available for those who need it. Faith does not demand some blind leap into the darkness. God has made it possible for the creature to believe with the full consent of all faculties—including the mind.

Faith: A Legitimate Assumption

Augustine (354–430 C.E.) Bishop of Hippo and early church father, noted in his writings that one must believe something before one can know anything. In essence Augustine was saying that basic assumptions or presuppositions are necessary to thought. All logical conclusions are drawn from basic assumptions from which we begin our thinking. The theorems of geometry, for example, are deduced from the axioms. The conclusions of behaviorism are derived from certain assumptions about the mind. Even scientists who take pride in their "objectivity" work with assumptions or presuppositions that govern their methodology and their thought. These original assumptions cannot be proved because they are the most basic beliefs from which we begin, the necessary starting points from which all thinking commences.

The Christian, Carnell argued, obviously cannot be denied what all other systems of thought require: a basic assumption from which to start. That assumption for the Christian is "the existence of the God who is revealed in Scripture."[8] Given that starting point, the Christian can solve both the practical and the theoretical human predicament. The meaninglessness and hopelessness that prevails in the modern world is directly related to modern humanity's departure from the controlling ideas of the Bible. Carnell totally agreed with Gordon Clark that Christians cannot be denied their right to their first principle:

> No philosopher is perfect and no system can give man omniscience. But if one system can provide plausible solutions to many problems while another leaves too many questions unanswered, if one system tends less to skepticism and gives more meaning to life, if one world-view is consistent while others are self-contradictory, who can deny us, since we must choose, the right to choose the more promising first principle.[9]

A return to biblical authority would not represent blind authoritarianism nor irrationalism but a return to an authority that would be unreasonable not to trust. What rational person would balk at giving his allegiance to a system of thought that solves the basic problems of epistemology and metaphysics, sensibly outlines the nature and destiny of man, and makes possible a personal encounter with God?

When he appropriates the implications that are found in the Bible for life's meaning, the Christian solves the problem of common ground, the relation between science and theology, the problem of miracles, the philosophy of history, the problem of evil, the ethical one and many, and the hope of immortality and the resurrection. Upon every important theoretical problem of life, the Bible has reliable, logical judgments to offer, judgments which, when accepted by the whole heart and soul, yield a system of thought which is horizontally self-consistent and which vertically fits the facts of life.[10]

Carnell did not feel that the Christian theist is under philosophical obligation to build up a belief in God through empirical sense experiences. On the contrary, he approached belief in God from his Reformed perspective that God has created within us the disposition (the *sensus divinitatis*) to believe in God. Knowing God by innate knowledge, we are reminded of God in His works (Rom 1:20). Belief in God is basic and is itself a totally rational act. It is just as rational to believe in God as it is to believe in the axioms of geometry. Faith in God does not require further proof in order to attain rational status. Most people do, in fact, come to believe in God apart from rational proofs or arguments.

Carnell was perfectly willing, however, to subject the Christian worldview to the canons of reason and experience because he was convinced that it fits what we know about one's inner and outer worlds better than any alternative world or life view. It is the ability of the hypothesis to stand up under the scrutiny of intense testing that makes it believable to the questioning mind.

Systematic Consistency: The Test for Truth

Carnell's understanding of the proper relationship between faith and reason reflected the curious interlarding of influences that shaped his own life. His evangelical background had rooted him in the authority of Scripture and the Reformed doctrine that the word of God is self-authenticating through the inner witness of the Holy Spirit. His philosophical background, on the other hand, led him to the conviction that there must be some way for truth to be verified. Otherwise, a genuinely true revelation could not be distinguished from an erroneous claim.

As noted, Carnell did not depend upon rational proofs for his belief in the existence of God. Since faith is not derived from rational argument, it cannot be dependent upon rational proofs. Reason cannot establish or prove what is basic to all Christian thought—the existence of God. Reason does play a valuable role in the life of faith, however, by helping to confirm what has already been presupposed. Carnell could agree with Gordon Clark that Christians are both dogmatists and rationalists. They are dogmatists in the sense that their belief in God is basic and does not require the assistance of rational support, but they are rationalists in the sense that they can apply the canons of reason to support the Christian claim that the Scriptures are the word of God. Even an alleged divine revelation must pass the test for rational consistency if it is to gain the acceptance of a rational man.

Carnell held to what is known as a correspondence theory of truth. "Truth," he insisted, "is correspondence with the mind of God." We have truth only so long as we say about facts what God says about these facts. "If man says that his chief end is to eat, drink, and be merry," Carnell noted, "he tells the truth only if that is what God says is man's chief end."[11] The criterion for truth is consistency with the Author of all facts and meaning. Scripture is how we know the truth precisely because Scripture is the primary means by which we know the mind of God. This is why the Christian starts with the hypothesis of "the existence of the God who is revealed in Scripture." The Christian's faith in the God of Scripture is not a blind faith, however, because God has established a means whereby the authenticity of the Bible can be confirmed.

The author of all truth and meaning has built a law of rational consistency into creation so that truth can be distinguished from error. It is through this law of rational consistency that God makes it possible for our minds to be fully convinced that God does exist and that God's revealed word is true.

The most basic law governing rational consistency, Carnell noted, is what is known as the law of non-contradiction. But he was careful to explain what this law of logic can and cannot establish. The law of non-contradiction, for instance, does not require that one see or understand all of the rational connections in things before accepting a given reality as true. Neither does the law of non-contradiction tell you what is true. That has to be established by other means.

What the law of non-contradiction can do is test for the presence of error. The law of non-contradiction means that something cannot be its opposite, in the same sense, at the same time. In other words, "A" cannot at the same time be "non-A." That would be a logical contradiction.

Applied to Scripture, or to any other truth claim, the law of non-contradiction allows us to know that error is present when there are such logical contradictions. When competing "revelations" such as the Bible and the Koran both claim to be true, for example, there must be some test for truth. The God who gives us a revelation of Himself and His will in the Holy Scriptures also gives us the means whereby we can recognize His Word as a true revelation.

Carnell was careful not to elevate reason above revelation as some kind of higher authority. It is not the purpose of reason to judge revelation—only to test for its authenticity. Once the authenticity of a purported revelation has been satisfactorily established, it stands to reason that one would come under the authority of that revelation. Reason then should not be construed as an enemy of God or as some kind of devilish competitor but as a tool that can and should be used in the service of God's truth. Reason is a part of one's spiritual endowment as a creature created in the image of God. There are, to be sure, truths that are beyond us and mysteries that our minds can never fully understand, but in the interest of our knowing God and His will, God has given us the mental equipment that allows us to "think His thoughts."

Every normal human being, Carnell believed, is born with a priori equipment, or innate knowledge, that allows one to know what is logically consistent and to make meaning out of the flux of experience. There must be standards established in the mind whereby good can be distinguished from evil, beauty from ugliness, and truth from error. Otherwise, one could not distinguish true faith from ignorance and superstition. The Christian faith was never meant to be an asylum for ignorance or an "ouija-board" variety of "respectable" superstition. God has established a way to test for truthfulness and to establish meanings so that the whole self can repose in the trustworthiness of God's word.

The proper balance must be struck. On the one hand, the Christian must never allow pseudo-intellectualisms to rob the Christian message and experience of its "wisdom and power." The truth of God is not bound by the limitations of human reason. There is mystery in much of what God reveals to us about Himself and His ways that our finite minds could never penetrate. But the presence of mystery does not mean that the Holy Spirit works contrary to reason or to the evidences that God has established in the natural order of things. We can be assured, Carnell insisted, that the Holy Spirit works to illuminate the evidences and not to contradict them.

Carnell was indebted to another of his mentors, Edgar Sheffield Brightman, for teaching him a proper respect for the total facts of experience—something that had not been fully appreciated in his fundamentalist background. Experience, in this case, was used in the broadest possible sense. It included humanity's entire empirical, rational, volitional, and emotional life, which, in effect, broadened the test for truth to include both *formal* and *material* truth. Carnell called this verification principle "Systematic Consistency." As a verification principle, systematic consistency appealed to the facts of subjective experience as well as the facts of logic and history. Christianity's truth claims would have to be internally consistent, but more than that they would have to make their peace with humanity's subjective experiences as well as historical, archaeological, and scientific data.

Could Christian truth claims meet the demands of systematic consistency? Carnell was fully convinced that they could. The facts of experience would only enhance the credibility of the Christian faith. Those who are honest with the facts and with their feelings would be in a better position to see that the Christian faith is the only world and life view that adequately answers to the complexity of humanity's external and internal world. If one objects to Christian claims on the grounds that many so-called revelations seek our acceptance, Carnell argued that one should apply the test for systematic consistency.

> Accept that revelation which, when examined, yields a system of thought which is horizontally self-consistent and which vertically fits the facts of history. . . . Bring on your revelations! Let them make peace with the law of contradiction and the facts of history, and they will deserve a rational man's assent. A careful examination of the Bible reveals that it passes these stringent examinations summa cum laude. Unlike all other religious volumes, the Bible speaks of, and gives a metaphysical basis to, the unity and solidarity of the entire human race under God. Christ's message has nothing clannish, tribal, esoteric, or racial about it. Christ was not only in sympathy with the building of a bridge of brotherhood that would wipe out all class distinctions, but he

expressly lived and died to make all men one in Him by His cross. . .
. He combines in Himself all of the best virtues of the East and the
West.[12]

Carnell was respected for his intellectual honesty. He was not one to
gloss over problems. He candidly admitted that Christianity too has its
intellectual difficulties, all of which cannot be easily resolved. But, he
noted, there are difficulties with any hypothesis. One must not insist upon
a perfect system of thought in an imperfect world. Rather, one must be
willing to accept that system that is most coherent, which best fits the test
for truth and for life. Carnell would have wholeheartedly agreed with
Francis Schaeffer that the Christian can at least live consistently with the
logic of his presuppositions. This is more than can be said for most non-
Christians.

When Christian apologists provide reasonable evidence that the
Christian faith is internally consistent, that it stands the test of historical
and scientific scrutiny, and that it works in practice—they have done all
that they can do. No worldview can rise above logical probability. Moral
certainty must be left to the work of the Holy Spirit. Rational evidence
cannot make anyone a Christian. The establishment of faith in the heart
and mind of the believer is a sovereign work of God. But we can rest
assured, Carnell believed, that God has removed as many of the obstacles
to faith as possible in order that we might believe with the consent of all
our faculties.

A Wise Choice

It goes without saying that a person is more than mind. We may be
creatures who know, but we are also creatures who make choices—ones
who choose values by which to live and die. In making choices, of
course, the possibility of making foolish as well as wise choices always
exists.

A foolish person's choices are generally characterized by a concern
for immediacy, for what will satisfy some aspect of life now. But a wise
person opts for those life values that are capable of satisfying the whole
person and can endure the passing of time. As Carnell noted, a wise
person will choose values by which one can both live and die. Anything
less would be foolish. If it is irrational to transgress reason, it is foolish

to disregard wisdom. In *An Introduction to Christian Apologetics* Carnell's burden was to convince his readers that Christianity is rationally coherent, that it fits the facts of human experience better than any other worldview. In *A Philosophy of the Christian Religion* he sought to establish the wisdom of choosing Christianity as the value option by which one may live and die. In the first work he persuasively argued that the unbeliever is rationally inconsistent; in the latter he shows that one is foolish for choosing values that are less than satisfying to the whole person and that will not endure.

While all humans by nature seek happiness, Carnell noted, it is a fact that some seek foolishly by making unwise decisions while others seek wisely by making decisions that will not bring regret. Like wholeness, wisdom is characterized by a full perspective; folly is characterized by its partiality. To choose that which is partial and merely satisfies the immediate is a misuse of one's freedom. In the end it can only bring regret. The Scriptures presuppose that a wise person will choose that which will bring wholeness and happiness to both the breadth and depth of life. To ignore the ultimate consequences of value choices is to court disaster. The pleasures of immediacy are real and may temporarily satisfy, but they ultimately fail because they cannot unite the self with the eternal God who alone is able to satisfy the needs of the heart as well as the head. The only way that persons can dignify their value choice is to choose that which is eternal and changeless. The wise person will be guided by those values that can satisfy the whole person for eternity. The tragedy of modern humanity's value system has been the willingness to choose values by which to live and die that offer so much less than what Christ offers. To illustrate his point Carnell evaluated some of the prominent values in the modern world.

Materialism and Pleasure: The Values of a Sensate Culture

At a retreat for evangelical university students a well-known evangelical leader was recently asked what he considered to be the greatest problem facing the church today. "It is not what you might expect me to say," he warned,

It is not liberalism or neo-othodoxy or wrong views of revelation or inspiration or other controversial points in theology. . . . Nor is it the sort of problems you hear discussed daily in your university classes in sociology. The most serious problem facing today's church is materialism—materialism not as a philosophical theory, but materialism as a way of life.

Half a century ago Carnell expressed a similar concern. He observed that materialism and pleasure were twin values that bred off of our sensate culture. They still lure us as the voice of the sirens near the Surrentine promontory lured Odysseus and his men, Carnell noted, but those who guide their ship toward them still experience the same destruction. Carnell was not, of course, referring to a normal desire for happiness or the basic material needs of life. He was referring instead to a naturalistic one-dimensional view of modern persons that reduces them to a mere product of nature and forfeits their dignity as creatures created in the image of God. All that is left for such creatures are the pleasures of the body.

Pitirim Sorokin, one of the eminent sociologists of this century, characterized the American culture as this kind of culture. He called it a "sensate culture" and described it as one that is dominated by sensate values. In short, those who make up a sensate culture have essentially reduced their world and life view to one that can be explained in terms of material factors and the pleasures of the body. People deny that they can know anything beyond that which can be known through the five senses and live as though this material world is all there is or ever will be.

In this kind of culture a person is expected to be motivated more by the stomach than by ideals. Their thinking and their behavior predictably reflect their materialistic assumptions. Psychologically, they reduce themselves to mechanistic animals, a mere combination of conditional and unconditional reflexes. Economically, they pursue wealth-for-the-sake-of-wealth as one of life's legitimate endeavors. Aesthetically, their art forms reflect their preoccupation with self and their lustful quest for sensual pleasure. Ethically, they view morality as a matter of personal taste and style. Sensate ethics can never logically be grounded in anything more than human-made rules for there is no divine being to whom humanity is ultimately accountable. Consequently, morals and ethics can be changed any time by social conditions or by popular opinion. All is relative and temporal. You only go around once, the sensate advertisements warn, so derive all of the pleasure that you possibly can from the game of life.

Spiritual values have no logical place in a sensate culture. As a result, Sorokin noted, all human relationships are affected. Contracts and covenants lose their binding power. Force and fraud are required to maintain moral order. Governments become more unstable and are more inclined to resort to violence. Families disintegrate. Gimmicks replace genius. Physical appearance is inordinately emphasized and the marketplace is glutted with sensually appealing materials. It is not the realities of life that are important, for we cannot be really sure what they are if they are at all, but the appearances. We must keep up the appearances. *The Emperor's New Cloths* becomes the contemporary classic. Little wonder, Sorokin noted, that levels of living grow worse and life in general becomes less secure in this kind of society.

Sorokin's descriptions of a sensate culture are pessimistic, but they accurately depict the drift of the modern secular society.[13] It is a long way, Sorokin noted, from the biblical ethics of the Apostle Paul to the contemporary sensate ethics of a Hugh Hefner. But it was a path that humanity was doomed to travel once it abandoned belief in absolute truths and values in favor of a materialistic view of things. If there are no spiritual, unchanging values by which to live and die, then modern persons are fated to live by their stomachs and their genitals.

Christian values, Carnell noted, depend upon a proper perspective of who we are and the purpose for which we were created. The beauty of the balanced perspective of the Christian view is that it affirms both the physical aspect of human nature and the spiritual essence from which persons derive their dignity and purpose. Any serious dialogue about selfhood cannot skirt the fact that humanity is bound to the processes of nature. Persons are complex physical organisms, unique animals who are, in a very real way, as much a part of nature as beaver dams, ant hills, and the nests of birds. But humans are more—infinitely more.

As a Christian, one can take humanity's natural and social dynamics with utmost seriousness without limiting one's self-understanding to natural or social processes. One can be true to the full content of one's experiences. One can acknowledge and account for the fact that a person is a mind, a consciousness—that a person is a bearer of hopes, fears, dreams, and aspirations that are as much a part of the reality of being human as blood pressure or the institutions and tools that humans create.

Natural facts alone do not explain humanity. Humanity would not be humanity without the depth of mind and spirit that it possesses. The point of the matter is not that we are not bodily creatures but that we are *more than* physical creatures. Having been created in God's image, we have been endowed with spiritual qualities that require spiritual values. Our moral and spiritual endowments anticipate more than an animal existence. God is our source and our fulfillment. The materialistic values of this world can never satisfy desires that have their source in another world. We instinctively aspire to a life and destiny that is appropriate for one who is a child of God. The immediacy of materialism and sensual pleasure can only satisfy partially and temporarily. Boredom and despair are their final end. The free self always seeks more. A wise person, Carnell contended, will never choose values by which to live and die that cannot satisfy one's spiritual needs.

Scientific Positivism: Worshiping a Method

Alfred North Whitehead, the Harvard philosopher and mathematician, correctly pointed out a generation ago that in the modern world science and technology have become the dominant agents of change. Major intellectual revolutions in the fields of biology and physics have completely changed the way we think about humanity and the universe, and technological advances have totally revolutionized the way we live.

Modern thought processes have been so shaped by the scientific method that modern persons scarcely acknowledge any kind of reality that cannot be known through the senses or subjected to methods appropriately deemed "scientific." Lifestyles have, in turn, been affected by the fruits of science and technology. We have come to expect science to provide us with an increasingly better and happier life. In many circles this scientism has come to be seen as a panacea for all our personal and social ills. Modern Western thought processes have been thoroughly baptized in the waters of scientific thought.

The point that needs to be made, however, is that the modern scientific enterprize has produced more than scientific conclusions and technological advances. It has resulted in a type of scientism that regards science as a cure for all of our problems and needs. For some, it has even become the model for an ideal society.

This optimism over what can be known and accomplished through science and its methods encouraged what has come to be known as the *positivistic* mind-set. Auguste Comte, the founder of modern sociology, believed that Western society had evolved through two stages of thinking before arriving at its present positivistic form. He called the first the theological stage. The second he called the metaphysical stage.

In the theological stage all forms of reality, including social institutions, were explained in reference to God or to divine beings. Virtually everything was explained supernaturally. That changed radically, however, during the Age of Enlightenment and the French Revolution. The philosophers of the Enlightenment sought to free humanity from what they regarded as the negative restraints of religion. They encouraged the people of their day to reconstruct their thinking about metaphysical and social realities on the basis of human reason. This so-called metaphysical stage remained dominant among the intelligensia until the nineteenth century when speculative reasoning gave way to empirically based methods in virtually all of the academic disciplines.

Western secular persons increasingly depended upon empirically based studies to establish the norms for what could be believed and practiced in every field of human endeavor. What could not be empirically based and verified was not generally accepted as true or even meaningful. The scientific method almost seemed to be messianic. It promised to deliver modern persons from the ignorance and superstition of the past and provide them a basis for building a better society.

Carnell's concern about modern humanity's devotion to scientific methodology had nothing to do with science as a legitimate means of inquiry or its capacity to improve the quality of human life. His contention was simply that science, for many, had proved to be much more than a vocation or an interest in bettering the quality of life. It represented a capitulation to a naturalistic worldview, a reductionist view of reality, and the worship of a method that could not even account for those things in life that count most. The positivistic mind-set had relegated qualities like love, joy, hope, friendship, peace, and faith to meaninglessness emotion because they could not be empirically verified or quantitatively measured. It is a poor bargain, Carnell warned, when one trades everything in life that counts for the anemic gain of being able to classify sentences according to those that can and those that cannot be empirically verified—referring, of course, to the logical positivists.

Whoever continues to repeat the stupid claim that sentences about justice, honor, chastity, self-control, piety, holiness and love are non-cognitive, Carnell said, should be laughed at—laughed at good and hard. Such a person shows not only a lack of education, but a lack of common sense. There are standards so ultimate to all meaning that all else must be judged by them. How can they be judged by a subordinate method? "If science is not 'good,'" Carnell asked, "what then is it 'good' for? If science is not 'true,' why should one believe it?" The whole scientific enterprize makes "no sense" if there is nothing more ultimate than science itself.

"A new religion has started—worship of the scientific method," Carnell warned, "and the faith that binds the members of this cult together is the blinding creed that man was made for the scientific method and not the method for man."[14] It is a poor value choice, Carnell noted, when one chooses to live and die for a method that cannot account for the ultimate realities of the heart.

Carnell had no interest in opposing true science or of reviving old hostilities between science and religion. He welcomed truth-seeking in any form and encouraged all technological advances that truly bettered human life. But he feared the prospect of any person's devotion to a form of science that refused to be governed by ethical standards. We are all at risk in a world where science is king. It is foolish and dangerous to labor under the constraints of a method that cannot acknowledge a supernatural realm of truth and value. Such a value option is dangerous and cannot possibly satisfy humanity's moral and spiritual needs.

Humanism: A Devotion to Humanity

Humanism has always been a strong contender for supremacy in the hierarchy of values. The reason is obvious: humanity has always been chiefly concerned about preserving its own uniqueness. Humanism is not so much a worldview as it is a devotion to certain insights and values that may or may not be incorporated into a system of thought. Humanists generally stand for the dignity, rights, and freedom of humanity and may align themselves with any worldview that can incorporate and preserve these values. What humanists are not willing to do is to be squeezed into any worldview or system that they feel will rob them of these cherished qualities. Man must be the measure.

Modern secular humanists, however, find themselves between the proverbial rock and a hard place. On the one hand, they want to align their humanistic values with the methods and conclusions of modern science because they respect the prestige and reliability of that method. But they also know the logic of Darwinian naturalism, which holds that humans are simply a part of nature, material entities, the "grand prize winner in the evolutionary sweepstakes." This view not only robs humanity of its unique dignity, it robs it of its freedom as well. If Darwinian naturalism is true, it stands to reason that human actions are as determined by natural forces as the ocean tides and the revolutions of the heavenly bodies. If we are merely material entities, there is not much basis for talking about our dignity, rights, or freedom. Naturalism, by virtue of its materialistic and its deterministic components, relegates us to the realm of what Bertrand Russell called "omnipotent matter" where we are restricted to the law-like regularity of natural processes.

On the other hand, humanists know that there is a basis for human dignity and freedom in theism, but they have generally rejected theism as an antiquated worldview that is no longer viable in the modern world. Furthermore, theism to humanists denotes authoritarianism, the debasement of self, and moral imperatives that they consider dehumanizing. What humanists choose to believe in is their own inherent dignity and the freedom to make of themselves what they choose, but they find themselves in a logical dilemma. This dilemma has been aptly described by William Halverson, a contemporary philosopher, in the form of a question.

> What is the status of honor, courage, and the passion for truth in a world where nothing exists but the elemental particles of which matter is composed? How can man abide a world that makes a mockery of his conviction that he is before everything else a conscious agent in the world, a being capable of doing deeds of worth and nobility?[15]

The humanist is right, Carnell acknowledged, in insisting that a devotion to humanity is a higher value option than materialism, pleasure, or the impersonal methods of science. A devotion to anything less than living personalities is an affront to human dignity. But humanists err in linking their humanistic values with the vision and methods of science. The humanists' contention that an essentially good person can combine a good method with the right values and reach almost infinite possibilities is tragically flawed.

Carnell's criticism of secular humanism was basically twofold. The first problem with humanism is that it harbors a contradiction at its center. Its value commitment is to the quality of human life, but its methodological commitment is to science—an empirical method that provides no basis for belief in God, no absolute code of moral law, or even those qualities that the humanist most admires and desires. Values that enhance human life—such as justice, honesty, love, etc.—that humanists claim *ought* to be preserved can only be gained by means that transcend the limitations of science. Secular humanists use the methods and claims of science to dismiss the existence of God while espousing values that science cannot possibly provide or even legitimate. This is the internal contradiction in secular humanism.

Consistency would require one to "either . . . break with science on the finality of human values, and so destroy the ideal of humanism; or he [the humanist] must at least leave open the possibility of God's existence."[16] This does not mean that one must disavow the importance of worthy human values but that one should gain his perspective for these values from a source that truly gives them their proper dignity and worth. That perspective, Carnell contended, can only be gained from the God of Scripture who gives persons their dignity and worth by creating them in God's own image. From the perspective of the Christian theist, secular humanism falls short as a value option because it mistakenly gives man an inherent value that can only be rightly derived from humanity's true source.

Carnell's other criticism of humanism was that it promises more than it can deliver. No respectable humanist, short of a complete egoist, would admit that he is only concerned about his own self-actualization. Virtually all humanists express a passionate concern for the kind of social order in which others can also have the opportunity to actualize their full humanity. The idea is a noble one, Carnell suggested, but there is an inevitable psychological problem involved when the good of others conflicts with the good of the self. Since it is psychologically impossible to desire one's own unhappiness, humanists lack the power (shall we say, grace) to choose others above themselves. They have, by reason of being created in the image of God, an inner sense of duty to care for the welfare of others. If they desire otherwise, they stand to lose their self-dignity, but therein lies their moral dilemma. Apart from God, which they refuse to acknowledge, humanists lack the moral power to fulfill their own ideal. They are doomed to guilt and condemnation before the self. Either God must be acknowledged as the means of filling the gap between the individual ego and the collective ego or else humanists must be content with their moral ideal without the power to fulfill it. Carnell succinctly pinpointed the dilemma and offered a solution:

> Humanism has tried to float the second table of the law without the dignifying foundations of the first, but the experiment has failed. Man has no dignity, and thus he is not worthy of our devotion, if he does not participate in a transtemporal, transpatial realm of values which give normative expression of the ideal law of life. . . . If nothing is timelessly obligatory, then it is meaningless to say that it is an obligation that we treat all men as ends and never as means.[17]

The solution to the humanist's dilemma is not through a denial of human dignity and freedom. That would only result in the inevitable disintegration of one's own person. The solution, Carnell insisted, lies rather in the need to press beyond humanism to theism where the needs of the former can find their true fulfillment in the reality of the latter.

Theism: Commitment to God

Carnell has strategically brought us to that point in the value system where God can be commended as the most logical value option and the only means of complete satisfaction for the whole person. Commitment to God is indeed a "wise" person's choice for God alone can satisfy the needs of the heart as well as the head.

The term "God," however, can obviously mean many different things. Carnell was careful to emphasize the fact that he was using the term "God" to specifically mean the God who is revealed in Scripture—the God who meets us and makes Himself known to us in Jesus Christ. The God we know in Jesus Christ is not an abstract deity, the "god of the philosophers," but the divine person who wills to know us through a heart-satisfying encounter.

Christianity does come to us as a worldview, but it is a worldview that has the person of Jesus Christ at its center. Without Christ there could be no satisfying solutions to the seeming contradictions of history or the ambiguities of human experience. When we look to the God of the Scriptures, Carnell believed, we find the God who satisfies our need for personal encounter and fellowship as well as the epistemological, meta-physical, and axiological demands of a coherent worldview. Jesus Christ is worthy of a wise person's commitment because he satisfies the needs of the whole person.

The old saying that "familiarity breeds contempt" is no where truer than Western society's tendency to simply ignore or overlook the profound truth of Christianity. Christianity is much more likely to be dismissed on the grounds that it is too simple a solution, or that it has been hopelessly distorted by denominational wrangling, than by sound logical reasoning. While each must judge the matter for himself, Carnell concluded that:

> It is the conviction of the Christian philosopher that men turn from Biblical Christianity more by the leading of prejudgment than by light gained from critical hypothesis. It is easy to misunderstand the simple system of biblical truth by confusing it with a dissatisfying denominational or institutional system which pretends to come in its name. Consequently, men comb the world for data with which to deliver them from the uncertainties of this present hour, while by-passing a copy of the Scriptures which may be purchased for a few cents in a variety store.

If a person rejects the solution to the riddle of the universe that Christ offers, and if one cannot believe in a system of philosophy that at least professes to answer the question of the rationality of the universe, to solve the dilemma of truth, and to provide a basis for personal immortality, Carnell asked, "how shall he answer Peter's question, 'to whom shall we go?' " (John 6:68)[18]

A Satisfied Heart

In his last major works, *Christian Commitment* and *The Kingdom of Love and the Pride of Life*, Carnell appealed to an even broader and higher principle of knowledge. He called it the third locus of truth, "truth in the heart." It is this more personal form of truth, Carnell insisted, that makes possible our "knowledge by acquaintance." In this form of knowledge the emphasis is on "fellowship" where spirit encounters Spirit in personal encounter. In contrast to the "I-It" relationships that characterize relations in our impersonal technocratic societies, the "I-Thou" form of "knowledge by acquaintance" offers a truly humanizing experience that modern persons crave. This is the kind of truth, Carnell noted, that biblical writers consistently invite one to enjoy. He described its superiority over other forms of knowledge:

> The apex in the pyramid of knowledge is personal acquaintance with God. When the creature finds his way to fellowship with God, the image and likeness returns to the center and source of its being, there to enjoy that perfection of love which human relations can enjoy only by finite degrees.
>
> There is no greater height of free potentiality, and thus no more conceivably perfect form of knowledge, than that enjoyed when the dust returns to the potter to experience fellowship and love.[19]

One should note that in his emphasis upon the environment of the heart and what he called "knowledge by acquaintance" Carnell never abandoned the canons of logic and reason. Christianity can satisfy the heart so completely, he insisted, precisely because it does not have to offend the mind in order to appease one's moral and spiritual needs. Contrary to thinkers like Søren Kierkegaard, the Christian existentialist, Carnell argued that a deserved emphasis on inwardness and subjectivity does not have to result in a divorce of "heart knowledge" from its objective grounding in Scripture or an abandonment of legitimate tests for truth.

Carnell believed with Kierkegaard that Christianity is a living truth and lamented the fact that the institutional church too often encourages "cheap grace" through sacramental rites and conformity to the organized church rather than challenging believers to a life of passionate existential commitment. But he disagreed with Kierkegaard's contention that God has intentionally made it intellectually difficult to become a Christian by making the Christian faith repulsive to the mind. Christianity cannot be reduced to some form of bloodless knowledge that can be known without it radically affecting one's life, but neither does commitment mean that one must pit faith against knowledge.

Carnell was impressed by certain aspects of Kierkegaard's understanding of Christianity. He admired the fresh pace that the Danish "gadfly" had set in the philosophy of religion, but he rejected his view that true inwardness is lost when the mind is satisfied with the consistency of objective rational evidences. That kind of either/or, Carnell insisted, is an unnecessary trade-off. Passion is not more important than eternal and objective truth, nor does faith amount to some kind of "leap" into the darkness. Jesus Christ is worthy of our faith precisely because his person and his doctrine are rationally continuous with the values that we have already accepted in ordinary experience. Whenever our spirit is satisfied that the evidences for faith are sufficient, it rests in truth. When insufficient evidence for belief seems to exist, the self will inevitably be divided by doubt.

The burden of *Christian Commitment*, Carnell's most creative work, was that God and humanity share common moral ground. Christian commitment goes well beyond "right belief" and "sound doctrine." It demands moral rectitude. While God is concerned that we know the truth, God is even more concerned that we "be" the truth. God's means of filling the gap between what we "are" and what we "ought to be" is the righteousness of Christ. The heart of the gospel is that one "becomes truth" as the moral and spiritual demands of one's moral and spiritual environment are met through the righteousness of Christ.

The self-giving love that motivated God to redeem us through the righteousness of Christ is the same love that is poured into our hearts by the Holy Spirit so that we too can live by the law of love. The realization that God lovingly accepts us in Jesus Christ is meant to be the basis for our loving acceptance of others as well as ourselves. The law of Christ is indeed the law of love. The only way to "knowledge by acquaintance," Carnell insisted, is through the experience of loving and being loved.

In his later writings Carnell made significant use of the insights of seminal thinkers like Søren Kierkegaard, Reinhold Niebuhr, Paul Tillich, and Sigmund Freud to show the correlation between humanity's moral anxiety and its failure to live by the law of love. He built his best case for love as the law of live in *The Kingdom of Love and the Pride of Life* where he employed the insights of psychotherapy to demonstrate that in the world of happy children—characterized by natural zest, simplicity, unconditional faith, and acceptance—there is a virtual kingdom of love. This is why Christ admonished us to become like little children in order to enter into God's kingdom. The world of happy children can teach grown men and women much about God's intentions for human happiness. Christianity has taught since the first century what psychotherapists now understand, that what every person needs most is to be loved and accepted.

Carnell's own background in fundamentalism intensified his understanding and appreciation for this great truth. Hardline fundamentalism had gone wrong, he believed, when it equated the possession of truth (i.e., the Bible) with the possession of virtue. Carnell never minimized the importance of believing the fundamentals of the faith. But the test of discipleship, he insisted, is not assent to fundamental doctrines but "works done in love." Fundamentalism never really understood that truth. It erred when it substituted adherence to dogmas and manifestos for a dynamic and demanding inner commitment of "being the truth" in love. It is infinitely more important to be sure of the sovereign God who can be known and experienced through simple trust, Carnell believed, than it is to rely upon any prideful pretension to complete biblical consistency in one's own theology.

Notes

[1]Alan Richardson, "Reinhold Niebuhr as Apologist," *Reinhold Niebuhr: His Religious, Social and Political Thought,* ed. Charles W. Kegley and Robert W. Bretall (New York: MacMillan Co., 1956) 220.

[2]Edward John Carnell, *An Introduction to Christian Apologetics* (Grand Rapids MI: Eerdmans Publishing Co., 1948) 121.

[3]Edward John Carnell, *The Kingdom of Love and the Pride of Life* (Grand Rapids MI: Eerdmans Publishing Co., 1960) 9.

[4]Edward John Carnell, Review of *The Defense of the Faith,* by Cornelius Van Til, *The Christian Century*(4 January 1956): 14-15.

[5]In particular Carnell noted the tendency among modern biblical critics, existentialists, and neo-orthodox theologians to separate faith from reason.

[6]Carnell, *Apologetics,* 23.

[7]Ibid., 353.   [8]Ibid., 354.

[9]Clark, *A Christian View of Men and Things,* 34.

[10]Carnell, *Apologetics,* 356. I do not treat these as individual issues, but Carnell deals with many of them at some length in *An Introduction to Christian Apologetics.*

[11]Ibid., 47.   [12]Ibid., 178.

[13]See "The Crisis of Our Age: The Views of Pitirim A. Sorokin," R. P. Cuzzart, *Humanity and Modern Sociological thought* (New York: Holt, Rinehart and Winston, 1969) 235-46.

[14]Edward John Carnell, *A Philosophy of the Christian Religion* (Grand Rapids MI: Eerdmans Publishing Co., 1952) 178.

[15]William Halverson, *A Concise Introduction to Philosophy*, 2d. ed. (New York: Random House, 1972) 466.

[16]Carnell, *A Philosophy of the Christian Religion,* 243.

[17]Ibid., 272, 273.

[18]Carnell, *Apologetics*, 357.

[19]Carnell, *Philosophy*, 181.

Selected Bibliography

Major Works by Carnell

The Burden of Søren Kierkegaard. Grand Rapids MI: Eerdmans Publishing Co., 1956.

The Case for Biblical Christianity. Grand Rapids MI: Eerdmans Publishing Co., 1969.

The Case for Orthodox Theology. Philadelphia PA: Westminister Press, 1959.

Christian Commitment. New York: Macmillan Co., 1957.

An Introduction to Christian Apologetics. Grand Rapids MI: Eerdmans Publishing Co., 1948.

The Kingdom of Love and the Pride of Life. Grand Rapids MI: Eerdmans Publishing Co., 1960.

A Philosophy of the Christian Religion. Grand Rapids MI: Eerdmans Publishing Co., 1952.

Television: Servant or Master? Grand Rapids MI: Eerdmans Publishing Co., 1950.

The Theology of Reinhold Niebuhr. Grand Rapids MI: Eerdmans Publishing Co., 1950.

Chapters in Books

"Niebuhr's Criteria of Verification," Chapter 18 in *Reinhold Niebuhr: His Religious, Social, and Political Thought*. Ed. Charles W. Kegley and Robert W. Bretall. Volume 2 of the Library of Living Theology. New York: Macmillan Co., 1956. 379-80.

"Reinhold Niebuhr's View of Scripture," Chapter 9 in *Inspiration and Interpretation*. Ed. John F. Walvoord. Grand Rapids MI: Eerdmans Publishing Co., 1957. 239-52.

"Fundamentalism," Chapter 37 in *Handbook of Christian Theology*, New York: Meridian Books, 1958. 142-43.

A Chapter in *How My Mind Has Changed*. Ed. Harold E. Fey. New York: Meridian Books, 1960. 91-104.

"The Government of the Church," Chapter 37, *Basic Christian Doctrines*, Ed. Carl F. H. Henry. New York: Holt, Rinehart, and Winston, Inc., 1962. 248-54.

"The Son of God," Chapter 14, *The Empirical Theology of Henry Nelson Wieman*, Ed. Robert W. Bretall. Volume 4 of the Library of Living Theology. New York: Macmillan Co., 1963. 306-14.

Other

Inaugural Address of Edward John Carnell, President of Fuller theological
Seminary 1954-1959, delivered 17 May 1955 (published as a portion of the
Carnell Memorial established in 1969–1970 by the Fuller Theological
Seminary Alumni Association, Pasadena CA).

Material about Carnell

Barnhart, J. E. *The Religious Epistemology and Theodicy of Edward John
Carnell.* Ann Arbor MI: University Microfilm, 1964.
Haines, Aubrey B. "Edward John Carnell: An Evaluation." *Christian Century* (7
June 1967): 751.
Hordern, William and Harold L. DeWold. Review of *The Case for Orthodox
Theology,* by Edward John Carnell, in *Journal of Bible and Religion*
(October 1959): 311-17.
Lewis, Gordon R. *Testing Christianity's Truth Claims: Approaches to Christian
Apologetics.* Chicago IL: Moody Press, 1976.
Marsden, George M. *Reforming Fundamentalism: Fuller Seminary and the New
Evangelicalism.* Grand Rapids MI: Eerdmans Publishing Co., 1987.
Nash, Ronald H. *The New Evangelicalism.* Grand Rapids MI: Zondervan
Publishing Co., 1963.
Nelson, Rudolph. *The Making and Unmaking of an Evangelical Mind: The Case
of Edward John Carnell.* New York: Cambridge University Press, 1987.
Ramm, Bernard. *Types of Apologetical Systems.* Wheaton IL: Van Kampen
Press, 1953.
Sailer, William S. "The Role of Reason in the Theologies of Nel Ferre and
Edward John Carnell." Unpublished S.T.D. dissertation. Philadelphia PA:
Temple University, 1964.
Sims, John A. *Edward John Carnell: Defender of the Faith.* Washington DC:
University Press of America, 1979.
Sims, John A. "The Problem of Knowledge in the Apologetical Concerns of
Edwin Lewis and Edward John Carnell." Unpublished Ph.D. dissertation.
Tallahassee FL: Florida State University, 1975.
Wozniak, Kenneth W. M. *Ethics in the Thought of Edward John Carnell.* New
York: University Press of America, 1983.

Part Three: Reinhold Niebuhr

Introduction

6. The Making of a Prophet

   A. Preparation for the Ministry
   B. The Detroit Experience
      1. The Making of a Preacher
      2. Writer, Lecturer, and Public Figure
      3. Niebuhr Challenges Henry Ford

7. The Shattering of Illusions and Pretensions

   A. Wisdom in Quest of Responsibility
   B. A Visible Sacrament
   C. The Marxist Challenge
   D. Toward Biblical Realism
   E. Religious Illusions and Pretensions
   F. Secular Illusions and Pretensions

8. In Defense of Biblical Realism

   A. A Realistic Appraisal of Human Nature
   B. A Christian Interpretation of History
   C. The Social Relevance of Christianity

Selected Bibliography

Introduction

The First World War had already begun when Reinhold Niebuhr went to Detroit to assume his duties as pastor of the Bethel Evangelical Church. His German speaking congregation had divided loyalties, but the courageous young pastor took a decisive stand in "americanizing" his parishoners and encouraging loyalty to what he regarded as the proper cause. The war and the aftermath of the Treaty of Versailles, however, pushed Niebuhr into a reconstructed world view. When the war began, Niebuhr noted, "I was a young man trying to be an optimist without falling into sentimentality." When it ended, "I had become a realist seeking to save myself from cynicism." The war, Niebuhr confessed, made him "a child of the age of disillusonment."

The vindictive Versailles settlement was a major disappointment, and the post-war revelations of false allied propaganda, driven by economic interests, added fuel to Niebuhr's growing cynicism. After a visit to the Ruhr Valley in 1923, where he witnessed first-hand the starvation, hatred, and sub-human conditions of the war victims, Niebuhr declared that he was "done with the war business." Even before the war ended he had sensed that American chaplains had "confused loyalty to Yahweh with loyalty to the war god Mars." But it was the uncritical patriotism of the churches that concerned Niebuhr most. He began to wonder out loud about the moral relevancy of organized religion.

Niebuhr's response to the "war business" was a courtship with pacifism. He became the head of a pacifist organization, The Fellowship of Reconciliation, but his commitment to pacifism was actually more pragmatic than ideological. His basic contention was that international conflicts should be avoided through wise statesmanship and by exhausting every possibility of accommodating competing interests. His reflections on the class struggle in *Moral Man and Immoral Society* (1932), and the rise of Nazi totalitarian aggression, marked Niebuhr's complete break with pacifist attitudes. After 1932 he became one of the sharpest critics of pacifism in America.

The Great War convinced Niebuhr that both secular and religious liberalism had been naively optimistic. All hope of automatic progress had been shattered. Human brutality had been revealed at its worse. International peace and prosperity was no longer realistic. The secular vision, based on the Enlightenment's faith in the goodness of humanity and the inevitability of human progress, had lost its appeal. The future course of Western civilization would need to be charted on more realistic assumptions.

The naive optimism of religious liberalism that good people could solve the social problems of the day by following the love ethic of the Sermon on the Mount was just as unrealistic. The belief that a love ethic, divorced from power, could bring social justice out of *laissez faire* capitalism was pure sentimentality. The social gospel had failed to plumb the depths of sin in either the individual or society. If the evils of self-interest, personified in industrial capitalists like Henry Ford, were to be faced realistically, there would have to be a return to biblical realism and its assessment of the human condition.

Karl Marx's radical criticism of Christianity, however, had convinced millions of oppressed people that Christianity was more of the problem than the solution. The Christian religion merely functioned to protect the economic interests of the rich and powerful. Niebuhr recognized that Marx's analysis and critique of religion could not be answered through traditional forms of apologetics or philosophical debate. Philosophical disputes were irrelevant to Marx's "social atheism." The only adequate response would have to be one in which it could be shown that Christianity's social function was radically different from the one described by Marx.

Niebuhr's apologetic interest was evident in the title of his first book, *Does Civilization Need Religion?* His conclusion was that civilization would always need those forms of religion that recognized and challenged social inequities. The socially sensitive, on the other hand, will always scorn those forms of religion that fail to challenge social injustice. It was no small task to persuade secular modernists that Christianity could play a positive role as an agent of change—especially in view of the fact that Marx's critique was the most serious and damaging in the long history of the Christian faith.

From 1929–1944 Reinhold Niebuhr faced the challenge from the position of a "Christian Marxist." He applied the Marxist analysis to the self-interests and inequities of a dehumanizing capitalist system but appealed to Christian insights to show that prophetic Chrisianity provided a more profound understanding of the nature and destiny of man. Even more important was the realism inherent in the biblical principles of love, justice, and power that he believed could empower the quest for social change.

Niebuhr always explored the options and had the courage to change as social and political situations dictated. The New Deal policies of

Roosevelt and the brutalities of post-war Stalinism in Russia, for instance, greatly altered his political alignments and loyalties. As he incessantly applied the truths of biblical realism to Marxian utopianism, he moved more and more optimistically toward democracy. Niebuhr's realistic appraisal of human nature, applied to democracy, resulted in his famous dictum that "man's capacity for justice makes democracy possible, but his inclination to injustice makes democracy necessary."

Niebuhr's social and political theory was always under the control of his theology, but he was not an armchair theologian. For four decades he applied his social ethic to flesh-and-blood situations around the world. His quest for social justice in the midst of changing times threw Niebuhr into political debates ranging from the New Deal to the Cold War, from America's involvement in World War II to its involvement in Vietnam. His wide ranging interests made Niebuhr known to Americans, and to many Europeans, as a religious thinker, political organizer, social critic, and professor at New York's prestigious Union Theological Seminary.

In the church world he was widely known as an ecumenical leader, seminary professor, theologian, and outstanding preacher who was in constant demand on the university chapel circuit. He did as much as any man of his time to articulate the interrelations between faith and culture. It was a fitting tribute to Reinhold Niebuhr that when he died on 1 June 1971 at his retirement home in Stockbridge, Massachusetts, he was viewed by many as America's greatest theologian since Jonathan Edwards—the man who had once been banished from Stockbridge for his "too-demanding" theology.

6.
The Making of a Prophet

Reinhold Niebuhr was born the fourth of five children to Gustav and Lydia Niebuhr on 21 June 1892 in Wright City, Missouri. The eldest child was Hulda, followed by Walter, and then Herbert who died six weeks after birth. Then came Reinhold and, two years later, Helmut Richard. Three of the children were destined to become well-known religious leaders. Hulda, the only girl in the family, became a practitioner and teacher of Christian Education at McCormick Theological Seminary in Chicago. During their lifetime, Reinhold and Helmut Richard would become the two leading Christian ethicists in America.

Gustav Niebuhr had immigrated to America from Germany in 1881 at the age of eighteen. He had not come to America for economic or religious reasons but to escape the stern autocratic ways of his father and compulsory military service in the Prussian army. For a while young Gustav worked in a sewing-machine factory in Chicago and then on a farm, owned by relatives, near Freeport, Illinois. During his stay on the farm Gustav's life took a turn, and he announced his intention of studying for the ministry. He entered Eden seminary, near St. Louis, and completed the three year program in two years.

In 1885, at the age of twenty-two, Gustav was ordained in the German Evangelical Synod of North America—a church of American origin that did not regard itself as either Lutheran or Calvinist. The church was, however, thoroughly German and heavily concentrated in the states of Illinois, Ohio, and Missouri. It was a "liberal" church in the sense that it stressed piety more than doctrine and pursued an accommodating pragmatism toward other denominations and the native American culture.[1] One of the things that Reinhold vividly recalled about his religious upbringing was "a vital personal piety combined with a complete freedom in his theological studies."[2]

Gustav's first church was a small congregation in San Francisco, California. It was there that he met and married Lydia. She was a talented and energetic worker in the church and proved to be the impetus that Gustav needed for success. The church was soon growing, and in a short while they moved to a larger congregation in Missouri where they stayed for ten years. Gustav was an ambitious and hard-working man. His boundless energy, together with his organizational abilities, attracted the attention of denominational leaders who appointed him to challenging tasks. During his pastorate at St. John's church in St. Charles, Missouri, Gustav traveled widely for his denomination creating new parishes and giving oversight to a number of denominationally sponsored welfare homes.

After a number of years "on the road" he was more than happy to settle down to the duties of a new church in Lincoln, Illinois, where he could spend more time with his family. There was a sizable German population in the town of Lincoln, and pastor Niebuhr soon emerged as a prominent public figure. In a short while he had become the director of a parochial school, superintendent of one of Lincoln's hospitals, and a leader of Lincoln's socially and politically active ministerial association.

Gustav was by temperament a no-nonsense kind of man, but he was not uncaring or autocratic, as his father had been. He exerted a powerful influence upon his children, particularly young Reinhold upon whom he lavished special attention. Reinhold's life-long admiration for his father was reflected in a story he recalled about an early discussion they had concerning Reinhold's future. According to the story, Reinhold was walking home with his father from a local event in which Gustav had taken a leading role when Gustav asked young Reinhold if he had thought about what he wanted to be. "A minister," Reinhold replied without hesitation. When asked why he wanted to be a minister, Reinhold quickly replied, "because you are obviously the most interesting man in town."

Gustav's religious views were both liberal and evangelical. He was liberal in his commitment to social issues and his preference for piety above doctrinal exactness, but he held firmly to his belief in the divinity of Christ, the supernatural inspiration of the Bible, miracles, and the importance of prayer. His relation to religious liberalism was reflected in his estimate of Adolf Harnack, one of the best known liberals of his time. He admired Harnack's love ethic and his openness, but he felt that he was much too subjective, wrong in his denial of miracles, and too liberal in his interpretation of Scripture.[3] Gustav was uncompromisingly liberal in his effort to relate his Christian faith to social and political issues. His own views were relatively moderate, but he never shied away from expressing them—even when his own parishioners sharply disagreed.

In many ways Reinhold Niebuhr proved to be the spiritual heir of his father, but in other respects he was much more liberal. He took Scripture and doctrine seriously but rejected virtually all literalistic and rationalistic interpretations. He embraced the historical-critical method and shared the naturalistic assumptions of modern science but warned against an over confidence in its methods or its conclusions. His universe was much more closed than Gustav's and offered virtually no place for miracles. He followed his father in his commitment to social issues and in his boldness.[4] Like Ernest Troeltsch, he refuted metaphysics and tried to keep his theology within the realm of human history. He understood theology as a response to human needs, human powers, and human responsibilities.[5] Theology was not a call to transcend the world but a resource for responding to human need.[6]

Preparation for the Ministry

Walter Niebuhr was the first-born son in the Niebuhr household. He grew up to become a handsome, athletic, and capable young man with a charming personality. It was well known among his friends that his goal in life was first to become a college fraternity man and after that a success in business. Hulda, on the other hand, was the only girl in the family. Gustav expected her to work in the home and the church until marriage. Fully aware of these expectations, Hulda did not feel free to continue her education beyond high school until after the death of her father. Because Gustav viewed Walter's and Hulda's careers differently from Reinhold's and Helmut Richard's, he allowed them to graduate from the local high school.

Reinhold and H. Richard, on the other hand, desired to follow their father into the ministry, so they left Lincoln High after the ninth grade to enter the denomination's boarding school for prospective ministers. Reinhold's respect and admiration for his father undoubtedly influenced his decision to prepare for the ministry, but he was also talented and gifted for that vocation. He was an energetic worker, made top grades, and excelled as a debater—a talent that later amplified his success in the pulpit, in the classroom, and the lecture circuit.

When he left home for Elmhurst College (1907), Reinhold was a mature fifteen-year-old boy. Elmhurst was actually not a college but a boarding school, sponsored by the synod, for the purpose of preparing young men for Eden Seminary and the ministry. It was not a first-rate school. Niebuhr found the classics-based curriculum at Elmhurst so stale and poorly-taught that he led a protest to have two of the teachers dismissed. He later recalled that it would have been a wasted three years had it not been for his frequent back-home visits with his father. His father, more than his teachers at Elmhurst, kept his critical faculties and his intellectual curiosity alive during his summer visits to Lincoln. He also enjoyed his summer visits to Chautauqua, an annual social and recreational event that was held during the summer about two miles outside the town. Campers gathered on the Chautauqua grounds for picnicking, ball games, lectures, music, and addresses by renowned orators. It was at Chautauqua that young Reinhold first heard impassioned speakers like William Jennings Bryan, "fighting" Bob Lafollette, and Billy Sunday expound the populist values of mid-America. The son of the German-immigrant pastor, who was still having problems with the English language, was getting a first-hand exposure to the intellectual and moral life of his adopted homeland.

In 1910 Reinhold began his three-year program of study at Eden Theological Seminary. His experiences there were more educationally rewarding. He especially enjoyed his relationship with Professor Samuel Press, a new member of the faculty who occupied the chair of English. Professor Press encouraged critical discussion and rewarded originality in his classes—something Niebuhr had missed in his earlier educational experiences. Press also taught his courses in English, another novelty for Niebuhr, and encouraged acculturation in a manner that the young German-American was anxious to pursue. Next to his father, Samuel Press exerted the strongest influence upon Niebuhr's formative development and forged a friendship with his young student that lasted throughout their lives.

At Eden Niebuhr had his first real opportunity to display his debating skills. He made the most of the opportunity and led Eden to its highest heights—a smashing victory over highly-regarded Concordia Lutheran College. Life at Eden was filled with extra-curricular activities, and Niebuhr's real interests began to show. He entered essay contests, wrote editorials for his brother Walter's newspaper, joined the Bachelor's Club, and impressed everyone with his debating skills. But what he remembered most about Eden was the positive influence of a good teacher. In his

"Intellectual Autobiography" Niebuhr paid high tribute to his old professor:

> The seminary was influential in my life primarily because of the creative effect upon me of the life of a very remarkable man, Dr. S. D. Press, who combined a childlike innocency with a rigorous scholarship in biblical and systematic subjects. This proved the point that an educational institution needs only to have Mark Hopkins on one end of a log and a student on the other.[7]

During his last year at Eden Reinhold and his father agreed that he should do graduate work at a major east coast university. Gustav wanted his son to have a first-rate university education, something comparable to what one would receive in a major German university. Reinhold was expected to be selected as valedictorian at Eden, but he knew this would not guarantee his acceptance at a major Ivy League university. The biggest obstacle, it was feared, was that he did not have a Bachelor of Arts degree from an accredited college. There was also the problem of financing his graduate work.

Reinhold, his family, and all those at the seminary were filled with pride when they learned that he had been accepted at Yale. He was the first student from the synod to be admitted to a prestigious eastern school. The problem of financing his education, however, turned out to be more serious than expected. In the Spring of 1913, just a few weeks before Reinhold was to graduate from Eden, Gustav Niebuhr unexpectedly became ill. He died a few days later. Everyone was shocked. He had just passed his fiftieth birthday, and his widow was only fourty-three. There were now new responsibilities for which Reinhold, or any of the children, had not been prepared.

The death of Gustav Niebuhr was deeply felt by his family, church, synod, and the town of Lincoln. Over a thousand mourners attended his funeral. Reinhold and Helmut were summoned home from Eden, and Reinhold was unanimously accepted by St. John's church council as its interim pastor. The son who had such a special place in his father's affections, and admired his father's vocation so highly, was now cast into his father's role. Nothing would have pleased Gustav more except Reinhold's continuing his education at Yale. The financial problems, however, now seemed insurmountable, and there was the added problem of persuading the denomination to release him from the ministerial obligation he owed the synod for the free education he had received at the seminary. Reinhold felt that he could, with good conscience, ask for a temporary release from his duties to the synod, but it was more difficult leaving the family.

Reinhold was pastor of St. John's for five months, but Fall found him in New Haven. He had, by that time, negotiated with synod officials about a successor for the church, found suitable housing for his mother, and made preparations for Yale. Reinhold had succeeded at virtually everything he had attempted in life, but he was more anxious than usual about going to Yale. This was the place where he had to make good, his personal proving ground, and he was keenly aware that there were deficiencies in his background. His command of the English language was limited, and he was sensitive about not having an earned bachelor's degree or the broad educational background that such a degree was meant to provide. In a letter to Professor Press, his confidant at Eden, he complained about the deficiency he felt: "I thought . . . that I lacked only the B.A.," he wrote, "but I have found that I lack the things that make up the B.A.—philosophy, ethics, science, and a real course in English."[8] His English was constantly improving, but he was very sensitive about his accent. He told Press that he felt like "a mongrel among thoroughbreds."

By the end of the nineteenth century secularization had already made its impact at Yale. The Divinity School had lost its doctrinal commitments to New England Congregationalism and was generally following the naturalistic assumptions of the day. The symbol of Yale's new commitments was Douglas Clyde Macintosh, a modernist, who was teaching systematic theology and philosophy of religion. During his first year Niebuhr struggled with his English and with his courses under Macintosh, but his final grades turned out well. He recalled that his favorite course was Macintosh's philosophy of religion, but he also enjoyed Professor Porter's course in New Testament theology.

Professor Macintosh supervised Niebuhr's Bachelor of Divinity thesis. He entitled the thesis, "The Validity and Certainty of Religious Knowledge," a significant piece of work in which he was trying to work out an epistemological position. Niebuhr had been, by this time, deeply influenced by biblical criticism, evolutionary assumptions, and Macintosh's conviction that theology could become an empirical science. His starting point, like that of his mentor, was not biblical authority but human experience. Theology, he stressed in his first theological endeavor, should be grounded in human need and experience. It was a theme that Niebuhr would emphasize throughout his theological career. His biographer would later note that Niebuhr always "hated absolutism of any kind. Life was an adventure in which people could create their own world if they had the courage and intelligence to do so."[9]

The thesis was actually an exercise in Christian apologetics from a liberal perspective. He built his case for "religious certainty" on two fundamental truths. The first was that we do not live in an impersonal universe where moral values and the moral struggle against evil are without merit or reward. The divine "personality" that has been revealed in Christ, Niebuhr argued, assures us that there are spiritual heights in human personality and freedom that transcend the brute forces of nature. In essence, the Bible does what naturalistic and idealistic philosophies cannot; it assures us that human life and experiences are morally meaningful. In true liberal fashion Niebuhr disavowed all forms of metaphysics and advocated the "back to history" motif.[10] But his aim was not to rediscover the old rational categories of thought or the "true man, true God" Christology of historic orthodoxy. He wanted somehow to inspire an encounter with the incomprehensible God through which modern persons could find an acceptable basis for human dignity and freedom.

The other nemesis that Niebuhr attacked was skepticism. In the spirit of William James's pragmatism he asserted his right to believe what he willed so long as it was not contrary "to established facts and desired consequences."[11] From Niebuhr's perspective, "truth was not something to be possessed once and for all, not a final apprehension of reality, but something to be worked toward, something approximated in action."[12] It was an epistemology with close affinities to the Ritschlian tradition, which grounded knowledge in value judgments rather than rationality, for Niebuhr insisted that, "in the main we may hold to our personal values and demand that the universe appreciate them."[13]

Paul Tillich once noted that

the difficulty in writing about Niebuhr's epistemology lies in the fact that there is no such epistemology. Niebuhr does not ask, "how can I know?"; he starts knowing. And he does not ask afterward, "how could I know?", but leaves the convincing power of his thought without epistemological support.[14]

Niebuhr did not seem to have a personal struggle with doubt, but he gave every other person the right to struggle with it as much as their experiences demanded. His biographer believed that was one of the factors from Niebuhr's own experience that "permitted him to speak to the intellectuals of his generation with a compelling force that few if any Christian preachers could match."[15]

The following year Niebuhr completed a Master of Arts thesis, also under Macintosh's supervision. It was entitled, "The Contribution of Christianity to the Doctrine of Immortality." The same epistemological and theological position that had emerged in the B.D. thesis was evident in the MA, but the most striking similarily was the dialectical method that Niebuhr had obviously adopted. In his B.D. thesis he had juxtaposed naturalism and idealism in order to show Christianity's superior view of personality. In the M.A. thesis he set the Greek against the Hebrew doctrine of immortality for the purpose of demonstrating that neither was adequate in itself but contributed to the superior Christian synthesis. Again, Niebuhr's real intent was not to speculate about the afterlife but to demonstrate that Christianity is the "religion of the person." Only "a God that loves the soul," Niebuhr believed, "could guarantee a universe that appreciates the individual." This kind of universe is necessary if one is to take heart against the forces of nature. It assures us that our struggles are real and meaningful. "What modern man needs," Niebuhr believed, "is the assurance that his personal struggles matter, that they are observed, recorded, appreciated in an ultimate scheme."[16]

The thesis readers were obviously impressed. They granted the MA to Niebuhr despite the fact that he lacked the customary BA. Macintosh liked Niebuhr's work and encouraged him to do the Ph.D., but he was not interested. Macintosh's interest in epistemology bored him, and he felt that it was now time to shoulder more of the family responsibilities and fulfill his duty to the synod and accept a church. He accepted his denomination's appointment to a pastorate at Bethel Evangelical Church in Detroit, Michigan. On 8 August 1915, Reinhold Niebuhr reported to Bethel ready to deliver his first sermon.

The Detroit Experience

The thirteen years that Reinhold Niebuhr spent in Detroit were probably the most important years of his life. It was a critical period of transition when the attention that had been paid to the intellectual problems of religion in academia was refocused on the ethical problems of the marketplace. It was also a time of personal and vocational development. During these crucial years Niebuhr became an outstanding preacher, a well-known writer for religious and secular journals, and an active participant in political and secular causes. But perhaps even more importantly, it was the time when he took up the prophetic mantle.

The Making of a Preacher

Soon after Niebuhr took the church, his widowed mother moved from Lincoln to Detroit. She remained with Reinhold until his marriage in 1931. Lydia Niebuhr was a remarkable woman. Her energy and organizational skills helped immensely in caring for the day-to-day tasks of the parish. In effect, Lydia became Bethel's assistant pastor.[17]

Bethel was a small congregation of about eighteen families when Niebuhr arrived, but it steadily grew into a large and impressive church. There were a number of factors that helped account for the growth. During the 1920s there was a rapid church growth pattern across America, and the Detroit area experienced a population explosion as workers poured into the city to work in the automoble industry. But the growth of Bethel was also due to other, more personal, factors as well; namely, Niebuhr's increasing reputation as a dynamic and challenging preacher. In a relatively short period of time Niebuhr was attracting listeners and readers who previously had not shown any interest in the Christian faith. His thought-provoking sermons were being heard and read throughout the country. Paul Scherer, a homiletics professor, commented on Niebuhr's growing reputation as a preacher during the decade of the 1920s:

> By the late twenties word had got around through the universities, and from such platforms as that of the Chicago Sunday Evening Club, that he was a preacher not to miss. Churches and auditoriums were crowded when it came his time to appear. Lectureships were opened to him. And from hearing him, professors and students alike, doctors, lawyers, politicians, authors, editors, long unaccustomed to take seriously anything that emanated from the pulpit, began to read his books and discuss his theology.[18]

Some twenty-five of Niebuhr's sermonic essays, representative of his university preaching, were eventually published under the titles of *Beyond Tragedy* and *Discerning the Signs of the Times.* His sermons were invariably set in the context of relevant social issues. He noted in *Leaves from the Notebook of a Tamed Cynic,* a journal that he kept while he was a pastor, that he started enjoying preaching more after he "stopped worrying so much about the intellectual problems of religion and began exploring some of its ethical problems."[19] The social and ethical relevance of Niebuhr's sermons, more than anything else, was the key to his success as a preacher.

The irony in Niebuhr's success at Bethel was that he was revulsed by ministers who were preoccupied with a "success" mentality. His *Leaves* are full of ire for ministers more interested in maximizing their salaries, expanding their church plants, and inflating their membership rolls than they were in their prophetic responsibilities. The dangers of power and privilege were no where more evident, he believed, than in the church. "May the good Lord deliver me," he wrote in his journal in 1922, "from ever being a popular preacher."[20]

His preaching was seldom, if ever, the straight-forward kerygmatic type. It was usually a curious blending of a prophetic and apologetic message. It was prophetic in the sense that he constantly tore away all pretense to self-righteousness and human achievement and challenged his hearers to face up to their personal and collective sins. He challenged all moral pretension, Alan Richardson noted, in the name of "an absolute, uncompromising, unattainable demand that left no room for self-satisfaction or ease of conscience."[21] It was apologetic in that Niebuhr invariably pointed his hearers and readers beyond themselves and their creaturely limitations. He was faithful to remind his audiences that they stood under the judgment of a God who forgives and empowers.

In *An Interpretation of Christian Ethics* (1935) Niebuhr defined prophetic preaching in a manner that deliberately incorporated the link between the prophetic and the apologetic task. "It is the genius and task of prophetic religion," he said, "to insist on the organic relation between historic human existence and that which is both the ground and the fulfillment of their existence, the transcendent."[22] Scherer rightly noted that his was not the preaching of old-fashioned evangelicalism or the this-worldliness of twentieth-century liberalism but a message addressed to the social, industrial, political, and international affairs of the day. It made what Niebuhr had to say of utmost significance to the secular person, but it always pointed the secular person beyond his or her own understanding and achievement.[23]

There was no inconsistency, in Niebuhr's mind, between being prophetic and being practical. He understood very well that even the prophet needs to be effective. The prophet who cannot effectively communicate his message will not be heard. Despite his aversion to revivalism, theatrics in the pulpit, and emotional appeals, he had a guarded admiration for popular preachers like Billy Sunday. He was critical of their extremism and their one-sided emphasis upon "personal sins," but he admired their enthusiasm and the personal magnetism that made their message effective. Most liberal preachers scoffed at Sunday's pulpit antics, but Niebuhr could appreciate the homiletical axiom that "religious enthusiasm is produced as much by the personal power of the prophet as by the power of the message."[24]

Despite his distaste for personality cults, institution building, and the temptation to upward mobility, Niebuhr managed to build one of the most opulent churches in Detroit and fill it—largely on the strength of his personal magnetism in the pulpit. His preaching was described as "a well-crafted blend of drama and argument, a constant dialectic of comfort and challenge."[25]

Niebuhr's biographer described the irony of what his congregation regularly experienced:

> However attractive the new church may have been to prospective members, Niebuhr's preaching was the chief magnet that drew people to Bethel. By the early 1920s he was an accomplished pulpit performer, the educated Protestant's Billy Sunday. One did not merely listen to Niebuhr: one watched him strut, gyrate, jerk, bend, and quake. He whirled his arms, rubbed his ears and his balding scalp, stretched his hawkish nose forward. His whole lanky frame was in motion. One did not merely listen to Niebuhr: to catch the stream-of-consciousness flow of analysis and anecdote . . . demanded a concentration that few could sustain during an entire sermon.[26]

Writer, Lecturer, and Public Figure

During his thirteen years in Detroit Reinhold Niebuhr remained a bachelor. Lydia Niebuhr, his energetic mother, assumed the domestic duties and helped immensely with the ladies groups and children's programs in the church. This gave Niebuhr more time to devote to his writing and the lecture circuit. He always suspected, however, that things could have been much different had there been family responsibilities. In one of his entries in *Leaves,* he wrote:

> The old Methodist preaher who told me some time ago that I was so cantankerous in my spirit of criticism of modern society because I am not married may be right. If I had about four children to love I might not care so much about insisting that the spirit of love shall dominate all human affairs. And there might be more value in loving the four children than in paying lip service to the spirit of love as I do.[27]

As it was, Niebuhr spent much of his time at the typewriter with correspondence and tediously pounding out article after article for leading magazines and journals across the nation. His reputation as a critical thinker with something to say had spread, and there was a growing demand for Niebuhr both as a speaker and a writer. He was rapidly becoming a public figure.

Niebuhr published his first article in 1916 in *The Atlantic Monthly* and some forty more during the remainder of his stay at Bethel—mostly in *The Christian Century, The World Tomorrow,* and *The Atlantic.* Writing helped supplement his meagre salary, but more importantly, it gave him the opportunity to share his thoughts with a broader public. Like Jeremiah, Niebuhr was a passionate thinker. His was like a "fire shut up in his bones"; he needed an outlet for his message. He enjoyed his pastoral ministry at Bethel, but it undoubtedly would have been difficult to stay there had his message been restricted to the four walls of his church. Few, if any, writers of the time were moving with more ease from such varied topics as social philosophy to ecclesiastical affairs and philosophy of religion. The widespread attention to his views, in turn, confirmed the public's interest in what he had to say.

Most of the members at Bethel were middle-class German-Americans. Ties with the old country were still strong as evidenced by the fact that worship services were conducted in the German language. The war had begun the year before Niebuhr went to Bethel, and many members in the congregation were having difficulties sorting out their loyalties. Niebuhr, however, was clear about his. He actively encouraged his parishioners to follow the best traditions of their homeland in embracing a progressive, liberal perspective on both religious and political issues. In practical terms this meant the use of the English language, unquestionable loyalty to America and its allies in the war effort, and an application of liberal theology and ethics to the problems of society. Given his persuasiveness and rapport with his congregation, Niebuhr soon gained their support on all counts.

His active role in encouraging loyalty to the allied cause brought public attention to Niebuhr that resulted in his appointment to the synod's War Welfare Commission. The commission served as a support group for the young men from the denomination who were serving in the military. Niebuhr's participation on the commission necessitated a great deal of travel, but it brought him into contact with many important leaders and organizations that would further enhance his influence—including The Federal Council of Churches. His abilities as a speaker and capable leader were not lost on his superiors. After the war he became the synod's major contact with an organization known as the Interchurch World Movment. The movement received major support from John D. Rockefeller, who was trying to reconcile some of the differences that were driving capital and labor farther and farther apart.

For a while Niebuhr tried to follow Rockefeller's vision of resolving the issues on religious and moral grounds. But Bishop Charles D. Williams and other church progressives saw through the vested interests of the movement and encouraged the churches to move beyond the role of moral umpire in the social struggle and come out openly for labor's cause. These men, particularly Williams, impressed Niebuhr with their moral courage. He always remembered Bishop Williams as a man whose moral convictions had given him the strength to radicalize his own. Together, Niebuhr and Williams worked to establish the Detroit branch of the Fellowship for a Christian Social Order (FCSO). The organization's avowed purpose was to work toward the reform of industrial capitalism. Niebuhr had declared war on industry.

His involvement in the FCSO took Niebuhr on a summer group-tour of Europe where he met some of the most important leaders in Europe. In England he met such diverse dignitaries as Labour Party leader Ramsey McDonald, writers Bernard Shaw and H. G. Wells, and the Archbishop of Canterbury. He was particularly impressed by the British Labour Party whose vision, he believed, combined the idealism of liberal Christianity with hard-headed practical wisdom. In Niebuhr's mind, the vision of British Labour was the viable alternative to Marxist cynicism. In the years that followed he often spoke openly of his admiration for the "organic" British society and the party that best embodied his own social philosophy. It was the model, he believed, for America and post-war Germany.

The church's limited involvement in social and political issues was a major disappointment to Niebuhr, but he always held out the hope that the church would become more involved as an agent for social change. Social justice, he believed, was a mandate for the church. Reason could analyze social and political problems, but religion was needed to provide the motivation and the moral resources from which spiritually sensitive persons could challenge unjust social conditions. It was this conviction that prompted a "yes" to the question that Niebuhr posed in his first major book, *Does Civilization Need Religion?* (1927).

Niebuhr Challenges Henry Ford

During the decade of the 1920s Detroit had become Automobile City, and the symbol of the automobile industry was Henry Ford. Actually, Henry Ford was more than an industrial magnate; he was the national symbol of America's consumer society. His "Model T," more than any other consumer good, was the symbol of middle-class success. As E. B. White recalled, "a man seated in the seven-foot tall automobile felt like 'a man enthroned.' "[28]

Niebuhr enjoyed the pleasures of the automobile as much as anyone. He had no argument with technological progress or the modern industries that made the fruits of science and technology available to consumers. What was disturbing was the "paganism of pleasure" that seemed to be everywhere in America. After a trip to California in 1925 Niebuhr remarked that "Detroit is typical of the America which works feverishly to get what it wants, while Los Angeles is typical of the America which has secured what it wants." He then asked, "Is it possible to preach the gospel in America where happiness is gauged in terms of automobiles and radios?"[29]

Niebuhr was deeply disturbed about the cost that the supposed "progress" was exacting from the industial workers and outraged over the moral pretensions under which Henry Ford was attempting to persuade the public that he was a model humanitarian. In 1914 Ford announced to the press that his company was inaugurating "the greatest revolution in the matter of rewards for workers ever known in the industrial world." Over the next few years Ford's public relations department created a Henry Ford image that resembled that of a moral hero. They accentuated the five-dollar-a-day wages, the reduction of the work week from six days to five, and Ford's egalitarian practices in hiring blacks, ex-convicts, and the physically handicapped at all levels of the manufacturing process.

Niebuhr, however, was chairman of the Interracial Committee in Detroit and had privileged access to unpublished findings on wage rates in Ford's plants. The findings showed that the average worker had lost wages after the reduction of the work week while Ford's efficiency engineers had sped up the assembly line and produced as many cars as before. Ford's claims to "big wages" were disgraceful in light of the company's profit margins and its total disregard for the unemployed. In 1926 Niebuhr attacked the "Ford myth" by exposing the fallacies in the Ford claim in a series of articles published in the *Christian Century.* In an entry from *Leaves* in 1927 he recorded his disgust for Ford's moral hypocrisy:

> What a civilization this is! Naive gentlemen with a genius for mechanics suddenly become the arbiters over the lives and fortunes of hundreds of thousands. Their moral pretensions are credulously accepted at full value. No one bothers to ask whether an industry which can maintain a cash reserve of a quarter of a billion ought not make some provision for its unemployed. . . . The cry of the hungry is drowned in the song, "Henry has made a lady out of Lizzy."[30]

The toll the industrial process took on the dignity and welfare of its workers was of particular concern. In another entry he described the despair and hopelessness that so often accompanied the misfortune or sickness of workers:

> Mother and I visited at the home of _____ today where the husband is sick and was out of employment because he was sick. The folks have few connections in the city. They belong to no church. What a miserable existence it is to be friendless in a large city. And to be dependent on a heartless industry. The man is about 55 or 57 I should judge, and he is going to have a desperate time securing employment after he gets well. . . . I promised _____ I would try to find him

a job. I did it to relieve the despair of that family, but I will have a hard time making good on my promise. According to the ethics of our modern industrialism men over fifty, without special training, are so much junk.[31]

If there was one thing that Niebuhr hated more than moral pretension it was moral passivity. He loathed moral platitudes and acts of charity that were meant to serve as substitutes for social justice. Acts of charity certainly had their place, particularly in agrarian societies where relations were more personal, but in urban societies like Detroit philanthropy could never be an adequate substitute for justice. Charity and philanthropy too often were self-serving and invested the benefactors with more of a religious and moral aura than they deserved. More profound and heroic changes were needed.

Niebuhr observed that the middle and upper-middle class churches in Detroit contributed to the injustices of industrial capitalism through their fear of social change and disorder. By solidly lining up against the collective labor movement they gave support to the self-interests of business and management. Religion in Detroit was functioning just like Karl Marx described it—as a servile form of sanction for those holding power. Middle class ethics played directly into the hands of the capitalist system. They idealized individual liberties, the slow-moving process of education, and law and order. Was it any wonder that the acculturated religion of the middle class served to perpetuate the status quo? The injustices inherent in industrial capitalism needed to be challenged in the name of a higher morality, but there were no prophetic voices to be heard.

The lower classes obviously had the most to gain from social change, and should have been in the forefront of demand for social justice, but the religion of blacks and poor whites instead focused on revivalism, personal salvation, and the hope of a better life in the world to come. In general, fundamentalist churches reckoned advocates of social change to be troublemakers, modernists, or communists and dismissed them out of hand.[32] Their lack of analysis of the human problem served the self-interests of factory owners, mining operators, and textile magnets throughout the country.

In 1926 the American Federation of Labor held its annual meeting in Detroit. It announced its intention of organizing the automobile industry and attempted to enlist the help of the churches. Business leaders branded the organization "communist" and exerted pressure on the churches to cancel invitations to labor leaders scheduled to speak in their churches. Virtually all of the churches caved in to the pressure and lined by solidly against labor and unionization. Niebuhr sadly concluded that, "Churches in America are on the whole thoroughly committed to the interests and prejudices of the middle class. I think it is a bit of unwarranted optimism to expect them to make any serious contribution to the reorganization of society."[33]

The real threat to Christianity was not intellectual attacks from philosophers like Bertrand Russell but the moral complacency of Christians. Modern industrial civilization called for a tougher response from organized religion. A religion that could not respond to the industrial challenge was, at best, anachronistic; at worst, it was an "opiate of the people." Marx's analysis of religion seemed painfully real to Niebuhr. The moral impotence of the ministers in the city was even more disgraceful than the moral pretensions of Henry Ford. A genuine Christian apologetic would have to advocate a more heroic type of religion—one that would begin by challenging the naive optimism of liberalism in both its religious and secular forms.

Notes

[1]Richard Fox, *Reinhold Niebuhr: A Biography* (New York: Pantheon Books, 1985) 4, 5.

[2]Charles W. Kegley and Robert W. Bretall, eds., *Reinhold Niebuhr: His Religious, Social, and Political Thought* (New York: Macmillan Co., 1967) 3.

[3]It should be noted that Gustav Niebuhr's thinking was in the tradition of German Pietism, not American Fundamentalism.

[4]Fox, 7.   [5]Ibid., 146.

[6]Niebuhr was critical of Karl Barth and his brother H. R. Niebuhr for placing too much emphasis upon the transcendent role of theology. This kind of emphasis, he believed, made theology too "other-worldly."

[7]Kegley and Bretall, 3, 4.

[8]June Bingham, *Courage to Change: An Introduction to the Life and Thought of Reinhold Niebuhr* (New York: Charles Scribner's Sons, 1961) 84.

[9]Fox, 165.   [10]Ibid., 30.   [11]Ibid., 32.
[12]Ibid.   [13]Ibid.   [14]Kegley and Bretall, 36.
[15]Fox, 33.   [16]Ibid., 38.   [17]Bingham, 102.
[18]Kegley and Bretall, 312.

[19]Reinhold Niebuhr, *Leaves from the Notebook of a Tamed Cynic* (Hamden CT: The Shoe String Press, 1956) 27.

[20]Ibid., 39.

[21]Kegley and Bretall, 220.

[22]Reinhold Niebuhr, *An Interpretation of Christian Ethics* (London: SCM Press LTD, 1948) 115.

[23]Kegley and Bretall, 315.

[24]Fox, 48.   [25]Ibid., 64.   [26]Ibid.

[27]*Leaves,* 49.   [28]Bingham, 132.   [29]Fox, 88.

[30]*Leaves,* 154, 155.   [31]Ibid., 149.

[32]Roger A. Johnson *et al, Critical Issues in Modern Religion* (2d ed.; Englewood Cliffs NJ: Prentice Hall, 1990) 250, 251.

[33]*Leaves,* 112.

7.
The Shattering of Illusions and Pretensions

In 1928 Reinhold Niebuhr significantly altered the course of his life. He resigned his church in Detroit and joined the faculty of Union Theological Seminary in New York as associate professor of Christian ethics and philosophy of religion. The decision to leave Bethel was not easy. His ministry in Detroit was rewarding enough, and he enjoyed preaching more than ever. But there was something about the opportunity at Union that he could not resist.

The new challenge, however, was tempered by two deeply felt concerns. One was his fear that life in academia might turn him into a professional, an academic specialist. Niebuhr viewed his ministry as a calling and feared the prospect of living out of the demands and resources of an institution. His other concern was that he was not adequately trained for the task. He had bypassed the opportunity to do a Ph.D. at Yale, and his heavy schedule in Detroit had not allowed much time for disciplined reading. Niebuhr felt embarrassed about not being better academically prepared to teach in the country's most prestigious seminary. He later recalled in his "Intellectual Autobiography" that it was a full decade before he could stand before a class and answer their questions at the end of a lecture without feeling like a fraud who pretended to a larger and more comprehensive knowledge than he possessed.[1]

Niebuhr would not have been at Union at all had it not been for Sherwood Eddy, a close friend who believed in him enough to fund his salary. Eddy was a wealthy YMCA leader who had traveled with Niebuhr on speaking tours during and after the war. He was so impressed with Niebuhr's speaking and leadership abilities that he was determined to help bring him to national prominence. In 1923 Niebuhr spoke to a student conference in Detroit where Henry Sloane Coffin, later-to-be president of Union Seminary, was in the audience. They became acquainted at that conference, and upon Eddy's instigation Coffin later offered Niebuhr a faculty post in the field of Applied Christianity. When Niebuhr asked, "What shall I teach?" Coffin responded, "Just teach what you think."

President Coffin's confidence in his young and inexperienced faculty member was not misplaced. In a relatively short time Niebuhr became Union's best known and most loved professor, at least among the students. With the likes of Reinhold Niebuhr and Paul Tillich on its faculty, Union Theological Seminary was entering into its "Golden Age."

Wisdom in Quest of Responsibility

Union Seminary's Gothic revival towers and the academic presence of its prestigious Ivy League neighbor, Columbia University, symbolized a world that contrasted starkly with that of nearby Harlem and Manhatten. Within a few short blocks of each other the interests of academia, the marketplace, and the church were all physically represented. The scenario was perfectly fitting for Reinhold Niebuhr was fully committed to bringing the intellectual resources of academia and the moral resources of the church to bear upon the social and political needs of the wider society.

Academic theology separated from ethical responsibility would be a farce. There had to be an ultimate frame of meaning, an overarching wisdom, that makes sense of human nature and destiny. But there must be a corresponding willingness to act upon what one knows. Life could have no meaning, Niebuhr contended, without responsibility. He once commented that there are two kinds of people: the "pure" and the "responsible." Niebuhr preferred the responsible.

He had no use for the kind of gnostic dualism that dichotomized the natural and the spiritual, the secular and the sacred, the world and the church. There needed to be a thoroughgoing encounter between the sacred and the secular that required serious dialogue between the biblical faith and all the modern disciplines. Niebuhr never claimed to be a specialist in any academic discipline and was certainly not presumptuous enough to believe that he could competently integrate them all. Yet he knew that the "big questions" of life could not be addressed without taking the risk that goes with invading the territory of other specialties. This invading of other discipline's territory was what Arthur Koestler, himself a political expert and literary man invading the field of science, called "creative trespassing." In the interest of discovering a collective "wisdom" Niebuhr was willing to become a creative trespasser.

At the height of his career Reinhold Niebuhr was in constant demand on the university lecture circuit, lecturing in virtually all the departments of the modern university. He was widely regarded as one of the most competent and effective synthesists of the twentieth century, giving and receiving wisdom from every source of truth he could discover. Niebuhr's quest for wisdom, however, was more than a search for knowledge and meaning. It was his way of critically and constructively engaging all forms of thought and practice that he believed were either inimical to, or had the potential to enhance, the human condition. The theological agenda, as Niebuhr understood it, was rooted in resistance to all forms of injustice and oppression and the positive task of making all persons more fully human.

A Visible Sacrament

Reinhold Niebuhr remained at Bethel as long as he did because his congregation understood his need to "keep one foot outside the doors of the church." The same was true at Union. Without neglecting his duties at the seminary, he constantly committed himself to outside issues and activities that kept his life on a frenzied pace. But neither the busyness of schedule or the seriousness of his concerns affected his seemingly less-than-serious demeanor among colleagues and students, particularly during his early years at the seminary. Niebuhr's biographer describes the strain that his unorthodox style created for some of the senior members of the faculty:

> Niebuhr's charging style, brash, outspoken, vehement, did not sit well with most of the senior faculty, who favored the clipped, understated, Scotch reserve of seminary tradition. Ernest Scott, professor of biblical theology, and William Adams Brown, professor of systematic theology . . . judged it improper for students to address a professor as "Reinie." They also shook their heads when Niebuhr turned up for a tuxedo affair in honor of a visiting dignitary in his everyday rumpled suit and carelessly knotted tie. They swallowed hard when they saw him eating an artichoke and a dish of Hollandaise sauce: instead of dipping the leaves one by one in the sauce, he dumped the sauce all over the artichoke. An uncouth country bumpkin with decidedly dubious scholarly credentials, an indecorous pulpit style, a nasal midwestern twang, and a growing reputation for political radicalism.[2]

President Coffin's faith in his young professor kept the old guard in check until his idyiosyncracies could be appreciated—even by his sternist critics. The students, on the other hand, liked "Reinie" from the outset. June Bingham, one of Niebuhr's biographers, recalls that when strangers called on Niebuhr the receptionist would tell them, if it was near the lunch hour, to go down the hall to the social room. "But how will I know which one is Niebuhr?" they would often ask. "That's easy," the receptionist would reply, "Just look for a crowd of students. He'll be the man in the middle of it."[3] Students were drawn to his ideas, his personality, and his power to evoke new thinking. As he became better known, students from Columbia and from universities throughout the country would make special trips to Union to talk with Niebuhr about pressing problems and issues of the time. He thrived on the exchanges. In later years, during his retirement, he often commented how much he missed his interaction with his students.

The academic environment and the research facilities at Union encouraged Niebuhr to write. He routinely cranked out article after article for leading journals, magazines, and newspapers just as he had in Detroit. It has been estimated that Niebuhr wrote as many as fifteen hundred articles and editorials during his career. He wrote regularly for *The Messenger, The Lutheran, The Episcopal Churchnews, The New Leader, Christianity and Crisis, Commonweal, Commentary, and The Christian Century.* His magazine and journal articles also appeared in such diverse sources as *The Atlantic, The Nation, The New Republic, Christianity and Society* (formerly called *Radical Religion*), and *Commonsense.* He also wrote for *Life, Fortune, Harper's, The Reporter, The Virginia Quarterly Review, The Yale Review, The Saturday Review, Partisan Review, Foreign Affairs, World Politics, The American Scholar, The Bulletin of Atomic Scientists, The Harvard Business Review, Mademoiselle,* and *The Saturday Evening Post.* In Great Britain most of his published work appeared in the *New Statesman and Nation* and *Spectator.* He also contributed regularly to the book review sections in the *New York Times* and the *New York Herald Tribune.*

His wide range of topics and sources reflected Niebuhr's broad interests, his refusal to make clear-cut distinctions between the sacred and the secular, and his belief that religious faith could not be separated from social and political activity. With the possible exception of Paul Tillich, Niebuhr struck more deeply into the heart and mind of modern secularists than any other Christian writer of his time. Because he believed that "common grace" was at work in secularists as well as Christians, Niebuhr insisted that their conversation should be a dialogue and not a monologue. He never worked for knockdown demonstrations that Christianity is true or for "leaps of faith." As Niebuhr once told a troubled doubter, he saw no reason why faith could not be bought "on the installment plan."

Enormous amounts of time were spent on articles and upwards of twenty full-length books, but Niebuhr still managed to remain deeply involved in political and social causes as well as the life of the church. In 1930 he helped establish the Fellowship of Socialist Christians and entered the race for Congress on the socialist ticket. He knew that he could not be elected, but it gave him a forum for speaking out on the issues. His interest in practical politics made Niebuhr as much at ease in working in New York politics, or participating in a worker's picket line, as he was in giving a lecture or preaching a sermon. In the words of one Niebuhr observer, he was a "visible sacrament," a unique kind of seminary professor who acted as well as thought.[4] Through precept and example Niebuhr challenged the common perception of the Christian scholar as that of a passive cloistered monk. Richard Fox described his frenzied pace:

> Niebuhr was always first a preacher, though he was always more than that: political organizer and commentator, religious thinker, social critic, seminary teacher. Students in his office on the seventh floor of Brown Tower at Broadway and 120th Street sat before an attentive listener but a frentic one: he paced with long strides through clouds of cigarette smoke while pondering their projects and problems. He had to be up and about. Forty or more weekends a year, for more than a quarter-century, he bolted from one state to another, preaching at colleges, addressing student conferences, conferring at political meetings. His hastily packed suitcase sometimes sat poised beside the lectern at his Friday class. A delayed train, or later a weatherbound plane, drove him to distraction. He constantly checked his watch. There might not be enough time.[5]

The one distraction that Niebuhr did not discourage was a Miss Ursula Keppel-Compton, an Oxford theological graduate who had come to Union for an extra year of study. She was the daughter of an English physician, intelligent, concerned about social issues, and drawn to the spirited demeanor of Professor Niebuhr. The fact that she was an attractive shapely blond in no way diminished her other virtues. It appeared to be a matter of Niebuhr's "pursuing Miss Keppel-Compton until she caught him," but in reality it turned out to be a mutual romance.

Ursula's conquest was Reinhold's victory. In 1931 they were united in marriage. For the rest of their lives they shared each others love and devoted support. Ursula was a competent woman in her own right. She assisted Reinhold in his writing and later chaired the department of Religion at nearby Barnard College. They enjoyed a long and happy life together and bore two children, Christopher and Elizabeth, who brought much joy into their home.

The Marxist Challenge

It was in Detroit that Niebuhr first felt the plight of the laborer in the sweatshops of the automobile industry and recalled Markham's poem, "The Man with the Hoe," which epitomized his seemingly hopeless condition:

Who made him dead to rapture and despair
A thing that grieves and that never hopes,
Stolid and stunned, a brother to the ox?[6]

It was there that he also came to a realistic appraisal of the role the religious community could be expected to play in social issues. He learned first-hand that most churches and churchmen were committed to the interests of the middle class. He did not doubt that the majority of religious liberals cared deeply for the oppressed and disadvantaged, but their ethic of love and optimism was ill-equipped to face the economic and political realities that perpetuated the plight of the poor. By 1928, when he went to Union, Niebuhr was turning away from all sentimental answers. He was actively looking for something more heroic, something with more teeth in it. Marxism was attractive but not in its extreme form. In 1930 Niebuhr helped establish The Fellowship of Socialist Christians, an organization whose stated purpose was "to explore and express a form of social Christianity independent of both pacifism and marxism."[7]

It should be noted that Niebuhr's interest in Marxism pre-dated the rise of the brutal Stalinist era in Russia and the onset of the cold war rhetoric that anathematized the word "communist" in most Western minds. Many were flirting with Marxism during the thirties. It was the era of the Great Depression, mass unemployment, bread lines, and general economic despair. It was also that period in American history that most closely resembled the social conditions of the mid-nineteenth century when Marx first issued his biting critique of industrial capitalism and the forms of religion that supported its exploitive practices. Many were struck by the accuracy of Marx's analysis and the hope that it offered the worker.

Karl Marx's critique of industrial capitalism focused on two competing classes: the middle-class capitalists, the industrialists, manufacturers, and merchants who were engaged in profit; and the workers, laboring men who were working for a wage, men whose labor made the profits for the capitalists. He deplored the manner in which the capitalists, the owners of the means of production, exploited the worker and his labor. He judged the whole process to be unjust in theory and completely dehumanizing in practice.

Friedrich Engels, Marx's close friend and collaborator, described the human cost of the industrial squalor in *The Condition of the Working Class in England* (1845). Without job security, and for subsistence wages, men and women worked twelve to thirteen hours a day, six days a week. Children began working six and one-half hours per day at age nine, and that increased to twelve hours at age thirteen. Most had no education and could not read or write. They lived in filthy, densely crowded slums. Dilapidated tenant houses were lined with unpaved roads, strewn with stinking rubbish. Industrial smoke hung over the towns like a cloud, and the rivers were black with refuse. Workers had little to eat, often eating spoiled food in order to escape starvation. Most dressed in rags. Women and children often had no shoes. Infant mortality rates were staggering and fatal or debilitating accidents were high in the factories. Medical care was virtually unknown. Many survived only through begging and petty theft.

Engel's conclusion was that the factory worker had been turned into "a soulless factor of production and . . . deprived of his humanity." In their famous *Communist Manifesto* (1848), Marx and Engels urged the workers to "rise up and throw off their chains." The only viable answer, they concluded, was for workers to unite in revolution against the economic and political system that oppressed them.

Marx was an economic determinist. He believed that all forms of consciousness are determined by socioeconomic conditions. Ideas (e.g., religion, politics) do not determine the society; rather, the society (i.e., socioeconomic conditions) determine ideas and values. In practical terms this meant that the bourgeois capitalist who controls the means of production also controls the consciousness of the proletariet, thereby perpetuating his own economic self-interest. Capitalist ideology not only legitimates and rationalizes its own self-interests, it also inculcates servile attitudes in the lower classes. The oppressed are made to feel that they are to blame for their sufferings and have no right to revolt against their conditions. They can only resign themselves to their fate and await a better life in another world.

Religion, Marx argued, is the greatest ally of the capitalist. It is his self-serving instrument because it holds together the social and economic edifice that he controls. By providing an ultimate sanction for the existing social order, religion legitimates the values and goals of the dominate class. Marx did not ascribe any form of transcendent reality to religion but saw it only as a man-made projection or form of wishful thinking. Out of intolerable oppression, Marx believed, desperate men create their fantasy world. It is generally one that offers heavenly bliss in a world to come and a rationale for their earthly sufferings, which they most often attribute to their own sins. In short, religion functions as a drug to relieve the unbearable suffering and pain of an exploited class. The real problem with religion, Marx taught, is that it fosters self-deception or false consciousness. It gives one a reason to accept what he ought to be struggling to overthrow.

This false ideological consciousness that determines and perpetuates the plight of the working class does not operate on the conscious level. It is an unconscious determination that can only be altered as the social and economic forces that impose it are eradicated. Marx's own critique of religion was meant to serve as a diagnosis so that the patient (i.e., the worker) could gain some insight into the unconscious factors that were determining his life. As workers unite and change their social and economic conditions the need for religion will "wither away." The world must not simply be interpreted; it must be changed.

Religion was such a negative force in Marx's thinking because he saw it as a major impediment to man's own humanity. "To find true fulfillment," Marx said, "humanity must take back and reintegrate its own powers that have been alienated in religion. Atheism is the prerequisite for salvation."[8] Marx's aim was not to attack religious people or institutions but to criticize religion so that there could be an insight into the social reality that makes religion necessary. What must be changed is the oppressive capitalist system. The need for religion would then be abolished and man could be restored to his humanity.

Once the critique of religion is complete there must be a focus on "law" and "politics," which are also socially conditioned ideologies. In *On Religion* Marx and Engels explained the necessary process:

> The abolition of religion as the *illusory* happiness of the people is required for their real happiness. The demand to give up the illusions about its conditions is the *demand to give up a condition which needs illusions.* The criticism of religion is therefore in *embryo the criticism of the vale of woe,* the *halo* of which is religion.
>
> *The task of history,* therefore, once the world *beyond the truth* has disappeared, is to establish *the truth of this world.* The immediate *task of philosophy,* which is at the service of history, once the *saintly form* of human self-alienation has been unmasked, is to unmask self-alienation in its *unholy forms.* Thus the criticism of heaven turns into the criticism of the earth, the *criticism of religion* into the *criticism of right*[i.e. law] and the *criticism of theology* into the *criticism of politics.*[9]

What Marx envisioned from this theoretical economic and political foundation was a communistic society. It would be a classless society where "the freedom of each is the condition for the free development of all."[10] Private ownership of the means of production would be abolished as would the profit motive. All would be rationally planned. Goods and services would be equally distributed, and the social and economic apparatus that had been necessary to dominate and oppress the working class would disappear because the conditions that had supposedly made them necessary would no longer exist.

Reinhold Niebuhr was much too independent of spirit and thought for any wholesale acceptance of Marx's views, but he did believe that Marx was profoundly insightful. Traditional Protestant religion, he believed, was particularly vulnerable to Marx's critique. As early as 1928 Niebuhr was bold enough to encourage clergymen to subscribe to journals that were critical of conventional religion. In *The Contribution of Religion to Social Work* (1932) he went so far as to encourage his readers to learn from the most "vital religion" of the day, which he identified as Marxism. Throughout the 1930s he appropriated Marx's analysis of ideology and ethics to his own critical analysis of religion.

Niebuhr believed that Marx's economic theory of history was basically sound, and he accepted his contention that ideologies are formed by socioeconomic factors. At one time he even favored the abolishing of the private ownership of the means of production. As for religion, he joined Marx in denouncing any form of religion that was willing to suspend the struggle for social justice out of deference for "rewards" in the world to come. Acculturated religion that perpetuated the socioeconomic interests of unjust power-mongering industrialists and political leaders was particularly despicable.

Toward Biblical Realism

In 1932 Niebuhr published *Moral Man and Immoral Society*. It was immediately received as a seminal work, rivaling Karl Barth's *Epistle to the Romans* (1919) as the most significant theological work published during the first third of the century. It clearly signaled Niebuhr's disenchantment with the liberal ethic and with pacifism.

The thesis of the book was that "a sharp distinction must be drawn between the moral and social behavior of individuals and that of groups (national, racial, or economic)." Niebuhr went on to deduce that "this distinction justifies and necessitates political policies which a purely individualistic ethic must always find embarrassing."[11] Through a wealth of historical detail he made a convincing case for his view that groups become more selfish and unjust as they increase in size and power. Social groups know the reality of power and never voluntarily give up their own. Consequently, Niebuhr deduced that the use of power in the interests of justice would always be necessary. An ethic that depended entirely upon an ethic of love, divorced from the realities of power, was pure sentimentality.

In *Reflections on the End of an Era* (1934) Niebuhr continued to argue for a realistic political theory. It was written during the throes of the Great Depression when many expected the collapse of capitalism and were looking for a solid basis on which a new social system could be built. Niebuhr's *Reflections* reiterated his conviction that, whatever the form of the system, power must be set against power in the interests of social justice.

Marxism was tempting, but it had serious deficiencies. It was by no means a panacea for society's ills. Economic forces obviously played a powerful role in shaping values and ideologies, but why were human beings capable of rising above class values? We know from human experience, Niebuhr maintained, that it is within human power to transcend the constraints of social and economic conditions. Marx's economic determinism simply did not give sufficient place to human freedom and responsibility.

If Niebuhr was more optimistic than Marx about humanity's capacity to transcend its social and economic conditioning, he was more pessimistic than Marx about its capacity for evil. Marx's assumption that humanity is essentially good and therefore capable of bringing forth a secular kingdom of classless altruistic persons, Niebuhr believed, was mere utopian thinking. Stalin's reign of terror during the 1930s made it increasingly apparent to Niebuhr that if human freedom allowed persons to rise to heights of goodness and justice it was also capable of descending to tragic levels of sin and selfishness. It was becoming increasingly clearer to Niebuhr that the human problem lay not in socioeconomic factors as much as it did the human condition. He was becoming, in the words of Robert McAfee Brown, "a pessimistic optimist —one who was aware that we are faced with indeterminate possibilities for good but also that we exhibit an infinite capacity to abuse these possibilities."[12]

Moral Man and Immoral Society marked Niebuhr's break with the moral idealism of Protestant Liberalism. The liberal hope that society could be transformed by the good moral intentions of individuals was totally unrealistic. Individuals may, on occasion, be responsive to a love ethic. But social groups, institutions, and nations only give up their power as they are confronted with greater power. The use of power, Niebuhr believed, is a necessary ingredient in the cause of social justice. What was needed were some realistic answers—answers that could account for humanity's capacity for both good and evil and, even more importantly, the answer as to how its capacity for good could be empowered for responsible social and political action. Those answers, Niebuhr believed, could be found through a more realistic assessment of human nature and destiny and the faith encounter with the God of Scripture.

Niebuhr was not advocating the retrieval of timeless moral principles and absolute truths as much as he was the fulfillment of moral commitments through existential encounter with God. The individual's moral choices must be exercised through the particularity of existential encounter, just as the determination of what is "right" and "just" must be made within the context of particular, historical situations. It is through encounter that the Christian appropriates the meaning of love, justice, and power to social, economic, and political issues. What verifies Christianity, Niebuhr believed, is not its rational coherence as much as its power to motivate action. In the second volume of *The Nature and Destiny of Man* Niebuhr explained the moral significance of an existential faith: "By its confidence in an eternal ground of existence which is involved in man's historical striving to the very point of suffering with and for him, this faith can prompt men to accept their historical responsibilities gladly."[13]

The Christian apologetic, Niebuhr believed, had a two-fold purpose. The first was to expose all religious and secular pretensions to moral aims that claimed to be untainted by sin and self-interest. Once that was done, the more realistic perspective of the Bible on the nature and destiny of man could be shown and the relevance of Christianity to social issues could be established. The strength of the Christian apologetic is not that it is rationally compelling but that it shows everything else to be inadequate.[14]

Religious Illusions and Pretensions

It has been said of Reinhold Niebuhr that he was "forever at war with oversimplification."[15] He believed that the truth about humanity "can never be plotted on a nice, neat, straight line." His thought seemed particularly relevant to the twentieth century because he was saying in theology what poets like W. H. Auden and Robert Frost were saying about poetry—that "the crooked way of life" must be distinguished from "inorganic, logical straightness," and that there is always a need for "the form that falsifies no ambiguities."[16]

Niebuhr's appreciation for the complexity of life was also in keeping with the discoveries of leading scientists like Niels Bohr. After a lifetime of search for consistency between two apparently conflicting concepts, Bohr concluded that both the wave and the particle theory of light were essentially true—thus, his Principle of Complementarity.[17] In a similar way, Niebuhr's struggle to understand rightly the nature and destiny of humanity led him on a pilgrimage back to the Bible and its paradoxical claim that man is both body and spirit, free and bound, majestic and tragic. After a lifetime of reflection on the matter, he concluded that the assessment of humanity that comes to us from the dramatic-historical account of the Bible was more realistic than any theory of coherence advocated by scientists or philosophers:

> Though I have meditated on these issues for some time, I have only recently come to realize fully why the dramatic-historical account of the Bible (about which an earlier generation of modern theologians have been unduly apologetic) should give a truer view of both the nobility and the misery of man than all the wisdom of scientists and philosophers. The fact is that the human self can only be understood in a dramatic-historical environment. Any effort to co-ordinate man to some coherence, whether of nature or of reason will falsify the facts; because the self's freedom, including both its creative and destructive capacities, precludes such co-ordination. [18]

The language of paradox did not mean contradiction; it only meant that the two sides of truth do not cancel each other out but enrich our understanding of the reality being described. Both liberal and conservative theologians, Niebuhr believed, were guilty of oversimplification. Liberals failed to understand humanity in the full dimension of its capacity for self-transcendence. They did not see that because persons are spiritual creatures, children of God, made in God's image, that they cannot be explained or contained by the harmony of nature or the prudence of reason.

The liberal had too optimistic a view of humanity. Niebuhr spoke of the "easy conscience" with which liberals outrightly denied the "fall" and the fact of human sinfulness—the most "empirically verifiable," he insisted, of all Christian doctrines. The liberal's faith in humanity's essential goodness led to the belief that humanity could exercise dominion over the forces of nature and achieve life's final good. Whatever was wrong with humanity, the liberal attributed the cause to some defect in human social organization or some imperfection in education that further social history and cultural development would correct. Liberals did not see that the real problem was the radical sin and evil in human nature. Because liberals had wrongly diagnosed the problem, they had no realistic cure for the evil and the injustices that they deplored in the realm of economics and politics. Liberals were quagmired in their moral idealism and sentimentality and hopelessly naive about the necessary relation of love, justice, and power in social ethics.

If Niebuhr had less to say about the more conservative "orthodox" position, it was because he had even less hope for that tradition. Orthodoxy, to its credit, took the Bible seriously and accepted its account of the "fall" and the tragic human condition. It rightly understood that the root of society's ills lay in the self, but the orthodox tradition had so set itself against secularism and the world that it had dropped out of the quest for social justice. Orthodoxy had tried to remain faithful to doctrine but had become tragically irrelevant to social need and concern. Its impulse was to pursue a more pietistic, individualistic ethic.

The major fault of the religions on the right, particularly fundamentalists, was obscurantism. Their negative attitudes toward science and philosophy made moderns reject them outright as obsolete relics of the past. Niebuhr wrote that the "Christian faith is still suffering from the obscurantist effort to guard its truths in an age of Darwinian science by defying the undisputed evidences that honorable and honest scientists have addressed. One still feels," he noted, "the force of Huxley's scorn against the dishonesties of the religious polemicists."[19] What Niebuhr disliked most about supernaturalists, however, was not their worldview but their insistence upon turning the salvation history of Scripture into a series of miraculous events, which they insisted must be believed, rather than appropriating the existential meaning of these events into responsible historical action. Conservatism had regretfully become a synonym for social irresponsibility. Institutionalized religion, particularly of the conservative variety, could hardly be expected to be a force for social change.[20]

The Billy Graham crusades in New York (1957) brought out Niebuhr's contempt for revivalism. He was particularly critical of Graham's passivity toward social issues. He urged Graham to take a tougher stand on civil rights and to "make his Christ a critic as well as a celebrator of culture."[21] Niebuhr was also critical of Graham's "Madison Avenue" methods in organizing the revival campaigns. He scorned his "frantic pursuit of religious success" as a pious form of secularism.[22]

The use of secular success tactics for religious purposes during the 1950s and 1960s led to the phenomenon described by sociologists of religion as the "cultural captivity of religion."[23] It was a phenomenon, Niebuhr recognized, that could work both ways. If Graham knew how to use secular tactics for religious ends, the Eisenhower administration knew how to use religion for political purposes. Niebuhr's new book, *Pious and*

Secular America (1957), revealed his deep concern about the new religious and political climate. It took up themes that had been expressed earlier in *The Irony of American History* (1952). Both works exposed the religious pretension that masked America's pride in its own virtue, wisdom, and power. He saw little evidence to support America's boast that it provided the "moral leadership in the free world." The liberal pragmatism of the Roosevelt Administration had raised Niebuhr's hopes for the future of the country, but he warned against any tendency to equate political and social success with virtue. The history of humanity, Niebuhr warned, had been anything but a "success story." The moral hypocrisy of the Eisenhower Administration, he believed, lay in its lack of courage to assume the moral role that it so proudly boasted. He was later critical of President Nixon and, to a lesser extent, President Kennedy for the same lack of moral courage.

Richard Nixon's policy of inviting clergymen to the White House for religious services was particularly irritating. Nothing would take the stinger out of a prophet more quickly, Niebuhr observed, than having dinner and giving a sermon at the White House. The Christian's role in politics must be "realistic" *and* "prophetic." In response to Hans Morganthau, a political scientist, who suggested that one could not be "a successful politician and a good Christian," Niebuhr replied: "I do not think we will sacrifice any value in the 'realist' approach to the political order . . . if we define it in terms which do not rob it of moral content." There ought to be a place in the kingdom of God for politicians like Abraham Lincoln, he noted, "who engage in the statesmanlike compromises that a sinful world demand, but who relentlessly subjects his actions to the test of the standard of justice." The Christian leader must "make use of the world's methods but not resign himself to the world's ways."[24] Above all, he must never cultivate the kind of moral pretension that leads to an easy conscience. The Christian politician sees the "moral ambiguity" in all of human action that befits the human condition and, for this reason, is always engaged in genuine self-criticism.

Niebuhr did not limit his critique of the illusions and moral pretensions within the "household of faith" to the modernists and conservatives. He was also critical of the two leading theologians of the day—Karl Barth and Paul Tillich. Both of these theologians, he believed, had abstracted their theology from the concrete realities and demands of the dramatic-historical message of the Bible. "If Karl Barth is the

Tertullian of our day," he wrote, "Tillich is the Origen of our period."[25] He regarded Barth as an obscurantist, a theological counterpart to the politics of Eisenhower whose "naive moralism threatened to lull American churchpeople into a disregard of historical struggles for proximate justice."[26] He was very uncomfortable with the "otherworldly" emphases in Barth's theology that removed it too far from "this worldly" responsibility.

Niebuhr also believed that Barth obscured the legitimate role of reason in the spiritual life. From Barth's point of view there was no real content in worldly wisdom, no commerce between the foolishness of the gospel and the wisdom of the world. The denial of any common ground between the two, Niebuhr believed, was disastrous.

> One could not, for instance, . . . engage in a debate with psychologists on the question of what level of human selfhood is adequately illumined by psychiatric techniques and what level of the self as subject and free spirit evades these analyses. Nor could one debate with social scientists on the possibilities and the limits of a rational justice in human society.

The Christian faith, Niebuhr argued, is always seeking "to be related to the wisdom of the world and to the cultural disciplines that seek to find the congruities and coherences, the structures and forms of nature, life, and history."[27] The truths of faith are always contrary to that which is false but not to principles known by reason. Barthian religion, Niebuhr remarked, was one "fashioned for the catacombs." It had little relation to the task of transforming the natural stuff of politics by the grace and wisdom of the gospel."[28]

Paul Tillich was the most popular theologian in America during the 1950s and 1960s. He was a professional philosopher and systematic theologian whom many regarded as a "theologian's theologian." Even Niebuhr was impressed by Tillich's erudition and imagination, but his theology, in general, deeply troubled him. He was particularly disturbed by Tillich's obsession with ontological categories of thought and his emphasis upon the sensual fulfillment of the self. The problem with defining the self in terms of its participation in the structure of being, as Tillich had in *The Courage To Be* (1952), was that the ontological categories too rigidly restricted human freedom. Niebuhr was much more comfortable with the biblical view of the self, interpreted in dramatic-historical categories, which presented the self as a creature that is in constant free dialogue with itself, its neighbors, and God. His public reply to Tillich appeared in *The Self and the Dramas of History* (1955).

Because Tillich's theology made ontology (i.e., the structures of "Being") prior to ethics, it had two disastrous effects. On the one hand, it moved the theological emphasis away from social and political responsibilities. If Barth was politically naive, Tillich tended to be fruitlessly abstract. The other problem with Tillich's existential understanding of the self was that it made the human self its own end. " 'Responsibility' for Tillich," Niebuhr noted, "was coming to mean responsibility to one's own self: adjust, develop, reach for fulfillment."[29] His popularity, at least in part, lay in the fact that he had become "the theologian for an era of abundance, ease, and self-satisfaction."[30]

Tillich's emphasis upon aesthetics and sensual fulfillment mirrored a sensate culture that delighted itself in two Kinsey reports that glorified sexual performance that could be measured in terms of "frequency of orgasm." The emphasis upon the self, undergirded and sanctioned by a theology, was indicative of a culture that was abysmally ignorant of the heights and depths of the human spirit. Its misfortune had been compounded by the fact that it had all been dignified by the prestige of "science." As Niebuhr carefully pointed out in *The Self and the Dramas of History,* a self that is devoted to its own self-realization inevitably fails. There can be no true fulfillment of the self apart from responsibility to others and to God. The self must be defined in terms of its three interactions. The sexual act itself affirms this biblical truth.

If Barth, the modern Tertullian, had too little interest in this world, Tillich, the contemporary Origen, had too much. What was needed was a modern-day Augustine who would steer the middle course. Niebuhr wanted to be that person. He desired to speak the word of God to the secular mind in a manner that would neither sacrifice the truth of the Christian message nor deny the true wisdom of human discovery. It was in this spirit that Reinhold Niebuhr turned his scrutiny in the direction of secular culture and took a critical look at modern man's view of human nature and destiny.

Secular Illusions and Pretensions

Reinhold Niebuhr began his Gifford Lectures by noting that "man has always been his own most vexing problem." His thoughts about himself and his place in the cosmos have always been filled with confusions and contradictions:

> If man insists that he is a child of nature and that he ought not to pretend to be more than the animal, which he obviously is, he tacitly admits that he is, at any rate, a curious kind of animal who has both the inclination and the capacity to make such pretensions. If on the other hand he insists upon his unique and distinctive place in nature and points to his rational faculties as proof of his special eminence, there is usually an anxious note in his avowals of uniqueness which betrays his unconscious sense of kinship with the brutes.[31]

The classical view of humanity, comprised primarily of Platonic, Aristotelian, and Stoic conceptions of human nature falls in the latter category. In this view humans were understood in terms of the uniqueness of their rational faculties. A dualism was set up between the mind or spirit, which was assumed to be essentially good, and the body, which was assumed to be inclined toward evil. Humanity's relation to the divine was thought to be through reason, which was at odds with the body and the mortality that the physical body entailed.

The modern view of humanity, on the other hand, emphasized humanity's relation to nature and its bodily, physical essence. The real difficulty was in how to explain the relation between nature, reason, and vitality. Was it the uniqueness of reason, this inseparability from natural processes, or nature's vitality that provided the real clue to humanity's essence? Idealism, naturalism, and romanticism, the three most prominent non-Christian anthropologies to emerge in the modern Western world, each understood humanity's uniqueness in terms of one of these dimensions. All of them understood the person as "creature," as a product of nature, but none of them acknowledged the Christian claim that persons are created in the "image of God" and thus enjoy a unique relation to the Creator.

Most forms of idealism in the modern world were derived from Kant or Hegel, both of whom emphasized humanity's capacity to transcend nature and exercize its freedom. Both understood humanity's involvement in nature but also acknowledged the capacity of the rational creature to transcend these natural processes. To their credit, they saw the problem of human freedom more clearly than the pure naturalists, but, Niebuhr noted, "they were never able to define sin in terms of a violation of the good within freedom itself. They cannot define sin as spiritual," he added, "because they regard spirit as essentially good. They fail to see the paradox of evil arising out of freedom not as an essential or necessary consequence but as an alogical fact."[32] The partial insight of the idealist is inadequate because it offers too simple a solution to humanity's dialectical nature and obscures the unpopular fact of its sinful nature.

Naturalism understands persons almost entirely in terms of their relation to nature. It is the physical person and the natural processes that explain the self. Naturalism understands even better than idealism that a person is creature, but it understands less that the person carries the image of God. Francis Bacon and Montaigne helped give rise to the naturalistic understanding of humanity, but the view came to fuller expression in the one-dimensional perspective of humanity in modern science and the various schools of psychology. "Every rigorous effort to remain within the confines of pure science," Niebuhr noted, "reduces psychology to physiology, and physiology to bio-mechanics." He concluded that

> only those schools which leave the confines of natural science and regard psychology as a cultural science, which means that their psychological investigations are guided and prompted by philosophical and therefore semi-religious presuppositions, . . . [can adequately account for] the real profundities of self-consciousness and the complex problems of personality.[33]

Naturalism cannot provide an adequate perspective on selfhood because it cannot take account of realities that transcend the realm of science. "An object which has both surface and depth," Niebuhr noted, "cannot be correctly interpreted in terms of one dimension when it has in fact two. This is why science which is only science cannot be scientifically accurate."[34]

The romantics recognized that a person could not be reduced to a physical machine nor the human spirit be made to conform to the patterns of rationality described by the idealists. There are vitalities in humanity, they insisted, that give rise to individuality and self-expression that defy naturalistic or idealistic explanation. These vitalities, described in terms like "feeling," "imagination," and "will," however, were thought of as having natural origins and were not ascribed to any transcendent source.

The romantics understood the goodness of creation in all of its particularity but had no perspective beyond creation from which to save the self from self-deification. This was what was potentially demonic in all forms of romantic self-glorification and its collective expression through race and nation. Nietzche's "superman" exemplified the former tendency; Nazi nationalism and racism expressed the latter. The fundamental error in romanticism, Niebuhr argued, was its attempt to provide a basis for individuality without the presuppositions of the Christian faith:

> Without the presuppositions of the Christian faith the individual is either nothing or becomes everything. In the Christian faith man's insignificance as a creature, involved in the process of nature and time, is lifted into significance by the mercy and power of God in which his life is sustained. But his significance as a free spirit is understood as subordinate to the freedom of God. His inclination to abuse his freedom, to overestimate his power and significance and to become everything is understood as the primal sin.[35]

All anthropologies that view humanity from only one dimension ultimately fail. They neither understand human nature or the answer to the human predicament. The idealist finds the root of evil in humanity's involvement in nature and seeks to increase its rational faculties. Naturalism and romanticism, on the other hand, seek to overcome evil through a return to nature and its harmonies. What they all lack is the wisdom to see that a person has a freedom of spirit that transcends both nature and reason. Consequently, they fail to see the real reason why humanity defies the laws of reason and nature. In short, they all fail because they do not see, or refuse to accept, the Christian dogma of original sin. Hence, they hope for some sort of redemption through social reorganization or scheme of education.

Non-Christian anthropologies err on another side, Niebuhr noted, when they seek to attribute the source of evil to factors outside the self. Holbach and Helvetius, for instance, insisted that evil could be located in religion. Hobbes, Locke, and Adam Smith traced evil to autocratic forms of government. Karl Marx believed that evil resided in the capitalist form of economic organization. The fact of the matter, however, is that the "easy conscience" of modern persons stems from their failure to understand the tragic consequences of their capacity for sinful choices.

They start from presuppositions that do not allow humanity to be measured in a dimension that is capable of adequately explaining one's capacity for both good and evil.

Modern humanity's difficulty, Niebuhr noted, is not that it finds the Christian drama of Creation, Fall, and Atonement "incredible" but that it finds it "irrelevant." People simply do not understand the wisdom and relevance of the Christian faith. An effective Christian apologetic, Niebuhr believed, must be one that provides deeper sources of insight into the meaning of life, and greater resources of power for the fulfillment of life, than any alternative view. Modern persons are not looking for a demonstration of logic as much as they are a demonstration of relevance. The test of validation, Niebuhr argued, is twofold:

> It consists of a negative and a positive approach to the relation of the truth of the Gospel to other forms of truth, and of the goodness of perfect love to historic forms of virtue. Negatively the gospel must and can be validated by exploring the limits of historic forms of wisdom and virtue. Positively it is validated when the truth of faith is correlated with all truths which may be known by scientific and philosophical disciplines and proves itself a resource for coordinating them into a deeper and wider system of coherence.[36]

Biblical realism, Niebuhr believed, meets the test.

Notes

[1]Charles W. Kegley and Robert W. Bretall, eds., *Reinhold Niebuhr: His Religious, Social, and Political Thought* (New York: Macmillan Co., 1967) 8, 9.

[2]June Bingham, *Courage to Change: An Introduction to the Life and Thought of Reinhold Niebuhr* (New York: Charles Scribner's Sons, 1961) 112.

[3]Ibid., 23.

[4]Bob E. Patterson, *Reinhold Niebuhr.* Makers of the Modern Theological Mind (Waco TX: Word Books, 1977) 147.

[5]Richard Fox, *Reinhold Niebuhr: A Biography* (New York: Pantheon Books, 1985) vii.

[6]Roger A. Johnson, *Critical Issues in Modern Religion*, 2d ed. (Englewood Cliffs NJ: Prentice Hall, 1990) 246.

[7]Bingham, 157.   [8]Johnson, 222.

[9]Ibid., 233, 234.   [10]Ibid., 215.

[11]Reinhold Niebuhr, *Moral Man and Immoral Society* (New York: Charles Scribner's Sons, 1932) xi.

[12]Robert McAfee Brown, ed., *The Essential Reinhold Niebuhr* (New Haven CT: Yale University Press, 1986) jacket.

[13]Reinhold Niebuhr, *The Nature and Destiny of Man*, 2 vols. (New York: Charles Scribner's Sons, 1943) 2:321.

[14]Kegley and Bretall, 17.

[15]Bingham, 33.   [16]Ibid., 32.   [17]Ibid.

[18]Kegley and Bretall, 11.

[19]Ibid., 21.

[20]The writings of H. R. Niebuhr brilliantly illustrate this point, particularly in *Christ and Culture*. Reinhold had hoped that Black churches would take more of a lead in the struggle for social justice but found, for the most part, a lack of rational analysis of the social situation and too strong an "other-worldly" emphasis to effectively facilitate social change. He did, however, welcome the Civil Rights movement led by Martin Luther King, Jr., during the later years of his life.

[21]Fox, 266.

[22]There seems to be some inconsistency between Niebuhr's early appreciation for Billy Sunday and his more negative attitude toward Billy Graham some years later. Niebuhr was not above the injection of personality into his own preaching and appreciated the fruits of "success."

[23]Gibson Winter, Will Herberg, and others interested in the sociology of religion were calling attention to this religious phenomenon during the 1950s and 1960s.

[24]Fox, 277.   [25]Ibid., 257.   [26]Ibid., 265.

[27]Brown, 230.   [28]Ibid.   [29]Fox, 258.

[30]Ibid.

[31]Reinhold Niebuhr, *The Nature and Destiny of Man,* 2 vols. (New York: Charles Scribner's Sons, 1941) 1:1.

[32]Ibid., 120.   [33]Ibid., 74.   [34]Ibid., 73.

[35]Ibid., 92.

[36]Reinhold Niebuhr, *Faith and History: A Comparison of Christian and Modern Views of History* (New York: Charles Scribner's Sons, 1949) 152.

8.
In Defense of Biblical Realism

Reinhold Niebuhr described his life-long interests as having been essentially practical and apologetic in nature. He said,

> I have taught Christian Social Ethics for a quarter of a century and have also dealt in the ancillary field of apologetics. My avocational interest as a kind of circuit rider in the colleges and universities has prompted an interest in the defense and justification of the Christian faith in a secular age, particularly among what Schleiermacher called Christianity's "intellectual despisers."[1]

Few would deny that Reinhold Niebuhr was a Christian apologist of the first rank, but he was not an apologist in the normal meaning of the word. He did not seek to defend the Christian faith by making sympathetic contact with the thought of his age or by drawing the *best* elements of modern thought into some kind of Christian synthesis. The "prophet" in Niebuhr, Alan Richardson noted, made him "far too critical of the presuppositions of our age to be a conventional apologist."[2]

If Reinhold Niebuhr had wanted to be a conventional apologist, he would have probably tried to convince modern readers that Christianity is intellectually respectable by appealing to the values and assumptions of liberalism. On the contrary, he deliberately cut the ground from under the very foundations on which the liberal apologetic had been constructed. The First World War, the Detroit experience, and his encounter with Marxism somehow aroused a prophetic spirit in Niebuhr that prompted a desire to sweep away all modern illusions and pretensions. It was not an easy thing for liberal Christians and secularists to be told that their ideals and aspirations were illusions that needed to be shattered:

> So far from serving an apologetic purpose, Niebuhr's earlier writings cut the ground from underneath all the Christian apologetical writers then in vogue. To many Christian readers Niebuhr's writings seemed to deny the very foundations upon which a Christian philosophy or apologetic could be built. Their dearest assumptions concerning man's perfectability, his kinship with the divine, his natural goodness, were all demolished with ruthless iconoclasm. *Moral Man and Immoral Society*

(1932) seemed to many Christian leaders, especially to those of the older generation, to be the outpouring of a cynical and perverse spirit, very far removed from the benevolent and sanguine serenity which was held to be the hallmark of a truly Christian mind.[3]

Niebuhr's early writings were all characterized by a critical attitude toward the liberal worldview, whether expressed in secular or in Christian terms. The two were strikingly similar in their commitment to the prevailing optimism of the time. Niebuhr's first task was to debunk the liberal interpretation of Christianity in favor of the more realistic biblical view. He then hoped to convince the secularist that the more realistic version of Christianity had more relevance for his life.

John C. Bennett, a close friend and colleague of Niebuhr at Union Theological Seminary, described Niebuhr as an "apologetic evangelist." Niebuhr, Bennett observed, "won people to the Christian faith and preserved them in it by showing them how it illumined the very issues that troubled them most and how it could be the commitment that might give form to their lives."[4] He had the rare gift of convincing moderns that "God is a necessary companion in the human pilgrimage, and that life makes better sense with Him than without Him."[5] Under Niebuhr's influence many secularists came to believe that what they had so easily dismissed as obsolete sentimentalism and bourgeois ideology could actually have an existential relevance for their personal lives and the hard problems of history in which their lives were set.

A Realistic Appraisal of Human Nature

In the first volume of *The Nature and Destiny of Man* Niebuhr returned to the dialectical method that he had employed in his B.D. thesis at Yale three decades before. This method was better adapted to the complexity of human reality, he believed, than methods employed by empiricists and rationalists that depended too heavily upon logical consistency and coherence. The truth about humanity and its history had to take account of mysteries and complexities that oftentimes seem contradictory to the logical mind. "The justification for this distinction," Niebuhr noted, "lies in the unique character of human freedom. Almost all the misinterpretations of human selfhood and the drama of history in the modern day are derived from the effort to reduce human existence to the coherence of nature."[6]

In the early chapters of *The Nature and Destiny of Man* Niebuhr surveyed the history of Western culture from the ancient Greeks to the modern period in an effort to glean any insights from human wisdom and experience that could illumine the human condition. The classical idealists and the modern naturalists both had insights that could not be ignored in any realistic appraisal of human nature. Modern naturalisms rightly understand that "man is a child of nature, subject to its vicissitudes, compelled by its necessities, driven by its impulses, and confined within the brevity of the years which nature permits its varied organic forms."[7] Idealism, on the other hand, understands better the less obvious fact that "man is a spirit who stands outside of nature, life, himself, his reason and the world."[8] But neither comprehends humanity in a dimension sufficiently high or deep to do full justice to the capacity for both good and evil. This is why the "dramatic" and "historical" method of the Bible offers a more adequate understanding of selfhood and humanity's historic existence than any alternative view. "When we deal with aspects of reality which exhibit a freedom above and beyond structures," Niebuhr noted, "we must resort to the Hebraic dramatic and historical way of apprehending reality."[9] This applies to both the divine and the human self.

Niebuhr used the term "myth" to describe the language of the Bible that points to truths that literalistic and logical language cannot possibly convey. In *Beyond Tragedy* (1937), one of his most insightful books, Niebuhr contended that mythological language can communicate the dynamic nature of history and humanity's encounter with God in freedom in a way that is impossible for literalistic propositional language. What may not be literally true (e.g., the Fall of Adam and Eve) can be profoundly true and meaningful on an existential level where the meaning of the event has been presented through the medium of myth. It is through the myth-medium, Niebuhr believed, that we grasp both the meaningfulness and the tragedy of life as it has been revealed through the Bible.

It is through the unique insight of creation *ex nihilo*, for instance, that we know the creator is the source of an order that is essentially good. Humanity is not to understand itself from the standpoint of its rational faculties or its relation to nature but in terms of its uniqueness before God. It is not enough to be told that humans are animals with a slightly "more complex central nervous system" than other brute creatures. This does not do justice to the real stature of the human spirit. We may be finite in body and spirit, but we have a capacity for self-transcendence that is unlike anything else in the created order. We are the "crown of creation"; the one creature that can relate to God, neighbor, and self through our unique power of freedom. It is in this freedom that we encounter God as creator, judge, and redeemer.

In this encounter with a "wholly other" at the edge of human consciousness one experiences a sense of reverence for majesty and a dependence upon an ultimate source of Being. This is our sense of God as creator. There is also a sense of moral obligation and of moral unworthiness before a judge. We long for forgiveness but refuse to acknowledge our own finite condition before God. In our freedom we refuse to acknowledge that we are weak, created, dependent, or insecure. On the contrary, Niebuhr notes, man in his freedom "transmutes his partial and finite values into the infinite good. Therein lies his sin."[10]

Sin is more than defiance of God. It is the misuse of the individual's freedom. Out of this insecurity we experience anxiety, which is the precondition of sin—the internal state of temptation. When this anxiety conceives, the individual falls into pride, the most basic form of sin. That is to say, we succumb to the temptation to raise our finite and contingent existence to unconditioned significance. This chief expression of sin manifests itself in various forms—the pride of power, learning, and goodness.

There is, of course, another side to sin. This other side is sensuality, humanity's attempt to escape from its unlimited possibilities of freedom and live according to the lower immediacies of life. This is the state of the sensualist, the drunk, the drug addict, and all who have resigned their free spirit to a mere bodily existence. To say that a person sins in freedom, however, is to know that one is responsible for one's actions. Nothing outside of a person can be blamed for making that person a sinner—not Adam, a bad environment, or even the devil. It is the misuse of freedom that turns us into sinners and makes us responsible before God for our own actions. The sin of pride, Niebuhr believed, "is not necessary but it is inevitable."[11] Sin and its moral correlative, guilt, are an inseparable part of the human predicament.

Sin has both vertical and horizontal consequences. On the vertical dimension it results in humanity's separation from God. Horizontally, it produces injustice to one's fellows and alienation from one's true self.

We cannot possibly complete our own incomplete life because human life always remains within the vicious circle of sinful self-glorification. Niebuhr emphasized, however, that sin is not a subject to be considered in isolation from God's gracious provision of forgiveness: "The good news of the gospel is that God takes the sinfulness of man into Himself and overcomes in His own heart what cannot be overcome in man."[12]

The Christian answer to the human predicament is a suffering divine love. The "foolishness" of the Cross becomes, in the eyes of faith, the key that unlocks the mysteries of life. It reveals the mystery of what humanity is and should be, and of what the repentant humanity can be through God's forgiveness. The cross is God's wisdom, but it is also God's power. It destroys all false systems of meaning in which the self has exalted itself against the knowledge of God, and it is the basis for the grace (i.e., power) through which the repentant person can be renewed.

Faith is not reason. "This faith in the sovereignty of a divine Creator, Judge, and Redeemer," Niebuhr noted, "is not subject to rational proof because it stands beyond and above the rational coherences of the world."[13] On the other hand, the coherences constructed by worldly wisdom point beyond themselves to a freedom that is not in them, which suggests a profounder mystery and meaning than can be accounted for by scientific and philosophical analysis. "The accusers and crucifiers," Niebuhr observed, "must always pay inadvertent tribute to the Kingdom of Truth which they seek to despise."[14]

A Christian Interpretation of History

Reinhold Niebuhr's views on history were scattered throughout numerous books and articles written over a lifetime of reflection on the meaning of history. *Reflections on the End of an Era* (1934) and *The Irony of American History* (1952) focused on Niebuhr's thoughts about America. *Beyond Tragedy* (1937) and *Discerning the Signs of the Times* (1946) contained essays that addressed more varied aspects of the subject. His more systematic treatment of the meaning of history was found in *Human Destiny* (1943) and *Faith and History* (1949). The common thread in all these works was Niebuhr's conviction that the Christian interpretation of life and history is truer to the facts of human experience than any other interpretation.

Classical philosophies erred in their denial of any disclosure of meaning in the temporal realm, while modern philosophies erred in their expectation of the fulfillment of history from within the process of history itself. The Christian view, on the other hand, claimed that "history provides a disclosure of meaning but not a fulfillment in history."[15] Through the revelatory events of Christ's life, death, and resurrection the meaning of history, the *telos,* has been disclosed. Through the eyes of faith the believer is able to apprehend the significance of these events and what they reveal about the meaning of history. They are the events that stand in judgment against all idolatrous centers of meaning, whether they be secular (e.g., bourgeois or Marxist) or Christian (e.g., Lutheran, Roman Catholic, Calvinist, or Pietist). History can disclose but it cannot redeem. It cannot be its own Christ. History has opened itself up to the worst of fanaticisms when it has projected its own redemptive solutions. To use one of Niebuhr's favorite analogies, "man is a Moses who has glimpsed the promised land from afar, and who has made some progress toward it on this earth, but who will not enter into it in history."[16] The eschatological symbols of the Bible all point to the fact that "man's reach will always exceed his grasp." The fulfillment of history will have to come from "beyond" history and human achievement.

Life is inevitably paradoxical and ambiguous because humanity lives in the unity of two dimensions—*time* and *eternity.* The biblical understanding of historical selfhood is superior to alternative views because it takes full account of both dimensions. Naturalistic and idealistic philosophies attempt to find an ultimate meaning for history by constructing some coherent system of nature or reason in time. Mystical doctrines, on the other hand, stress the capacity of the self to transcend the processes of nature and reason and stand above the structures and coherences of this world. Both falsify the human experience by either making too little, or too much, of the eternal dimension in the human spirit. The former tries to make faith acceptable to the intellectual scruples of modern thought by reducing humanity to ontological categories or to some "essence" from which one can derive ethical truisms. The latter simply try to escape from history and find meaning in some transcendent realm.

The Christian view starts with the historical character of humanity. "Man is primarily a historical character," Niebuhr emphasized. "His real milieu is history."[17] Existentially, however, we live in both time *and* eternity because we carry the image of God. Reason is our mode of expression for the dimension of time and history. Myth is the mode of expression that allows us to break through the barriers of time and reason and talk about the realities of the eternal and the mysterious in the realm of time. The "genius of myth," Niebuhr said, is "that it points to the timeless in time."[18] In a sense the Bible "deceives" by speaking of the eternal in historical and temporal terms. Yet, it is "true" and realistic in what it says about the "tragedy of life" and God's provision of new life and hope from "beyond history."

The biblical myth of the "Fall" teaches what is continually confirmed in human experience—the tragedy of life. But the cross and resurrection of Christ, as well as the eschatological symbols, affirm the meaningfulness of history. This is the source of the Christian transvaluation of all values. "The Christian knows." Niebuhr argued, "that the cross is the truth. In that standard he sees the ultimate success of what the world calls failure and the failure of what the world calls success."[19]

The good news of the gospel, expressed in the Christian symbols of incarnation and atonement, is that Christ is "for us." We are the recipients of God's benefits of truth and power. In Christ and his cross the "wisdom of God" is revealed; the wisdom that stands in judgment against all partial perspectives. Moreover, Christ's cross makes available to us the mercy and power to continue on in the struggles of history. As "suffering Messiah" he both judges and completes our moral efforts so that the fulfillment of history, like the fulfillment of self, depends upon that grace that impinges upon human experience. All human attempts to find the norm for life in some source other than Christ turn out to be inadequate centers of truth and hope. It is only when our old life has been shattered, our egos and pretensions "crucified," that the power of God is able to renew us, overcome our sin, and fulfill our lives. The Christ norm that was impossible now becomes possible through the grace of God that works within us. The sacrificial love of Christ, which is the norm for human life, always remains the "impossible possibility." This is the paradox of grace that the Apostle Paul expounded in Galatians 2:20. "I am crucified with Christ, nevertheless I live, yet not I; but Christ lives in me."

Justification by faith, Niebuhr believed, is the doctrinal corollary of the "impossible possibility." It is the acceptance of the fact that we cannot set our own norm or fulfill our own lives. We must accept by faith the divine mercy and forgiveness that is offered through the Cross. The Reformation, he suggested, is the historical and cultural expression of this same truth. It understood very well the limits of human goodness and inability of humans to fulfill their own nature and destiny. All of the reformers taught that life must be completed by a power outside of the person.

The gift of the Holy Spirit (i.e., sanctification), on the other hand, empowers the new person to strive after the agape norm. Even though the grace of sanctification is never perfected in this life, Niebuhr emphasized, it does enable the diligent to pursue proximate answers and solutions to the problems of life in the here and now. The grace of sanctification, like that of justification, shows us the inadequacy of our own power, but it also bespeaks the necessity of an unrelenting cooperation with God on our part to fulfill the law of life that has been revealed in Jesus Christ. If the doctrine of justification by faith was needed to preserve the integrity of divine sovereignty, a proper emphasis upon sanctification was needed to insure that the church rightly understood the need for human responsibility. The Renaissance, Niebuhr believed, was the cultural expression of this same truth. The Renaissance thinkers emphasized humanity's capacity for goodness and the role that it must play in the fulfillment of one's own life and destiny. What the Christian and the secularist both need is a synthesis of the truthful insights contained in these doctrines (justification by faith/sanctification) and historical movements (Reformation/ Renaissance). Sin always prevents the completion of human nature and destiny from human effort alone, but the possibilities of divine grace always keep the hope and the struggle alive.

The essential message contained in the eschatological symbols of the Bible, Niebuhr believed, is that what cannot be perfected from within history will be fulfilled from "beyond." The return of Christ expresses the hope that the triumphant, suffering Messiah will "come again" with power and glory to fulfill the meaning of history and overcome the contradictions of sin. His return will insure the promise of final grace and complete the moral struggle. The last judgment speaks of the true norm of history, the "sacrificial love of Christ," by which all human norms and efforts will be judged. Christ, the true norm of humaneness and history, will judge all partial realizations and approximations by the ideal possibilities of his own sacrificial love. The moral ambiguities that have characterized human action will be clearly illumined and judged. All illusion and moral pretension will be exposed. While Niebuhr did not claim to know "either the furniture of heaven or the temperature of hell," he was confident that the testimony of the heart teaches humankind the inevitability of judgment.[20]

The resurrection of the body points to the meaningfulness of human effort to redeem and sanctify life. But it also expresses the "condition of finiteness and freedom . . . from which there is no solution by any human power."[21] Only God can solve this problem. The resurrection assures us that the God who is revealed in Christ cannot be separated from us by life or death. God's love gives meaning to the limits and ambiguities of human existence. The hope of resurrection paradoxically implies that "the meaningfulness of history is the more certainly affirmed because the consummation of history as a human possibility is denied."[22] The final victory, which comes at the end of history, represents the perfect fulfillment of nature through grace.

The Social Relevance of Christianity

Reinhold Niebuhr's mind held no doubt that the Christian faith provided a superior insight into the dynamics of human society. Prophetic religion, based on biblical realism, had proved its worth as a resource for social criticism. The key question, however, was could it do more? Could it be an effective instrument for social change? Could it provide a responsible approach to concrete social problems? This was its true test of relevance.

The central message of Christianity, Niebuhr emphasized, is Christ's self-giving *agape* love. This love, revealed through the cross, is not the kind of love that is concerned for reciprocity but is directed toward the good of others. The social significance of agape love is that it is the norm for human social and personal existence. The application of the agape norm to social and political relations, however, is not a simple solution to the complex problems of society. Niebuhr described the agape norm as an "impossible possibility." It is an "impossibility" in the sense that one always falls short of the agape ideal; it is a "possibility" because the grace of God's love provides the moral undergirding to continue the struggle for a better life and a better world. The cross is central; it shows us the self-sacrificing love of Christ that is the only answer to the self-interest that permeates all social relations. The paradox of this "perfect love" is that it is always crucified in history by humanity's self-serving interests, but it continues to define the ultimate heroic possibilities of human existence.

The relevance of agape love to social life is that it provides the norm for critiquing all secular and religious perspectives that pretend to altruism, absolute moral goodness, and divine sanction. Agape should not be confused with a mere feeling of benevolence toward others. The cross is not a symbol for sentimentality or passivity. Its moral ideal functions as a *protest* against all forms of sinful self-interest. The prophetic tradition—stretching from Amos, to Jesus, the Anabaptists, Marx, Gandhi, and Martin Luther King, Jr.—attests to the power of love to challenge all social inequities. The law of love saves society from dispensing with all ethical standards and falling into nihilism or cynicism. It "provides foundations for a final standard against which interest and power can be measured, beguiled, harnessed, and deflected for the ultimate end of creating the most inclusive possible community of justice and order."[23]

The struggle for social and political power reflects on the collective level what every person struggles with in the attempt to gain security over the anxious insecurities of one's own self. Our capacity to transcend our empirical self allows us to move beyond the mere need for physical survival and seek security by enhancing our own individual and collective power. Groups, Niebuhr contended, are even more motivated than individuals to seek dominion over each other. Self-giving love, as an ethical ideal, is for this reason even less attainable in collective life. But it must, nonetheless, live in constant tension with power. Without agape there would be no ultimate standard for which to strive or any power that could enable the loving person to seek the good of others.

The ideal of love and the realities of power, Niebuhr argued, necessitate a mediating norm. That norm is social justice. Justice is not the ultimate norm, but it is usually the best that one can hope for under the "conditions of sin." The dialectical relation between love and justice serves to draw justice toward higher and higher levels of expression while the constant demand for justice saves love from sentimentalism and paralysis. In the interest of human equality it pushes and shoves and makes use of creative power and coercion to achieve its ends. The struggle for justice in society often consists of the need to redistribute power to those who have become the victims of injustice. This need to redistribute power takes place in social relations, but it also has to occur in social institutions. The struggle is an ongoing one through legal systems, governmental structures, the popular will, economic resources, and even force of arms. When these fail to achieve justice in society, people resort to more violent means.

Niebuhr did not agree with Karl Marx that violent revolution was an inevitable ingredient in social justice. But neither did he agree with bourgeois sentimentalists that violence was "intrinsically immoral." Civil disobedience in the cause of social justice, even in its more violent forms, was not necessarily an expression of hatred nor did it impose more suffering than passive obedience to unjust laws and structures. The necessary virtue in any use of force, he believed, must be reason and prudence. There are no easy solutions, nor should there be any moral pretension to self-righteousness in the difficult arena where the struggle for justice takes place. The one thing about which Niebuhr was certain was that Christians are called upon to get their hands dirty. Moral responsibility was to be preferred over moral purity.

Christians need to "stop fooling themselves," Niebuhr wrote. If they want to help create a more just society they must recognize "the perennial necessity" of a this-worldly involvement.[24] He personally embodied that conviction. Reinhold Niebuhr was as likely to be found on a picket line or at a political rally as he was behind a pulpit or a lectern. He constantly supported structures of power that he believed would enhance the welfare of workers, the poor, women, blacks, Jews, and ethnic minorities. On the international level he argued for a pragmatic balance of power among the superpowers and policies of humanitarian concern toward weaker nations. He advocated the virtues of wise statecraft, the benefits of compromise, and the folly of miscalculations like Vietnam. Niebuhr was a principled pragmatist. The principles of justice, he argued, must always prudently take account of the human factor.

The fact that humanity inevitably falls from the agape ideal back into selfish interests does not mean that Christianity is a failure. On the contrary, it points to the grace that must meet humanity at the point of *its* failure. Christianity is relevant to the social order, as it is to one's personal life, precisely because it adequately diagnoses one's predicament and prescribes the proper cure. One must not equate true prophetic religion with the failures of the institutional church. The fruits of the Christian faith have always been evident when people have been renewed by grace and blessed with reason and wisdom to make intelligent and compassionate use of love, justice, and power.

Notes

[1]Charles W. Kegley and Robert W. Bretall, eds., *Reinhold Niebuhr: His Religious, Social, and Political thought* (New York: Macmillan Co., 1967) 3.
[2]Ibid., 216.   [3]Ibid., 218.

[4]John C. Bennett, "The Greatness of Reinhold Niebuhr," *Union Seminary Quarterly Review* 27 (Fall 1971): 4.

[5]Bob E. Patterson, *Reinhold Niebuhr*. Makers of the Modern Theological Mind (Waco TX: Word Books, 1977) 152.

[6]Robert McAfee Brown, ed., *The Essential Reinhold Niebuhr* (New Haven CT: Yale University Press, 1986) 233.

[7]Reinhold Niebuhr, *The Nature and Destiny of Man,* (New York: Charles Scribner's Sons, 1941) 1:3.

[8]Ibid.   [9]Kegley and Bretall, 433.

[10]Niebuhr, *Nature and Destiny of Man,* 1:122.

[11]Ibid., 1:242.   [12]Ibid., 1:142.   [13]Brown, 1:236.

[14]Ibid.   [15]Kegley and Bretall, 294.

[16]Ibid.   [17]Ibid., 18.

[18]Reinhold Niebuhr, *An Interpretation of Christian Ethics* (London: SCM Press LTD, 1948) 82, 83.

[19]Reinhold Niebuhr, *Beyond Tragedy: Essays on the Christian Interpretation of History* (New York: Charles Scribner's Sons, 1937), x.

[20]Brown, 238.

[21]Reinhold Niebuhr, *The Nature and Destiny of Man*, (New York: Charles Scribner's Sons, 1943) 2:295.

[22]Ibid.

[23]Kegley and Bretall, 169.

[24]Roger A. Johnson, *Critical Issues in Modern Religion*, 2d ed. (Englewood Cliffs NJ: Prentice Hall, 1990) 259. Also, see Kegley and Bretall, 135.

Selected Bibliography

Major Works by Reinhold Niebuhr

Does Civilization Need Religion?—A Study in the Social Resources and Limitations of Religion in Modern Life. New York: Macmillan Co., 1927.

Leaves from the Notebook of a Tamed Cynic. New York: Meridian Books, 1959.

The Contribution of Religion to Social Work. New York: Columbia University Press, 1932.

Moral Man and Immoral Society: A Study in Ethics and Politics. New York: Charles Scribner's Sons, 1932.

Reflections on the End of an Era. New York: Charles Scribner's Sons, 1934.

An Interpretation of Christian Ethics. New York: Meridian Books, 1956.

Beyond Tragedy: Essays on the Christian Interpretation of History. New York: Charles Scribner's Sons, 1937.

Christianity and Power Politics. New York: Charles Scribner's Sons, 1940.

The Nature and Destiny of Man: A Christian Interpretation. Two volumes in one. Volume 1, *Human Nature.* Volume 2, *Human Destiny.* New York: Charles Scribner's Sons, 1953.

The Children of Light and the Children of Darkness: A Vindication of Democracy and a Critique of Its Traditional Defense. New York: Charles Scribner's Sons, 1944.

Discerning the Signs of the Times: Sermons for Today and Tomorrow. New York: Charles Scribner's Sons, 1946.

Faith and History: A Comparison of Christian and Modern Views of History. New York: Charles Scribner's Sons, 1949.

The Irony of American History. New York: Charles Scribner's Sons, 1952.

Christian Realism and Political Problems. New York: Charles Scribner's Sons, 1953.

The Self and the Dramas of History. New York: Charles Scribner's Sons, 1957.

Love and Justice. Edited by D.B. Robertson. Philadelphia PA: Westminster Press, 1957.

The World Crisis and American Responsibility. Ed. Ernest W. Lefever. New York: Association Press, 1958.

Pious and Secular America. New York: Charles Scribner's Sons, 1958.

Essays in Applied Christianity. Ed. D. B. Robertson. New York: World Publishing Co., Meridian Books, 1959.

The Structure of Nations and Empires: A Study of the Recurring Patterns and Problems of the Political Order in Relation to the Unique Problems of the Nuclear Age. New York: Charles Scribner's Sons, 1959.

Reinhold Niebuhr on Politics. Ed. Harry H. Davis and Robert C. Good. New York: Charles Scribner's Sons, 1960.

A Nation So Conceived: Reflections on the History of America from Its Early Vision to Its Present Power. With Alan Heimert. New York: Charles Scribner's Sons, 1963.

Man's Nature and His Communities. New York: Charles Scribner's Sons, 1965.

Faith and Politics: A Commentary on Religious, Social, and Political Thought in a Technological Age. Ed. Ronald H. Stone. New York: George Braziller, 1968.

The Democratic Experience: Past and Prospects. With Paul E. Sigmund. New York: Frederick A. Praeger Publishers, 1969.

Justice and Mercy. Ed. Ursula M. Niebuhr. New York: Harper and Row, 1974.

Books about Reinhold Niebuhr

Bingham, June. *Courage to Change: An Introduction to the Life and Thought of Reinhold Niebuhr.* New York: Charles Scribner's Sons, 1961.

Brown, Robert McAfee, ed. *The Essential Reinhold Niebuhr: Selected Essays and Addresses.* New Haven: Yale University Press, 1986.

Carnell, Edward John. *The Theology of Reinhold Niebuhr.* Grand Rapids MI: Eerdmans Publishing Co., 1950.

Fackre, Gabriel J. *The Promise of Reinhold Niebuhr.* Philadelphia PA: J. B. Lippincott Co., 1970.

Fox, Richard. *Reinhold Niebuhr: A Biography.* New York: Pantheon Books, 1985.

Guthrie, Shirley Caperton, Jr. *The Theological Character of Reinhold Niebuhr's Social Ethic.* Winterthur, Switzerland: P. G. Keller Verlag, 1959.

Harland, Gordon. *The Thought of Reinhold Niebuhr.* New York: Oxford University Press, 1960.

Hofmann, Hans. *The Theology of Reinhold Niebuhr.* Trans. Louise Pettibone Smith. New York: Charles Scribner's Sons, 1956.

Kegley, Charles W., and Robert W. Bretall, eds. *Reinhold Niebuhr: His Religious, Social, and Political Thought.* The Library of Living Theology, volume 2. New York: Macmillan Co., 1956.

Landon, Harold R., ed. *Reinhold Niebuhr: A Prophetic Voice in Our Time.* Greenwich CT: Seabury Press, 1962.

Merkley, Paul. *Reinhold Niebuhr: A Political Account.* Montreal, Canada: McGill-Queen's University Press, 1975.

Patterson, Bob E. *Reinhold Niebuhr.* Makers of the Modern Mind Series. Waco TX: Word Publishers, 1977.

Scott, Nathan A., Jr., ed. *The Legacy of Reinhold Niebuhr.* Chicago IL: University of Chicago Press, 1975.

Stone, Ronald H. *Reinhold Niebuhr: Prophet to Politicians.* Nashville TN: Abingdon Press, 1972.

An exhaustive bibliography on Niebuhr will probably never be compiled because some of what he wrote cannot be identified. The indispensable guide to Reinhold Niebuhr's published works, however, is D. B. Robertson's *Reinhold Niebuhr's Works: A Bibliography* (rev. ed .), published by University Press of America in 1983.

Reinhold Niebuhr's collected papers are at the Library of Congress and recordings from oral history interviews, conducted in 1953 and 1954, are kept at the Columbia University Oral History Research office.

Conclusion

Apologetics: The Continuing Imperative

The Christian religion cannot be fully comprehended for it transcends what our finite minds can grasp and all that we have ever experienced. It cannot possibly be accepted on the grounds that its incomprehensible mysteries and paradoxes be laid open and explained. Becoming a Christian always involves a risk in the sense that it requires a commitment that can only be validated by subsequent events. "Understanding is the reward of faith," Augustine said; "Therefore, seek not to understand that thou mayest believe, but believe that thou mayest understand."[1] Christian orthodoxy has always held that it is necessary for one to accept an unfathomable mystery before one can become a Christian.

Christian belief, however, is more than a mere leap into the ultimately incomprehensible and ineffable truth of the Christian religion. It is also a graced response to a divine call. "No one can come to me," Jesus said, "unless the Father who sent me draws him" (John 6:44 RSV). No amount of reason or evidence can make one a Christian apart from the calling and regenerating work of the Holy Spirit.

A sound apologetic must always operate within the bounds of these considerations. The effort to establish solid theological grounds upon which the Christian faith commitment can be considered a prudent, humanly responsible act, however, is no violation of these sacred realities. Augustine's conviction that faith must lead the intellect does not mean that faith is the end of thought but simply its presupposition. "I believe," Augustine said, "in order that I may know." Faith and reason, revelation and philosophy, cannot be ultimately antithetical to each other for true theology must be true philosophy. "Far be it," Augustine added, "that we would have faith without accepting or demanding reasons for our faith."[2]

Dogmatic theology is an attempt to state what faith believes. Its task has traditionally been to structure the truth of faith and explain the inner coherence of the Scriptures. Until recent times apologetics was viewed as a subsection of dogmatic theology. It functioned to prepare the hearer to receive that which was being proclaimed, and closed the theological loop against all anticipated incursions of criticism and unbelief. Apologetics in this context was more oriented to the thing being proclaimed than it was to the hearer of the proclamation. The foundations of Reformed apologetics, for instance, were laid by John Calvin in the first few chapters of his *Institutes of the Christian Religion.* In these early chapters Calvin prepared the reader for what followed by making a case for the view that human intelligence, human moral sense, and one's very existence were a witness to the existence of God. The logic of the matter then was that faith is an eminently reasonable act as well as a graced response to God's call. Faith, from this perspective, was grounded in the divine initiative, but it was also set forth as an act that no reasonable person could refuse. Apologetics done from this theological perspective aimed to close the circle of faith without assuming an offensive posture. What this kind of apologetic lacked was a positive and aggressive style.

Faith has to live and express itself in a world that changes and is culturally diverse. The shape and style of Christian apologetics has always mirrored that change and diversity but never more dramatically than in the twentieth century. Apologists in this century have not been able to presume a Christian culture or homogeneous beliefs. Consequently, they have had to move out of the arena of dogmatics where faith commitments were safe and expected into an unbelieving secularized world where the real situation is one of decision and doubt.

The new situation has transformed the apologetic task. In an era that is secular and ecumenical it is no longer popular, or effective, to do confessional apologetics. Doctrinal and confessional differences are more and more relegated to discussions among those who already share the same faith while apologists concentrate their efforts on establishing intellectually defensible grounds with those who do not yet share the Christian perspective.

The apologetic imperative today is defined in terms of a continuing need for theologies that do not divorce systematic from apologetic aims but that are distinctively apologetic in their point of view. Systematic and apologetic aims in theology are not contradictory but complimentary and interdependent. Theology, as a systematic expression of Christian faith and knowledge, seeks to communicate the message of the church. The apologetic goal, on the other hand, is to speak this message to a secular world in a manner that can be understood and appreciated. A theology that is functioning apologetically must aspire to make its message as convincing as possible by making itself intelligible and relevant to the universal human experience that Christians share with all other persons.

The church must extend its message beyond its confessional and doctrinal commitments to the broader needs of a secular society. A Christian apologetic that is worthy of the name never surrenders its faith commitments, but neither does it abandon its obligation to articulate the intellectually responsible grounds for the faith commitment that Christians have already made. The apologist is always concerned to establish the reasonableness and relevance of faith. The Christian faith is by its very nature something that was meant to be shared. The gift has become the task. Christians sometimes need to be reminded that the line between the faithful and the secular must not be drawn too tightly. After all, Arthur Holmes has noted, "Christianity does not exempt us from the creation mandate with its cultural and 'secular' responsibilities but brings us to it with all the perspective and grace that Jesus Christ provides."[3]

The Apologetic Point of View

The First Vatican Council (1870) was one of the first instances of theological militancy in the modern era. In an atmosphere of skepticism and doubt the council declared that God could be known from the world of created reality through the natural light of reason, and in 1910 the anti-modernist declaration spoke of the possibility of proving God's existence. The apologetic significance of this bold venture on the part of the Catholic church was twofold. It showed a willingness on the part of Catholic theologians to confront the anti-faith forces of the nineteenth century and it reaffirmed the church's position that faith was not restricted to the ghetto of dogmatics or inward piety. It was the beginning, however successful or unsuccessful one may deem it to have been, of a new apologetic offensive that refused to divorce the claims of faith from the canons of reason.

During the decade of the 1920s an attempt to build a platform for discussion and encounter with critics of faith began to emerge at the Free University of Amsterdam. Bavinck, Hepp, and Dooyeweerd attracted attention as bold and aggressive apologists by attempting to move Reformed theology beyond dogmatics and into the center of spiritual and cultural conflict. The conviction underlying the new theological venture in Amsterdam was that while faith is a miraculous gift it is also an objective truth that is open to the investigations of reason. The truth of faith is more than that which can be known through subjective experience. It is an objective truth that is capable of persuading and convincing others.

A. H. de Hartog, Dutch philosopher and theologian, was a crusading apologist of this same era. He did not work entirely out of the Reformed tradition, but de Hartog tirelessly labored to demonstrate the harmony between faith and science. New discoveries and the prospect of change never threatened de Hartog's faith. De Hartog celebrated all new discovery as if it would all somehow fit into the deeper rationality of divine truth. New questions only spurred him on in search of the eternal synthesis that he believed would adequately account for all change and progress.[4]

Karl Heim, a Lutheran theologian in Germany, was another key figure of the time who was moving away from dogmatics to a study of the questions that were being posed by science and philosophy. Heim was intrigued by the questions themselves, but he was more impressed by the adequacy of the answers that his own faith provided. He never attempted to prove the affirmations of his faith, but Heim remained convinced that the Christian faith was the answer to the questions modern persons were raising. The Christian, Heim argued, does not ask the scientist to listen to the dogmatic conclusions of faith; the Christian simply invites the scientist to interrogate his own perspective and discover the need for the meanings that are inaccessible to science. Heim carefully weighed the tough questions raised by empiricism, positivism, and relativism and emerged convinced of the certainty of the faith that can be known through encounter with Christ. His book, *The Certainty of Faith,* proved to be a significant work in Lutheran apologetics.

Heim was definitely moving in the direction of the new apologetic approach. He was not arguing for an apologetic that was independent of special revelation but for one that was faithful to the Christian's responsibility to preach the gospel to the world. A Christian apologetic would of necessity be informed by the substance of the faith but its form would be patterned after the issues of the time. An apologetic, Heim argued, has three obligations. The first, the offensive phase, is to unmask the idols which the world destructively reveres. The second is to preach the positive Christian message, and the third is to meaningfully consolidate a Christian view of life into the total environment in which the Christian lives.[5]

The two major figures responsible for summoning theology to its apologetic task were Emil Brunner and Paul Tillich. Neither drew an absolute distinction between apologetics and dogmatics, but their entire theology had a definite apologetic character. Brunner's intent for his apologetic was that it follow the path that the Christian revelation follows in God's self-disclosure to humanity. Since divine revelation is absolutely transcendent and unavailable through the reason of the natural person, the comprehension of divine truth must be a personal act—a divine-human encounter that takes place through a concrete situation. It is in this situation of the encounter that the inner contradiction of the sinner, who has entrenched himself against God's claim, is graciously overcome through the "decision for faith" that makes faith intelligible. Natural reason could never accept what the "gift of reason" now grasps through the divine self-disclosure. Through this personal act of faith, the being who is created in the image of God is claimed as subject and gifted to see what the person whose image is still spoiled cannot yet see. Brunner did not argue for a "pure reason" but for a reason that can believe because it has accepted the revelation. The reason that is dominated by sinful self-assumption, on the other hand, is blinded by the contradiction in its own nature. The distinction between the two is recognizable only to the person of faith.[6] Brunner held out no hope for a peaceful co-existence. The sinful self-understanding, he believed, will inevitably rise up against the reason of faith in science, secular ideologies, and varied cultural expressions.

The purpose of apologetics, Brunner insisted, is not to defend the message of the revelation for the message is always embedded in sociological, historical, philosophical, and scientific conceptions that are not essential to the message itself. What apologetics must do is attack the strongholds of sinful human reason and the "-isms" that it has spawned. Unlike apologists like de Hartog and Heim who sought for a synthesis between faith and reason, Brunner's theology of "crisis" demanded a Yes or a No to God in either faith or revolt. An unholy alliance between the reason of faith and the self-destructive reason of unbelief was unthinkable. Brunner called for an "eristic" theology (*eris* means "dispute") that would enter into the problematics of science, philosophy, and culture with the aim of confronting the irrational forces of unbelief. Brunner's aim was not to "prove" the truths of faith but to invite the natural man to "taste and see" that the gospel does have an answer to the contradictions and despair of his life. He could only hope to expose the false steps by which sinful reason had advanced to autonomy and made itself absolute. Like Pascal and Kierkegaard before him, Brunner's intent was not to defend the citadel of faith but to attack the unreasonable claims of the natural person. He wanted to shake the foundations of unbelief, to help the unbeliever see that unbelief is not derived from true reason but from a particular *Zeitgeist*, a secret dogmatics, or one's own metaphysic.

Paul Tillich's theology, like Emil Brunner's, was thoroughly apologetic in character. Tillich's approach to apologetics was to follow a method of correlation that attempted to give answers, drawn from the standpoint of the Christian faith, to answers raised by the "modern mind." He rejected the notion that the gospel could be thrown at the unbeliever's head like a stone. He believed that the Christian kerygma, to be effective, had to speak to the situation in which modern humanity exists. The form of the questions, as well as the answers, had to be determined by the language of modern philosophy, science, pyschology, and art. He presumed to draw the substance of the answers, however, from the Christian tradition.[7]

Tillich rightly held that revelation is spoken *to* humanity; it is not humanity speaking to itself. But he also emphasized that answers are meaningful only when they are relevant to the questions that are being asked in concrete historical situations. Tillich's analysis of the contemporary culture convinced him that the questions being asked were *existential* in character. He consequently couched his theology in existential ontological categories that were intended to speak to the contemporary situation.

Paul Tillich was hailed by many as a master theologian, but there were many others who were not impressed by the kind of bridges that he attempted to build between the modern mind and the Christian faith. The major criticism from evangelicals was that Tillich had been so intent upon correlating his apologetic theology with the contemporary situation that he had not allowed the Bible to speak for itself. Scripture did not carry the normative authority acknowledged by historic orthodoxy but was adapted to the existential and antisupernatural bias of his thought. It was a theology informed more by the philosophies of Schelling, Kierkegaard, and Heidegger than the biblical text. John Jefferson Davis, an evangelical theologian, rightly noted that Tillich's apologetic aims were noble, but his philosophical assumptions were alien to the historic message of the Christian faith. His attempt to correlate the Christian faith with existentialist philosophies, current scientific views of the physical universe, comparative studies of world religions, and a view of human nature informed by modern psychology, sociology, and anthropology was hardly a success. Its major weakness was that it made modern culture rather than the Christian tradition the controlling factor.[8]

Christian apologetics must help to raise the right questions as well as provide honest answers to honest inquiries. Diogenes Allen, Princeton Seminary philosopher and theologian, has noted that there are two ranges of needs that are satisfied by the gospel. There are those needs that are understood in light of the human condition, and there are those needs that cannot be understood in light of the human condition. These needs must be awakened in us by a scriptural understanding of God and ourselves. "That men die is an obvious fact, but that men die because of God's wrath over sin is not something that is evident from the fact of death nor from a study of the human condition." Allen has further noted that "while one might escape death is a distinct hope in man, the hope that the gospel offers far exceeds the hope that men shall escape death."[9] The gospel promises the penitent and faithful eternal life as sons and daughters in fellowship with God. To have a strong desire to be good and moral, and then suffer the frustration and guilt over one's failure to be so is yet another yearning of the human heart. But only the gospel can create the yearning for a clean heart and then comfort us with the assurance that the answer to that yearning is the righteousness of Christ. The point that Allen has made is that the gospel of Christ is the most practical and relevant truth known to humanity, but it must be received on its own terms. When its full integrity is acknowledged, the gospel addresses itself to us in such a way as to make our knowledge of God inseparable from a true knowledge of ourselves and our needs.

Karl Barth was the leading dogmatic theologian in this century who denied any basis for a real and mutually understood dialogue between faith and faithless reason. There is no "point of contact," he insisted, between the gospel and the natural person. Contrary to all who advocated an analogy of being or believed in rational continuity between God and humanity, Barth insisted that there were no possibilities in humanity's historical or psychic experience that could lead one to God. Barth never tired of emphasizing the "infinite qualitative distance" between the

Creator and the creature. Barth argued that it is not the task of theology "to lighten heaven with earth's searchlights, but to let the light of heaven be seen and understood on earth."[10] That was his way of saying that God's answers cannot be determined by humanity's questions. Revelatory answers are inevitably distorted when the questions are structured by human experiences and thoughts. Through his castigation of the apologetic enterprize Barth emptied more apologetics classrooms than any other theologian in this century.

Apologists have always known the dangers inherent in the effort to make the Christian faith relevant to human need. Liberal theology was an obvious case in point. Out of the liberal concern for relevance, liberal theologians tended to surrender essential truths of the Christian message in an effort to find common ground with those outside the church. But the opposite danger of isolating the faith from those to whom it was meant to speak was just as serious an error. Theological obscurantism has always been a failure. Fundamentalism exemplified this extreme. Out of a concern to preserve faithfulness to a timeless message, fundamentalist theologians failed to address the life and thought situations of modern persons. As a result, most moderns assumed that fundamentalist theology was obselete and irrelevant to human need. The fact of the matter was that both liberals and fundamentalists tended to be right in what they affirmed but wrong in what they denied.

Edwin Lewis, the great Methodist theologian of a generation ago, put the apologetic task in perspective by emphasizing that while theology must guard against the tendency adventitiously to mistake the word of man for the Word of God, it must not insist upon an absolute mutual exclusiveness between God and humanity. There is indeed a vast "qualitative difference" between God and human beings, Lewis admitted, but the beauty of the paradox is that the middle wall of partition is not absolute. God is in actual fact on both sides of the line that meta-physically divides God from humanity. God's special revelation is preceded by an implanted quest to which the revelation can appeal. Lewis noted that, "If God sought humanity but humanity did not seek God, or if humanity sought God and God did not seek humanity, the quest would be fruitless. God begins the quest for humanity by first inciting persons to a quest for God."[11] It is a mistake, he argued, to ignore the apologetic point of view that there is a unity of revelation that centers in God the Creator as well as God the Redeemer:

Barth's attempt to limit revelation to Christ and the historical preparation for him is a profound mistake, even from the standpoint of Christian apologetics. Of a God who reveals himself at only one point it may well be asked what good reason we can have for supposing that he is revealed even there. To ignore outside of one narrow stream the fact of creation, the fact of history, the fact of one's own distinctive nature, especially his reason and his conscience, the fact of ethical activity, and the fact of universal religion, is to weaken rather than to strengthen the case for revelation in Jesus Christ and in all that of which he was the climax.[12]

C. S. Lewis, Edward John Carnell, and Reinhold Niebuhr all believed that apologetics must follow the path of Christian revelation, but they did not understand the authority or revelation to mean something akin to "an order is an order" or "God has spoken and that is the end of it" mentality. On the contrary, they held that revelation is meaningful because it is able to make contact and take root in lives that are already filled with human searching.

In a similar vein, all three apologists welcomed meaningful religious experiences but warned against the fideist claim that faith is such an irrational or esoteric mystery that one can only *witness* to one's faith. The problem with this kind of claim is that it closes all doors to open discussion by appealing to private experience. The fideist who argues for God's existence on the grounds that "he just talked to him this morning" is more likely to engender scorn than belief from the skeptic. More sophisticated appeals to "mystery," "paradox," and even the "absurdity" of faith may be more intellectually respectable, but they have the same effect of walling faith off from real and mutually understood dialogue.

All of our apologists admitted that many Christian truths are incomprehensible and inaccessible to human reason. But they rejected the kind of mysticism that makes the faith impervious to human thought and isolates it in a ghetto of irrational, privatized experience. Mysteries are not something to be believed without benefit of any insight or connection with thought. Reinhold Niebuhr, in particular, stressed the importance of mystery, but argued that there is "meaning in mystery" just as there is "mystery in meaning."

It is important, as well, to acknowledge that the truth of Christian revelation often comes to us in the language of paradox. Paradox is a significant form of truth because it calls attention to the tension between

God's truth and the limitations of human wisdom. But paradox should not be construed as a form of credulity that mandates the sacrifice of the intellect. Faith may elude a finished reasoned synthesis, but it does not follow that God's truth is absurd or irrational. God does not reveal Himself to us by breaking all our rules of thought or by denying all truth in worldly wisdom. G. C. Berkouwer rightly warns that there is an important distinction to be made between the "foolishness and weakness" of God's methods and the "positing of absurdity as the esential content of faith."[13] Luther's "theology of the cross" makes this distinction but the advocates of "faith as absurdity" do not. The unfortunate consequence of this failure is an irrational faith that is fated to live in cultural isolation from those who need to hear its message.

A theology that speaks from an apologetic point of view must make communication a central concern. The Christian imperative, on this matter, is clear. The apologist is to "speak the truth in love." C. S. Lewis, E. J. Carnell, and Reinhold Niebuhr were exemplary Christian apologists in this regard. Despite the fact that they were all prophetic-type apologists who were aggressive and militant in their attacks on the self-destructive assumptions of modern humanity, their apologetic endeavors were not waged in the spirit of a "fight" or a "lust for victory." The message they presented to the skeptics was always in the spirit of an *invitation* to share in the joy and hospitality of the household of faith. In *New Accents in Contemporary Theology* Roger Hazelton has described an apologetic style that is reminiscent of the styles employed by these apologists. He wrote:

> Apologetics is the theology of invitation, and as such it is but the logical development of the Christian gospel itself. The good news of God, who identifies himself with us and imparts himself to us in Christ, belongs not to Christians but to the world. It is not ours to keep but to give. Moreover, says the apologist, this news is not too good to be true, and he makes it his business to show just how true it is. The gospel not only constitutes and orders his thought but controls his purpose and shapes his task. As God extends his invitation in Christ, so the Christian adds his own. If he does his thinking in the spirit of the gospel, he will soon learn that he too must identify himself with those to whom he would impart the truth of faith. When all is said and done, the apologetic theologian remains a message bearer from God to this world, and his message is in the form of an invitation to faith.[14]

Hazelton has further noted that just as systematic and apologetic aims are complementary and interdependent, the aims of apologetics cannot be separated from those of preaching and evangelism. This is not to say that there are no functional differences between apologetics and evangelism— only that apologetics, by its very nature, strives to be evangelical. Apologetics, Hazelton argued, "sets the whole enterprize of evangelism in the context of an engagement with the world."[15] In effect, apologetics is a missionary theology, and apologists like C. S. Lewis, Edward John Carnell, and Reinhold Niebuhr were the missionaries to the skeptics and "intellectual despisers" of their time.

Revelation and Reason

No standard set of issues or topics comprises Christian apologetics. But there are key issues that differentiate the thought and strategy of one apologist from that of another and help us understand them better. The problem of knowledge is this kind of issue. The meaning of revelation and its relation to reason, or philosophy, is a central concern for the Christian apologist. Much has already been said about the similarities of these apologists with respect to their commitment to an apologetic point of view. A more critical look at their understanding of the character of revelation and their understanding of the relationship between faith and reason should provide a basis for better understanding some of their fundamental differences.

Lewis, Carnell, and Niebuhr were all committed to the view that the Christian apologist must follow the path of Christian revelation. It would hardly be acceptable for Christians to think that they could talk intelligibly about the Christian faith apart from the Christian revelation. All three apologists were in essential agreement about that, but there were fundamental disagreements among them concerning the *character* of Christian revelation and the direction they believed that apologetics should take.

Niebuhr's concept of revelation, like that of Emil Brunner's, centered in the view that revelation has to do with a personal meeting or encounter with God—not a communication of divine truths or facts that can be known through a reading of the Bible. From Carnell's perspective this was a disturbing view of revelation because it undermined the orthodox understanding of the authority of a divinely inspired Bible by making it authoritative only as a *means* (i.e., as a witness to the revelation of God in Christ) and not as the *ground* of the Christian faith. This meant that the Scriptures have the authority of a norm only in the sphere of *salvation-history* (*heilsgeschichte*), not in the realm of *ordinary history* (*geschichte*) where critics hold that the Scriptures may err and should simply be viewed as a human, fallible book. Such a view, Carnell argued, undermines trust in the Bible. If the Bible cannot be trusted in matters of science and history, why should it be trusted in matters of salvation. Revelation commends itself to a thinking person because it fits all of the facts of human experience, not just because it is subjectively meaningful and satisfying.

It is well to remember, however, that Niebuhr's interests lay primarily with the practical, ethical, and social problems of his time. He was not nearly as concerned with assumptions about truth and revelation as with real life situations. There was a basis for apologetics in Niebuhr's thinking, "a *logos* in man to which the divine *logos* may be commended by human words,"[16] but he recognized that the human situation is far more complex than can be comprehended through any scheme of rational meaning. The strength of his apologetic lay in the fact that he recognized the incoherences as well as the coherences of life and never attempted to rationalize the ambiguities and mysteries of life that defy rationalization.

It was his perspective on the coherences and incoherences of human experience that saved Niebuhr from subjective irrationalism, on the one hand, and the attempt of naturalists, on the other, to reduce the vitalities of human selfhood to the coherences of nature. Niebuhr felt that the incoherences of life point up the disillusionment of liberal utopianism while life's coherences teach us the errors of the "fanatical idolatry of Marxism and the cynical despair of nihilism."[17] The grace and wisdom that comes through encounter with God in human history save us from such extremes because they presuppose both the meaning and mystery of life.

Niebuhr made much of the fact that *history* is the sphere of the saving encounter with God and the locus of the biblical revelation. History is the "personal" realm that cannot be predicted nor controlled by the coherences of nature. The natural realm, however, is more closed to miraculous intervention than assumed by the pre-scientific understanding of the biblical writers. Consequently, Niebuhr tended to disassociate the account of miracles from the historical Christian faith. This reserve regarding miracles did not escape the attention of more conservative evangelical critics for it meant that Niebuhr was commending to the world a Christ of faith who was not the Jesus of history, who was not born of the Virgin Mary, who did not heal the sick, or raise the dead, who was, in fact, not himself raised from the dead on the third day.[18] The same criticism was made of Niebuhr that was earlier made of Tillich. His apologetic aims were noble and many skeptics were drawn to his point of view, but his naturalistic assumptions were inimical to a truly evangelical perspective.

Niebuhr was the first to admit that his real interests were practical rather than theological. He was always turned more toward social and ethical issues than toward epistemological concerns, which Niebuhr admitted "bored him."[19] The task of human reason, as he understood it, was not to probe into questions concerning ultimate aims, values, and truths but to search for solutions to immediate practical problems. His interests in systematic and theoretical constructions of theology, apart from their practical and ethical implications, were virtually nonexistent. In this sense, Reinhold Niebuhr was a thoroughgoing American pragmatist. What the biblical picture points to, Niebuhr believed, is a "mystery of divine freedom beyond all schemes of rational intelligibility that has an existential relevance to the human condition and to the condition of society in which our lives are set."[20] It is all true but not in a literal historical sense. What needs defending is not a set of propositional truth statements grounded in historical and supernatural events but a biblical picture of creation, judgment, and redemption that is not dependent upon concepts of natural or rational causation.[21] Niebuhr could commend the unique emphases of biblical faith above those of idealism, naturalism, Marxism, or any other competing view because he was convinced that these "myths" provide a truer view of both the nobility and misery of humanity, as well as the meaning of history, than all the wisdom of the scientists and philosophers.

More conservative apologists like Alan Richardson and Edward John Carnell were deeply disturbed by this kind of apologetic perspective. Because Niebuhr began with naturalistic assumptions, Richardson noted, he ended "by disassociating the historical basis of Christianity from any divine miraculous interventions in the realm of natural causation." One cannot surrender the factuality and historicity of Creation, the Fall of Man, the Virgin Birth, and the physical Resurrection, he argued, without turning the historic Christian faith into a modern form of gnosticism or making it a pale truism for a mere theistic philosophy.[22] In a critique of Niebuhr's apologetic, Richardson wrote:

> If the Resurrection of Christ is not a historical event but only a profound myth, that is, a representation created by the poetic imagination of the true meaning of life, then a kind of Christian philosophy and a kind of Christian religion might still conceivably be true, even though the original apostolic witnesses were mistaken about the very facts around which the poetic imagination played and out of which it built its myth. But then Christianity would be an imaginative religious interpretation of the world, which would differ from the historic Christian faith as poetry differs from history and as religion differs from Gospel.[23]

Niebuhr's defense of the Christian faith rested upon the radical distinction he drew between the natural world and the more "personal" world of human history. In the realm of natural history all events occur in accordance with fixed natural laws, but in the realm of human history the matter of free human choice makes events more unpredictable. An apologetic done from this point of view releases itself from the burden of defending miraculous truth claims. The emphasis falls instead upon the depth of meaning that is revealed through the "mythological" events of the Bible and the analogy we have for revelation in our relations with other persons. William Hordern has explained the rationale behind this more "personal" form of verification:

> The events of history come to the believer as given; they cannot be anticipated by some rational theory. Among the events of history are those that reveal God. We find an analogy for revelation in our relations with other persons. We have evidence that there is in the other person a depth of reality that is more than just a physical organism. We have evidence that we are dealing with a "thou," not just a thing . . . . This other person can only be understood when he speaks to us and reveals something of the underlying depth of his being. The word which he speaks is at once a verification of the fact that we are dealing with a different dimension than that of physical existence alone, and it is a revelation of the precise character of the person with whom we are dealing. The same is true of God. We have intimations that this world points beyond itself, that it is not self-explanatory, that there is a depth

of reality which does not meet the eye. But we cannot know this other dimension of reality unless it speaks and reveals itself to us. Christianity is based on the faith that God has spoken in the events of the Bible and particularly in the life of Jesus.[24]

The truth of Christianity then is verified by the actual fruits of the new life in Christ that issue from this personal encounter. Any attempt to transmute this experience into philosophical and historical propositions that can be intellectually verified and propagated, Niebuhr warned, "rob the experience of its resource of 'wisdom and power.' "[25]

Carnell valued the personal character of Christian revelation, but he insisted that no wedge should be driven between the "thou-truth" and "it-truth" distinction. He took his case for Christianity into the arena of nature and history as well because he believed that Christianity could account for all the facts of existence, including science and history. Faith as trust and commitment is a resting of the mind in the total sufficiency of the evidences. It cannot authenticate itself through personal experience alone; it must make peace with the law of non-contradiction and empirical facts. The truth of the Christian faith should not be made to stand or fall entirely on the basis of existential encounter. Truth is one, Carnell insisted, whether it be in philosophy, science, or theology. The theologian has no right to violate criteria for truth that God has established. To do so is to violate the canons of logic resident in the *Logos* and in the common sense that governs our daily lives.[26]

C. S. Lewis's apologetic perspective, on the other hand, was neither governed by conservative or modernist assumptions. His sole intent was to commend and defend what he called "mere" Christianty. As Peter Kreeft notes, "Lewis was neither a Christian conservative nor a Christian radical, but a radical Christian. His 'mere' Christianity is radical for the same reason it is orthodox: it returns to its root rather than putting forth new branches."[27] The "middle way" perspective of Lewis's Anglican background pervaded his thought. His Christianity was dogmatic, but it was almost always imaginative. He vigorously affirmed the supernatural but managed to do so in a manner that did not bifurcate the natural and the supernatural into separate and unrelated realms. His faith was rooted in the texts of the Bible and the creeds of the church, but he was never seriously accused of being a fundamentalist in either spirit or doctrine.

Lewis rejected as an a priori bias all theology of the liberal type that denies the miraculous and the historicity of nearly everything in the Gospels. It is pure presumption, he believed, for modern critics to claim that their interpretations, based as they usually are on a priori naturalistic assumptions, are superior to those of Jesus's closest contemporary followers. "The canon 'If miraculous, unhistorical,' " Lewis noted, "is one that scholars bring to their study of the texts, not one they have learned from it. If one is speaking of authority, the united authority of all the biblical critics in the world counts here for nothing. On this they speak simply as men, men obviously influenced by, and perhaps insufficiently critical of, the spirit of the age they grew up in."[28]

Like Carnell, C. S. Lewis was concerned to defend biblical Christianity in its historical, supernatural form. He had no use for what he called "Christianity-and-water." But he was not a fundamentalist or even a standard-issue evangelical. His nonpenal view of the Atonement, his nonmention of justification, his belief in purgatory, prayer for the dead, and regular confession to his priest was definitely Anglicanism with a Catholic leaning.[29] His understanding of the *imago Dei* and the Fall did not discount an evolutionary perspective,[30] and, like Niebuhr, Lewis commonly used the term "myth" to describe the primordial form through which divine truth was first communicated.

Unlike Niebuhr, however, Lewis did not use the term "myth" to mean a symbolic representation of non-historical truth. He rather used it to mean an account of what may have been the historical fact, though he realized that some memoirs and stories were obviously less historical than others. Lewis defined myth as "a real though unfocused gleam of divine truth falling on human imagination."[31] The Hebrews, he believed, like all other ancient people, had their mythology. But theirs was the chosen mythology that ends in the New Testament where truth becomes completely historical. The form, Lewis stressed, governs the response. What is often called for is an imaginative as well as a religious and historical response. Scripture, Lewis said, "is directed to the child, the poet, and the savage in us as well as the conscience and the intellect. One of its functions is to break down dividing walls."[32]

It is this many-sidedness appeal that makes Christianity morally compelling, imaginatively moving, and rationally convincing. Lewis admitted that there are no demonstrable proofs for the Christian faith, but he believed that its claims may be so overwhelmingly probable as virtually to exclude all psychological doubt.[33] The one claim that must be settled for the Christian is the person of Jesus Christ, for he is the basis for our reason, our morality, and our hope for happiness. It is not unreasonable, Lewis claimed, for one to believe in a faith claim that makes more sense out of the universe and the human experience than any alternative view. The upshot of C. S. Lewis's apologetic is that "a universe without God is a universe without meaning, a universe in which reason is not to be trusted, the moral law has no force, and the hope of happiness is doomed to frustration."[34]

Lewis knew the value and power of reasoned argument. He also knew that it must not be overemphasized. It is possible, as Martin Luther warned, to "defend the faith until it collapses." Most religious knowledge comes through means other than rational persuasion. Faith cannot be the product of apologetic argument for God cannot be known through a detached and speculative attitude of reasoned indifference. This does not mean, however, that apologetic arguments have no legitimate function. The apologist's task is to help those who are struggling with faith to see that it is not a lack of reason but perhaps a biased attitude, an impoverished imagination, or a dogmatic belief that blocks their acceptance of the Christian faith. What apologists can do most effectively is attack the citadels of unbelief, unsettling the dogmatism and removing the barriers that hinder a genuine hearing of the Christian message. C. S. Lewis, Edward John Carnell, and Reinhold Niebuhr were among the great apologists of this century because they helped to remove these barriers to faith.

Notes

[1] *On Christian Doctrine,* I:10.

[2] *Letters,* I:3.

[3] Arthur F. Holmes, *All Truth Is God's Truth* (Downers Grove IL: Intervarsity Press, 1977) 25.

[4] See G. W. Berkouwer's chapter entitled, "The Era of Apologetics" in *A Half Century of theology* (Grand Rapids MI: Eerdmans Publishing Co., 1977) 28-31.

[5] Martin Marty and Dean Peerman (eds), *A Handbook of Christian Theologians* (Cleveland OH: World Publishing Co., 1965) 288.

[6] See the chapter on "Brunner as Apologist" in Kegley and Bretall's *The Theology of Emil Brunner* (New York: Macmillan, 1962) 289-301.

[7]John Jefferson Davis, "Tillich—Accurate Aims, Alien Assumptions," *Christianity Today* 20 (27 January 1976): 7, 8.

[8]Ibid.

[9]Diogenes Allen, *The Reasonableness of Faith* (Washington DC: Corpus Publications, 1968) 54, 55.

[10]Berkouwer, 149.

[11]Edwin Lewis, "Where is Barth Wrong?" *Christian Century* 50 (22 March 1933): 385.

[12]Edwin Lewis, "From Philosophy to Revelation; Twenty-first Article in the series 'How My Mind Has Changed in This Decade,' " *Christian Century* 56 (14 June 1939): 762.

[13]Berkouwer, 149.

[14]Roger Hazelton, *New Accents in Contemporary Theology* (New York: Harper and Brothers, 1960) 118.

[15]Ibid., 120.

16Charles Kegley and Robert Bretall, eds., *Reinhold Niebuhr: His Religious, Social, and Political Thought* (New York: Macmillan, 1967) 223.

17Ibid., 225.   [18]Ibid., 226.   [19]Ibid., 4.
[20]Ibid., 438.   [21]Ibid., 225.   [22]Ibid., 226.
[23]Ibid., 228.

[24]William Hordern, *A Layman's Guide To Protestant Theology* (New York: Macmillan, 1976) 155.

[25]Kegley and Bretall, 443.

[26]John A. Sims, *Edward John Carnell: Defender of the Faith* (Washington DC: University Press, 1979) 33.

[27]Peter Kreeft, *C. S. Lewis: A Critical Essay* (Front Royal VA: Christendom College Press, 1988) 33.

[28]Walter Hooper, ed., *Christian Reflections* (Grand Rapids MI: Eerdmans Publishing Co., 1967) 158.

[29]J. I. Packer, "What Lewis Was and Wasn't," *Christianity Today* (15 January 1988): 11.

[30]C. S. Lewis, *The Problem of Pain* (New York: Macmillan, 1978) 77.

[31]C. S. Lewis, *Miracles* (New York: Macmillan, 1978) 134.

[32]Ibid., 34.

[33]Richard L. Purtill, *Reason to Believe* (Grand Rapids MI: Eerdmans Publishing Co., 1974) 75.

[34]Ibid., 111.

Index of Persons